The Human Tradition in America

CHARLES W. CALHOUN
Series Editor
Department of History, East Carolina University

The nineteenth-century English author Thomas Carlyle once remarked that "the history of the world is but the biography of great men." This approach to the study of the human past had existed for centuries before Carlyle wrote, and it continued to hold sway among many scholars well into the twentieth century. In more recent times, however, historians have recognized and examined the impact of large, seemingly impersonal forces in the evolution of human history—social and economic developments such as industrialization and urbanization as well as political movements such as nationalism, militarism, and socialism. Yet even as modern scholars seek to explain these wider currents, they have come more and more to realize that such phenomena represent the composite result of countless actions and decisions by untold numbers of individual actors. On another occasion, Carlyle said that "history is the essence of innumerable biographies." In this conception of the past, Carlyle came closer to modern notions that see the lives of all kinds of people, high and low, powerful and weak, known and unknown, as part of the mosaic of human history, each contributing in a large or small way to the unfolding of the human tradition.

This latter idea forms the foundation for this series of books on the human tradition in America. Each volume is devoted to a particular period or topic in American history and each consists of minibiographies of persons whose lives shed light on that period or topic. Well-known figures are not altogether absent, but more often the chapters explore a variety of individuals who may be less conspicuous but whose stories, nonetheless, offer us a window on some aspect of the nation's past.

By bringing the study of history down to the level of the individual, these sketches reveal not only the diversity of the American people and the complexity of their interaction but also some of the commonalities of sentiment and experience that Americans have shared in the evolution of their culture. Our hope is that these explorations of the lives of "real people" will give readers a deeper understanding of the human tradition in America.

Volumes in the Human Tradition in America series:

Ian K. Steele and Nancy L. Rhoden, eds., *The Human Tradition in Colonial America* (1999). Cloth ISBN 0-8420-2697-5
Paper ISBN 0-8420-2700-9

Nancy L. Rhoden and Ian K. Steele, eds., *The Human Tradition in the American Revolution* (2000). Cloth ISBN 0-8420-2747-5
Paper ISBN 0-8420-2748-3

Ballard C. Campbell, ed., *The Human Tradition in the Gilded Age and Progressive Era* (2000). Cloth ISBN 0-8420-2734-3
Paper ISBN 0-8420-2735-1

Steven E. Woodworth, ed., *The Human Tradition in the Civil War and Reconstruction* (2000). Cloth ISBN 0-8420-2726-2
Paper ISBN 0-8420-2727-0

David L. Anderson, ed., *The Human Tradition in the Vietnam Era* (2000). Cloth ISBN 0-8420-2762-9   Paper ISBN 0-8420-2763-7

Kriste Lindenmeyer, ed., *Ordinary Women, Extraordinary Lives: Women in American History* (2000). Cloth ISBN 0-8420-2752-1
Paper ISBN 0-8420-2754-8

Michael A. Morrison, ed., *The Human Tradition in Antebellum America* (2000). Cloth ISBN 0-8420-2834-X
Paper ISBN 0-8420-2835-8

Malcolm Muir Jr., ed., *The Human Tradition in the World War II Era* (2001). Cloth ISBN 0-8420-2785-8   Paper ISBN 0-8420-2786-6

THE HUMAN TRADITION IN THE
WORLD WAR II ERA

Pvt. Paul Oglesby, 30th Infantry, standing in reverence before an altar in a damaged Catholic church. Note that the pews at left appear undamaged, while parts of the bomb-shattered roof are strewn about the sanctuary. Acerno, Italy, July 23, 1943. *Courtesy of the National Archives and Records Administration, College Park, Maryland*

THE HUMAN TRADITION IN THE
WORLD WAR II ERA

No. 8
Human Tradition in America

Edited by
Malcolm Muir Jr.

A Scholarly Resources Inc. Imprint
Wilmington, Delaware

Scholarly Resources Inc.
104 Greenhill Avenue
Wilmington, DE 19805-1897
www.scholarly.com

Library of Congress Cataloging-in-Publication Data

The human tradition in the World War II era / edited by Malcolm
    Muir Jr.
        p. cm. — (The human tradition in America ; no. 8)
    Includes bibliographical references and index.
    ISBN 0-8420-2785-8 (alk. paper)—ISBN 0-8420-2786-6 (pbk. :
alk. paper)
        1. United States—History—1933–1945. 2. United States—
Civilization—1918–1945. 3. World War, 1939–1945—United States.
4. World War, 1939–1945—Social aspects—United States. I. Muir,
Malcolm, 1943– II. Series.

E806.H8657   2000
973.91—dc21   00-029700

About the Editor

Malcolm Muir Jr. is a military historian who received his degrees from Emory University in Atlanta, Georgia, Florida State University in Tallahassee, and Ohio State University in Columbus. Since 1977 he has been on the faculty of Austin Peay State University in Clarksville, Tennessee, where he served as chairman of the Department of History and Philosophy from 1990 to 2000. He has also held the Secretary of the Navy's Research Chair in Naval History and visiting positions at the U.S. Military Academy at West Point and the Air War College at Maxwell Air Force Base in Alabama. His publications include *Black Shoes and Blue Water: Surface Warfare in the U.S. Navy, 1945–1975* (1996), winner of the John Lyman prize for books in U.S. naval history.

I believe in aristocracy, though—if that is the right word, and if a democrat may use it. Not an aristocracy of power, based upon rank and influence, but an aristocracy of the sensitive, the considerate and the plucky. Its members are to be found in all nations and classes, and all through the ages, and there is a secret understanding between them when they meet. They represent the true human tradition, the one permanent victory of our queer race over cruelty and chaos. Thousands of them perish in obscurity, a few are great names. They are sensitive for others as well as for themselves, they are considerate without being fussy, their pluck is not swankiness but the power to endure, and they can take a joke.

—E. M. Forster, *Two Cheers for Democracy* (1951)

Contents

Introduction
Americans in Total War

Malcolm Muir Jr.

Pearl Harbor—that dramatic slap in the face—shocked Americans; it also brought them together. Never before or since have Americans been so united as they were on that Sunday afternoon, December 7, 1941, when they learned of the Japanese bombing of the U.S. Navy's Pacific Fleet at its base. Pearl Harbor was a watershed: unmistakable and profound. Virtually all adult Americans would remember for the rest of their lives exactly where they were and what they were doing when they heard the news of the surprise attack. When Nazi Germany and Fascist Italy declared war on the United States four days later, most Americans realized that their nation was fully engaged in a struggle for survival against powerful and ruthless enemies. Most Americans also sensed that their personal worlds would be permanently altered in significant, if unknowable, ways. For the war's duration, private lives would be subsumed in the national emergency.

These initial perceptions were accurate. World War II, more than any other conflict in modern history, was a total war. Beginning with Adolf Hitler's assault against Poland on September 1, 1939, the struggle, lasting six years and a day, ended half a world away with the surrender of Imperial Japan aboard the USS *Missouri* in Tokyo Bay. Before the war ran its course, nearly every important nation on the globe except Argentina became an active belligerent. Fighting took place on or immediately off the shores of every continent save Antarctica.

Without question, the United States was essential to the ultimate defeat of the Axis coalition of Germany, Italy, and Japan. However, to focus too closely on the United States in the war is to lose sight of the fact that this country was one of many making up that great Allied partnership dubbed the United Nations. Numbered among its members were most Latin American countries as well as governments and armed forces in exile from nations suffering Nazi occupation, such as Poland, France, Norway, the Netherlands, and Greece. Of very substantial weight were Great Britain and the members of its Commonwealth (including Australia, Canada, India, New Zealand, and South Africa), which had entered the war at its outbreak in 1939.

From the beginning, most Americans sympathized with the Allies. Commercial and ancestral ties added to the memories of shared sacrifices in World War I. Many Americans were concerned about the blatant militarism of the Nazi regime, Italian ambitions in the Mediterranean, and Japanese aggression in East Asia. Although the United States proclaimed its neutrality, President Franklin D. Roosevelt saw the Axis as threatening the most basic values of Western civilization. He extended help to the hard-pressed Allies by such measures as "cash and carry" and the "destroyers for bases" deal.

Major Axis successes in the summer and fall of 1940 influenced voters enough to elect Roosevelt to an unprecedented third term. The next February, the United States edged further away from neutrality with the famous Lend-Lease Act whereby the nation began loaning war materials to "victims of aggression," most notably Britain and China. In the summer of 1941, the president extended Lend-Lease aid to the Soviet Union when Nazi Germany attacked that country. From that time, the titanic struggle on the Eastern Front consumed approximately 75 percent of the German war effort. When Japan struck Pearl Harbor in December of that year, the United States fully joined Great Britain and the Soviet Union in what Prime Minister Winston Churchill later termed the "Grand Alliance."

The global nature of the struggle and the collective contribution of the Allied powers to the final victory can perhaps best be illustrated by the pivotal battles of 1942 that reversed the tide against the Axis. In a certain neat symmetry, of the three key military turning points, one (Midway) was a complex naval engagement won over the Japanese northwest of Hawaii by the United States. The second (El Alamein) was fought in the deserts of North Africa with British and Commonwealth forces the victors over the Germans and Italians. The third (Stalingrad) was waged on the southern steppes of Russia where the Soviets crushed an entire German army. These far-flung triumphs were made possible in part by the efforts of ordinary citizens on the home front. By definition, a total war demands of the nations involved a maximum commitment of resources for their fighting forces with a corresponding cutback in the bare necessities for their civilians. For Americans on the home front, the watchword became "Use it up; make it do; wear it out." "The home front"—the very words are evocative of the critical place that civilians in the United States held in the war effort. President Roosevelt and his advisers made the deliberate decision that the United States would focus on war production instead of trying to field armies as massive as those of Germany or the Soviet Union. When America became, in Roosevelt's words, the "great arsenal of democracy," its industry and agriculture prepared to provide weapons and supplies—the guns, trucks, ships, aircraft, Spam, and boots—not only to equip Americans on distant fighting fronts but also to help sustain America's allies.

The scale of the domestic effort was huge, especially considering that the country was coming out of the Great Depression, the worst economic convulsion in its history. At rock bottom, unemployment had reached one-quarter of the workforce. Many adults counted themselves lucky to earn the New Deal minimum wage of twenty-five cents per hour. Some Americans had suffered real want during the 1930s; newspapers frequently ran ads for tonics guaranteed to make individuals *gain* weight. When young American men were called up for military service during World War II, the results of dietary deprivation became glaringly apparent. Almost 30 percent of volunteers and draftees were rejected early in the war, most because they weighed less than 105 pounds, had fewer than one-half of their natural teeth, or suffered from uncorrectable vision problems.

The war put Americans back to work and food back on the table. The government poured $186 billion into the economy; the gross national product grew 36 percent during the war—its greatest jump ever in such a short period of time. No longer did unemployment percentages run into double-digit figures; instead, the burgeoning war industry was hard-pressed to find workers. People formerly barred from better jobs because of prejudice or social convention now found their services eagerly sought. Even handicapped Americans were able to contribute to the effort. (The deaf, for instance, could work in unusually noisy areas on the plant floor; midgets could turn bolts in the tight crannies of aircraft on the assembly line.) Prior to Pearl Harbor, many states had legislated against companies hiring anyone over thirty-five for the first time on the grounds that older people were too slow to learn. But once the country was at war, "seniors" given a second chance proved on average more productive in factory jobs than young men.

Many black Americans seized the opportunity to escape from Jim Crow segregation in the South and to seek well-paid jobs by heading for the industrial cities of the North and West. Congress furthered this mass migration by establishing the Fair Employment Practices Commission, which tried with some success to stamp out racial discrimination in war work. As in World War I, large numbers of blacks served their country in uniform, although still in segregated units and mostly in support roles. Symptomatically, the two black infantry divisions, the 92d and 93d, saw little action until late in the war.

Racial segregation, which had been accepted by most Americans as the natural order, now came under sharper scrutiny. Those who doubted that blacks could fight effectively were confounded by the fine performance of the 332d Fighter Group (the famed "Tuskegee Airmen"). Some military leaders concluded that segregation was wasteful of resources and damaging to morale in black units. With the United States battling for human rights against two of the most racist regimes in history, Nazi Germany and Imperial Japan, discerning people became increasingly uncomfortable with restaurants that would seat German prisoners but not their black American guards in uniform. Ultimately, the war energized many Americans to fight for both efficiency and justice; between 1940 and 1946, membership in the National Association for the Advancement of Colored People (NAACP) jumped from 50,000 to 450,000. The following decades would see the triumph of the Civil Rights movement; its foundation had been laid from 1941 to 1945.

In analogous ways, women entered the public and economic life of the nation more fully. They also joined the military in large numbers. During the conflict, 333,000 women put on their country's uniforms, thereby taking over essential support duties and freeing male soldiers and sailors for combat. Women ferried aircraft, nursed the wounded close behind the front lines, and worked in a host of other areas, including intelligence, communications, meteorology, mission plotting, and photo interpretation.

Certainly one of the most beneficial—and ironic—consequences of the greatest war in history was the marked improvement in American health. With the revival of the economy, people could afford better food; many could afford to visit a doctor for the first time. Of course, those in uniform received free medical care, as did their dependents. Blue Cross and Blue Shield programs became commonplace for war workers. By virtually every index, Americans were healthier in 1945 than they had been four years earlier. In that short period, life expectancy rose by a remarkable three years, even if one counted the deaths of almost 300,000 young Americans in combat. Diseases resulting from dietary deficiencies, such as beriberi and pellagra, which had been all too common during the depression years, virtually disappeared. Military needs spurred on such innovations as blood banks. Penicillin, developed in Great Britain, was little more than a medical curiosity in the summer of 1942 when existing American stocks were large enough for only one hundred patients. Two years later, military doctors possessed adequate supplies of the "miracle drug" to treat all major casualties. By the end of the war, the drug had reached the civilian market in quantity. At the same time, major advances were also made in heart and lung surgery. Although surgeons previously had been reluctant to operate on or even to touch the heart, grim war wounds required drastic measures. It is no exaggeration to say that modern cardiac surgery was born on the battlefields of World War II.

The pressure-cooker atmosphere generated by the war emergency also fostered major changes in the country's scientific establishment. In direct contrast to the relatively feeble efforts of Imperial Japan and even Nazi Germany, the U.S. government expanded its research laboratories and mobilized scientists at more than four hundred civilian institutions, including such bastions of scientific inquiry as the Massachusetts Institute of Technology, Johns Hopkins University, and the California Institute of Technology. Little publicized at the time, the work of more than seventeen thousand scientists refined aircraft design and produced or improved such militarily useful devices as antiaircraft fuses, sonar, radar, and the atomic bomb. In a broader sense, these efforts led to major advances in fields as disparate as electronics, oceanography, and nuclear particle physics.

To produce weapons and war goods on the scale envisioned by U.S. planners called for the widespread conversion of peacetime industry to war production. Supplementing existing facilities were entirely new plants, the most noted of which were Henry J. Kaiser's shipyards on the West Coast; the Boeing plant built specifically at Renton, Washington, for the production of B-29 bombers; and Henry Ford's gigantic aircraft factory at Willow Run, outside Detroit. Dubbed in its early difficult stages "Willit Run?" run it did, producing B-24 bombers faster than the Army Air Forces (AAF) could train crews to fly them.

One of the inevitable concomitants of such industrial expansion was ecological pollution as factories were thrown up with little concern for the surrounding environment. Another was large-scale social dislocation. Entire trainloads of workers headed for the Kaiser yards in Washington. Large numbers of southerners from the Appalachians headed north and west, spreading their country music across the nation. With civilian needs taking a back seat to military requirements, housing shortages frequently plagued the workforce. In response, at places such as Oak Ridge, Tennessee, the government resorted to mobile homes, which brought that industry to prominence. Housing aside, family life suffered as "latch-key children" or "eight-hour orphans" became common. The rapid increase in juvenile delinquency concerned many sociologists.

Shortages abounded; rationing was a constant aggravation. Civilians paid for most products twice—in cash and in ration coupons, thereby equalizing the sacrifices and heading off the age-old lament of "a rich man's war and a poor man's fight." Civilians could purchase only two pairs of shoes annually; auto dealers sold no new cars after 1942. To save gas and tires, authorities imposed a nationwide speed limit of 35 miles per hour. Critical commodities such as sugar and gasoline were always in short supply and were rationed separately. At certain times, smokers had to get by on four cigarettes per day, and motorists on two gallons of fuel weekly (although doctors and those in critical occupations enjoyed larger allotments). Strict government controls on prices and rents kept inflation to below 2 percent.

American agriculture changed in similar, often wrenching ways. To fill in for men absent from the fields, the government employed prisoners and, with more permanent impact, imported substantial numbers of workers from the Caribbean and Mexico. Gender roles so common in farm homesteads began to melt away with the labor shortage and the increasingly widespread availability of labor-saving machinery. In the face of virtually limitless demand and with cash at their disposal, farm families rushed to mechanize; farm income leaped during the war by 250 percent. Such measures paid remarkable dividends. Agricultural production increased 45 percent from 1939 to 1945.

The net result of the mobilization of the home front was nothing short of phenomenal. To cite only a few examples, in 1942 President Roosevelt publicly set a production goal of 50,000 military aircraft for 1943, a year in which Nazi Germany built 15,556 and Japan, 8,861. Confounding Hitler's gibes, in 1943 the American aircraft industry built 92,196 warplanes. Similar startling figures highlighted the strength of American industry in virtually every area of war production. U.S. shipyards built 103 aircraft carriers; the Axis nations commissioned 17.

Numbers can sometimes be eloquent. By the end of the war, 1,300 new war production plants and shipyards supplemented existing facilities that had been converted from peacetime production. The yards turned out 5,400 merchant ships, including one, the *Robert E. Perry*, constructed in four days, fifteen and one-half hours at Richmond, California. In 1944 the automobile industry manufactured 86,000 tanks, 2.5 million trucks, and 660,000 Jeeps. Ford Motor Company alone produced more military goods than the entire Italian economy.

In terms of quality, much of this matériel set the world standard. The P-51 Mustang was the finest fighter aircraft produced in quantity by any nation; for bombers, the same could be said of the B-29 Superfortress. The GI carried the M-1 Garand, a semiautomatic rifle that was markedly better than the bolt-action weapons issued to German or Japanese infantrymen. American submarines with their great range and deep-diving capability were ideally suited for operations in the vastness of the Pacific.

Not all American equipment excelled. The navy's torpedoes were notoriously defective—a problem that was not solved for almost two years. The standard American tank, the M-4 Sherman, was cursed with a weak gun and thin armor compared to its most formidable German opponents. Still, U.S. industry built 48,000 Shermans while the Germans turned out 7,300 of their powerful but cantankerous Panthers and Tigers. As a later saying put it, "Quantity has a quality all its own."

For the United States, World War II placed novel demands on its human as well as its material resources. Ultimately, of its sixty million males, almost sixteen million enrolled in the military. Thus, approximately one out of every four American males of all ages and conditions wore a uniform. Many were volunteers, especially early in the war; the others were conscripts. Congress set the draft age from twenty to forty-five (although those from eighteen to twenty could volunteer). Some divisions wore a surprisingly mature appearance with their soldiers averaging up to thirty-two years of age.

The army was built almost from the ground up because the prewar force was shockingly small. In 1939 the U.S. Army counted only 137,000 soldiers on its rosters; its larger formations, the divisions and corps, existed only on paper. In size, the army ranked nineteenth in the world, behind that of Portugal, among others. Fortunately, far-sighted army planners, such as Gen. George C. Marshall, had laid the groundwork for rapidly expanding the force by developing mobilization plans, prototype weapons, leaner combat formations, and standardized training procedures. To turn enlistees into soldiers and to meld individuals into smoothly functioning units, the army formulated a training regimen to build each of its 15,000-man divisions from raw recruits within one year. Forty-six new camps were created, mostly in the South where land was cheap and the weather conducive to year-round training. Paren-thetically, the effects of mobilization on that region of the country were pronounced as federal dollars brought a measure of prosperity to what had been for generations the most economically backward section of the United States.

As the infantry, armor, and airborne divisions were being built, so were the Army Air Forces and the navy. Although not in the public eye to the degree that the army was, the navy had a task that was equally as essential to a successful prosecution of the war both in Europe and the Pacific. Because virtually all men and matériel traveled to the war the-aters aboard transport and cargo vessels, the navy had to defeat German submarines in the Atlantic and the potent Japanese navy of aircraft car-riers and surface warships in the broad Pacific. Fortunately, the U.S. Navy was reasonably well prepared for war. Although having placed too much emphasis on the battleship and too little on antisubmarine war-fare, the navy nonetheless had experimented with many of the weapons and techniques that would bring victory, such as the fast aircraft carrier and the long-range submarine. Little publicized but of cardinal impor-tance was the fleet train of support ships that allowed the combatant vessels to operate at great distances from fixed bases.

Following serious defeats in the early stages of the war in the Pacific and against German submarines, especially in American waters during 1942, the navy made the requisite adjustments in fighting techniques while U.S. shipyards quickly replaced combat losses. For the remainder of the war, it played a major role in helping the British and Canadians defeat the German U-boats and in transporting troops and supplies across the Atlantic. Similarly, after a succession of reverses at the hands of the Japanese early in the war, in 1944 the U.S. Navy effectively destroyed the excellent Japanese fleet in the largest naval battles of all times: the Philippine Sea and Leyte Gulf. By the end of that year, the U.S. Navy was bigger than all the rest of the navies in the world put together; its sailors numbered almost 4 million.

A welcome addition to navy strength during the war had been the Coast Guard, transferred to the U.S. Navy by executive order in late 1941 from the Treasury Department. The larger cutters gave good ser-vice shepherding merchantmen; Coast Guardsmen—241,000 served during the war—crewed many navy transports and escorts. As America went on the offensive in the latter half of 1942, Coast Guard expertise in handling boats proved especially useful in the manning of the thou-sands of landing craft joining the fleet.

Another key element in carrying out America's offensive strategy was the U.S. Marine Corps. A part of the navy, the Marines prior to the war had gone against prevailing military thought by adopting the mission of amphibious assault. Despite widespread predictions that landings on hostile shores would be impossible in the face of enemy aircraft and submarines, the Marines (and the army) attempted more than one hundred such operations in World War II. Not one failed. During the conflict, the Marine Corps grew to its largest size ever, numbering more than 669,000 men and women.

In the prewar view of some enthusiastic advocates of air power, large ground units, whether army or Marine, were unnecessary because the war would be won from the skies. At the beginning of the struggle, the army's aerial component (the Army Air Corps; after July 1941, the Army Air Forces) had in very limited production a fine bomber design, the B-17 Flying Fortress. Planners believed that these bombers, flying in large numbers in close formation, could fight their way through enemy defenses to deliver precise and war-winning blows at enemy industry.

Bitter experience showed these hopes unrealistic. After suffering prohibitively high losses, the aviators were forced to employ long-range fighters to escort the bombers on their raids. In the end, this dark cloud's silver lining was that enemy fighters in turn suffered prohibitive losses to the guns of the escorting fighters. This unexpected bonus proved most valuable in clearing the skies above Allied invasion forces.

Late in the war, forced by high losses and other operational considerations, the bombers shifted from attacking enemy industry to aiming at cities. The incendiary attacks on Japanese cities proved horrifyingly effective. Thus, the closing nuclear strikes against Hiroshima and Nagasaki represented for airmen a difference in scale but not in kind.

Like the ground army and the navy, the Army Air Forces ballooned enormously. As one index, in 1938 the Air Corps had trained 300 pilots; by 1942 the figure reached 30,000. At its peak in 1944 the AAF numbered 2.4 million airmen and 80,000 combat aircraft. Its Air Transport Command was by any measure the largest airline in the world with close to 15,000 aircraft. On the debit side of the ledger, the AAF lost 22,948 planes in combat during the conflict. In the final analysis, strategic bombing did not deliver victory by itself. Yet it was one key element in the Allied success in both theaters. After the war, its importance was recognized when the air force was detached from the army and established as a separate, coequal third service.

Long before the aerial campaign reached its height, top strategists concluded that it was unlikely, by itself, to bring victory. Thus, the United States would need to employ its army to help the Allies defeat the enemies' forces in the field and to occupy their homelands. By 1945 the army numbered more than 8 million. Its combat troops made up ninety divisions (of about 15,000 soldiers each), by far the largest army the United States has ever raised. By way of contrast, the army in 1999 comprised 10 active divisions. More pertinent, during World War II the Japanese fielded about 100 divisions; the Germans, close to 300; the Russians, about 700 (although Soviet divisions were smaller than their peers).

One reason that the American combatant force did not reach a greater size was the manpower devoted to the home front. Another was the large support element backing up the fighting units. For every soldier on the front line, three soldiers in the Army Service Forces supported him. Although this arrangement deprived the United States of some fighting troops, it multiplied the effectiveness of those on the "cutting edge." For instance, every U.S. division was completely motorized whereas the standard German infantry division used 4,000 horses. By 1945 the U.S. Army was so lavishly equipped with vehicles that theoretically all the men and women in it could have hopped rides in Jeeps and trucks simultaneously. One observer wryly contrasted the three sheets of toilet paper issued daily to the British soldier with the GI's allowance of twenty-two sheets. Famed German Field Marshal Erwin Rommel, the "Desert Fox," called the U.S. Army "fantastically well equipped." Many wondered if American soldiers would fight well—or at all—if deprived of their accustomed level of material support.

In one important way the U.S. Army of World War II differed from earlier versions: it fought in diverse theaters in a wide array of climatic and topographical conditions against foes who also varied quite markedly in weapons and fighting style. American troops battled in areas as disparate as the deserts of North Africa, the mountains of northern Italy, the hedgerows of France, the jungles of the southwest Pacific, and the muskeg of the Aleutians. Against skilled and tenacious troops defending terrain of their choosing, the soldiers of the U.S. Army compiled an enviable record indeed. After losing their first campaign of the war to the Japanese in the Philippines and their first battle against the Germans at Kasserine Pass in Tunisia, the U.S. Army did not suffer another significant defeat. Rommel remarked of American troops that they knew less but learned faster than any other fighting men he had ever opposed.

And to the dismay of their Axis foes, when American soldiers were deprived of their elaborate support structure, they still stood and fought tenaciously. After the excellent performance of U.S. troopers in the terrible cold of the Ardennes during the Battle of the Bulge, a German army intelligence report concluded its assessment of the American soldier: "a first-rate, well-trained, and often physically superior opponent."

This high praise came at a high cost. In one of his more eloquent addresses, President Roosevelt concluded, "We, born to freedom and believing in freedom, are willing to fight to maintain freedom. We and all others who believe as deeply as we do would rather die on our feet than live on our knees." For 292,131 soldiers, airmen, sailors, and Marines who died in combat, these words proved prophetic. In terms of lives lost, World War II was the second most costly conflict in U.S. history. Another 115,187 Americans lost their lives to noncombat causes; 671,801 were wounded; and 139,709 suffered as prisoners of the enemy. Only the Civil War drew more American blood. Even for the majority of those Americans who came home whole, the war exacted its price in interrupted careers and disrupted families.

These sacrifices by men at the front, the service forces behind them, and the civilians at home brought the greatest of prizes: deliverance from two of the most predatory, brutal, and racist regimes in history. The contrast between the behavior of American soldiers in occupied Germany or Japan stands in sharp contrast with that of soldiers from those nations in Russia and China. Can anyone doubt for a moment that the world would have been a much worse place had the vanquished been the victors?

This volume presents the American experience in World War II by looking at the conflict through the ordeals of a broad array of men and women. All the services are represented: U.S. Army, Army Air Forces, U.S. Navy, and Marines. So are the principal theaters of war: Europe and the Pacific. The critical home front comes to life through such diverse figures as a Kansas farmer, a famous Hollywood actor, women workers in the Iron Range of Minnesota, a Mennonite conscientious objector, and a congresswoman. The varied experiences of a Japanese American couple, a Jewish policymaker, and a black leader flesh out the trials and accomplishments of American minority groups. Of course, this portrayal—like any other—cannot claim to be complete; yet by focusing on a wide variety of Americans, the volume illustrates how the greatest of human conflicts changed the lives of all Americans, whether in uniform or at home.

I
The Home Front

1

Ralph A. Lee
Farmer and Service Station Operator

R. Alton Lee

Ralph A. Lee typified the rural American who struggled through years of desperate trial and wrenching change. On his small farm in Kansas, Lee mirrored in his life some of the great shifts in American agriculture during depression and war. Having plowed with horses as a young man, Lee moved into town during the Roaring Twenties to take advantage of the automobile boom. When economic collapse forced him back onto the land, Lee soon swapped his six-horse team for a tractor and electrified his operation with the help of New Deal government programs.

One great ordeal followed another as the war placed an enormous strain on couples such as Ralph and Alice Lee who rented small farms. Although crop prices rose, Ralph encountered shortages of key commodities such as tires and gasoline. As a consumer and then as the operator of a service station, Lee coped with rationing from both sides of the regulatory fence. Another experience that the Lees shared with so many Americans was the loss of a child. Their daughter Ruth, an army nurse, suffered frostbite during the Italian campaign and died of its complications.

Ralph Lee's story is told by his son, R. Alton Lee, who earned his Ph.D. at the University of Oklahoma. Rising to the rank of professor at the University of South Dakota in Vermillion, Alton Lee has published extensively on twentieth-century America. Among his eight books are studies of Presidents Harry S. Truman and Dwight D. Eisenhower as well as the edited volume *Agricultural Legacies* (1986).

Ralph Albert Lee's ancestors were part of a large number of people who migrated from economically depressed Virginia and moved through Kentucky and Tennesee after the War of 1812. The family eventually came to Stone County in southern Missouri. Ralph's grandfather Thomas E. Lee married Phoebe Goff, also of Virginia, by whom he had three sons. Thomas enlisted in the Confederate army in 1861 and died in December 1862, not in glorious battle but from yellow jaundice. One of his sons, Robert Franklin, married Laura Beasley and they had five children. Their second child, Ralph, born on May 16, 1889, at Ponce de Leon, Missouri, was given the middle initial "A" and,

3

according to the custom in southern Missouri at the time, he chose the name Albert when he was thirteen.

The Robert Lee family homesteaded in Oklahoma when the Indian Territory opened up soon after Ralph was born. He was raised on a farm, and working the soil became his life's ambition. At maturity he stood 5' 10" tall, weighed 180 pounds, and had a muscular physique from a boyhood of hard work. He migrated northward into east-central Kansas where he met and married Alice Butts, the daughter of English emigrants who had settled in Morris County, Kansas. Ralph and Alice had seven children, five daughters and two sons, one of whom died in infancy.

Ralph and Alice began married life on a rented farm but he soon envisioned economic affluence in the nearby bustling town of White City. He opened a horse-drawn taxi and drayage venture there, which met with moderate success. The town of Alta Vista, in the adjoining county, soon beckoned and he established a drayage service there, becoming one of the first to use a gasoline-powered truck in his business. Three of their daughters were born in Alta Vista.

The decade of the 1920s brought widespread use of the automobile, and in 1930 Ralph moved his family back to White City where he constructed a service station on one of the busy corners of the commercial area on the main street. At the rear of his station he built a miniature golf course, one of the fads that was sweeping the nation at the time; he briefly enjoyed financial success. But the Great Depression that engulfed the nation soon reached the hinterlands and his gasoline business declined as customers had less and less money for purchasing fuel beyond that required by their vocations.

During the depression decade, Lee leased his service station to a number of people who sought, unsuccessfully, to make it profitable. Returning to farming, his first love, he supplemented his meager farm income during the depression by buying and selling cattle. Each Saturday afternoon at the livestock pavilions in Council Grove, Herington, and Junction City—towns approximately twenty-five miles away—livestock was sold on commission. Farmers, however, lacked the means of transporting their stock to the markets. Ralph had a truck and a financial arrangement with his banker, who trusted his judgment and approved loans in advance to make purchases during the week. Farmers across the county would telephone Ralph, offering a steer for sale or a dozen hogs ready for market. Lee would drive to the farm, appraise the animals, estimate the weight, guess what the price per pound would be on Saturday, and negotiate a purchase.

He kept the animals on his farm during the week and then hauled them to Junction City on Saturday morning. The salespeople pasted a number on the hip of each animal for identification as they occasionally sold several similar ones in the same lot. The animals were driven into the ring, viewed by buyers while the auctioneer chattered his offers, and sold to the highest bidder. At the end of the day, Lee paid his commission fees and drove home, hoping he had a little more than enough money for the Monday morning reckoning with his banker. This enterprise was a risky art that could be disastrous if he incorrectly guessed weights or if the market shifted downward by a half-cent during the week.

When the United States became involved in World War II, farming on the Great Plains was still characterized by social and financial divisions based on ownership of land and wealth. At the bottom of the economic ladder stood the farm laborers. The wealthy farmers who dominated the top rung had large acreages that required hired men, as they were then called, to do the manual labor. In the middle were farmers such as Lee who might own the minimum number of acres required for diversified farming or who, usually, owned their livestock and machinery and rented a farm.

Lee's farm work was similar to that of his grandfather, except that his implements were larger, were mounted on wheels, and had seats on which the operator could ride. Electricity and the internal combustion engine were the major developments after the Civil War that decisively affected agrarian methods, and farmers were beginning tentatively to use tractors during the Great Depression. Electricity did not reach many farms until the end of the 1930s—in most cases, after the New Deal's Rural Electrification Administration (REA), which was established in 1935, had approved cooperatives to run power lines into the rural areas.

Agricultural labor at that time was divided between the farmer and his wife. This dichotomy held that the man's income from crops financed the farm, and his wife's "pin money" (income from sale of eggs, butter, and cream) ran her household. The average housewife usually raised one hundred chickens each year, and nature provided a rooster for Sunday dinners and fifty hens for laying eggs. Most middle-class farmers milked a few cows by hand and separated the cream. Alice churned some of the cream into butter and sold it and the surplus cream and eggs for credit to purchase food not grown on the farm and the necessary dry goods for the family. She and her friends chose the store they patronized; hence the expression, "Who do you trade with? I trade with the Stewarts." The housewife also maintained a large vegetable garden and canned several hundred jars of fruits and vegetables each year.

In the winter, Lee's day began before dawn. He first started fires in the wood-burning cook and heating stoves and broke the ice in the drinking-water pail in the kitchen. He then went to the barn and, by lantern light, milked seventeen cows with the help of his son. The cows had to be milked twice per day without fail, which meant that the Lees never took a vacation. After separating the cream from the milk, he fed the calves the skimmed milk and then was ready for breakfast before a hard day's work in the fields.

Lee farmed with six horses, and, by World War II, he had managed to purchase a used Farmall F-12 tractor with steel wheels and lugs for the heaviest work, such as plowing. Gasoline tractors were not widely used until World War II when the resulting severe shortage of labor forced mechanization. There were two reasons for the delay in employing tractors. It was not until 1925 that International Harvester introduced its high-wheeled, row-straddling Farmall, the first all-purpose tractor that could be used to cultivate row crops and cotton. The depression struck soon after, and many farmers who wanted to mechanize did not have the necessary funds to purchase a tractor. Meanwhile, there was inadequate evidence to prove to farmers who diversified their crops on their small acreages that the price of a tractor was low enough and the increased productivity great enough to justify the purchase. Western wheat farmers with larger farms on the High Plains and cotton planters of the South began to use tractors much earlier than their counterparts to the east and north, who had smaller farms. The agricultural prosperity that accompanied World War II provided the necessary capital, but all automobile and some implement production was converted to the war effort to manufacture tanks, guns, Jeeps, and aircraft. New farm machinery was rationed until November 1944.

Farmers at the time believed that "deep plowing" was vital for success—low tillage and no tillage were postwar concepts. Lee and his neighbors turned over the soil with a tractor if they had one or, if not, with a six-horse team that pulled the two-bottom plow. A two-horse team was used for cultivating row crops. Successful farmers planted a band of less valuable cane around the fields of row crops to entice the

Ralph Lee on his first tractor, a Farmall F-12. *Courtesy of the Lee family*

chinch bugs away from the milo or kafir (varieties of grain sorghums). The row crops were harvested in the late summer, and the cattle were turned out to forage on the stubble. In the late fall, corn was picked by hand and loaded in a team-drawn wagon. After World War II these techniques were revolutionized by the development of mechanized pickers and combines.

During periods of inclement weather or when the fields were muddy, Lee rebuilt fences or made repairs. There were always sickles to sharpen, harness to repair, or implements to be readied for use. He never purchased new machinery but bought second-hand at auctions of farmers who lost their property because of the depression and had to sell their machinery and livestock before seeking employment elsewhere. When a machine grew so old that parts were no longer available for it, he bought a newer one at a farm sale, but all the equipment was in constant need of repair. After he completed the plowing, disking, or drilling, the shears and disks (which were stored outdoors) needed to be greased heavily to prevent them from rusting. The axes, hoes, and sickles, both hand and for horse-drawn mowers, were sharpened with a large circular grindstone complete with a seat and foot pedals for power. A tin can with a hole in the bottom was suspended above it to drip water on the stone.

Most lessors required that weeds be controlled on the farm, which meant spraying for bindweed. The county commissioners provided financial assistance for spraying because these weeds were a widespread problem. Lee destroyed cockleburrs, sunflowers, marijuana, and other noxious weeds with hoes wielded by his children. Larger tasks (such as haying and threshing) required collaboration between neighbors. Harvests—like all other aspects of farming—were governed by the weather. As the wheat, oats, and barley crops began to turn golden, Lee cut them with a four-horse binder that tied the sheaves with twine and dumped them in long rows. He and the children collected them in neat round shocks to ripen further. Six or eight neighbors joined together and contracted with a man who owned a steam- or gasoline-powered thresher. The thresherman, who made his schedule largely on the basis of whose crops were the ripest, usually spent two or three days on each farm. The cooperating farmers brought their teams and hayracks to haul the shocks to the thresher. The grain was shoveled into the granary for future use in feeding livestock or as next year's seed, or it was hauled to the town elevator to be sold. The straw stack provided forage for the cattle and bedding for the barn animals. Every day during the harvest season, Alice Lee and the other wives prepared a large dinner meal at noon and a hearty snack at the midafternoon break. Even Lee's young son could be part of the enterprise by hauling drinking water to the workers, and his sisters helped their mother with the cooking chores. Harvesting was hard, dirty work but it was satisfying to see the granary filled before a summer storm struck, as it often did at that time of year.

The New Deal sought to preserve the family farm. To reduce surpluses and to raise farm prices, the second Agricultural Adjustment Administration (AAA) of 1938 placed an acreage limit on production of several basic commodities. Farmers' incomes would be brought up to parity (meaning the same purchasing power they had enjoyed in the prosperous years from 1909 to 1914) by higher prices resulting from the elimination of surpluses and by subsidies for reducing acreage in production. The cash payments were welcome during the depression but the program failed to eliminate surpluses as farmers, conditioned to produce as much as possible, poured on more fertilizers and herbicides to keep overall production high. Poor farmers were also assisted by the Farm Security Administration (FSA), which sought to help those who were losing their mortgaged farms by refinancing them at long-term, low interest rates.

The outbreak of World War II, and the subsequent need for unlimited farm production, ushered in great changes in these farm programs. In early 1941 the administration committed the United States to the Allied cause when President Franklin D. Roosevelt persuaded Congress to enact the Lend-Lease Act to make American military and agricultural production available to nations fighting the Axis powers. The question was how should American agricultural policy be reversed to implement this remarkable plan of assistance to the Allies.

The AAA was not welcomed by many farmers because, as implemented, it tended to favor the large producers. In the Cotton Belt, for example, owners kept the subsidy checks that were supposed to be shared with their tenants, used the money to purchase tractors and machinery, and ejected most of their tenants, keeping only a few as day laborers. Middle-class farmers such as Ralph Lee opposed the AAA because the large farmers were better able to take advantage of it, while its controls and subsidies offered little to the smaller, diversified farmer who might not receive subsidies because his acreage fell below the maximum. Hence, the wealthier farmers and southern planters backed their organization, the Farm Bureau Federation, which lobbied for the program, while the poorer farmers sought protection through the Farmers Union, which supported the FSA, an agrarian division that still exists.

During the defense crisis, the basic question of how to increase farm production had at least three possible answers. The first, which was favored by the Farm Bureau, proposed raising the prices of all farm products. The AAA, however, wanted to raise prices only on those commodities most in need for the defense effort. Both of these options came up against the price stabilization policies of the Office of Price Administration (OPA), an agency created immediately after the bombing of Pearl Harbor. Another option, promoted by the FSA and its ally the Farmers Union, would be to improve yields and increase agricultural services for the smaller producers. The Farm Bureau emerged victorious. In 1941 it forced through Congress the Price Stabilization Act, which raised parity supports to 85 percent (from the then-current 72) and the following year bumped the percentage up to 90 and added five more commodities to the support list. In 1943 the Bureau successfully pressed for 110 percent parity, which covered most agricultural commodities. The Price Stabilization Act was amended to extend this coverage for two years after the war ended. Throughout its history, the Farm Bureau opposed the FSA as its aim was to assist poorer farmers in acquiring financial independence. By 1940 the FSA claimed to have helped 850,000 farm families. Most of the country's agricultural production was labor intensive and required a large source of cheap labor for the wealthy farmers who dominated the agrarian scene and who were members of the Farm Bureau Federation. The Farm Bureau lobbied strenuously and persuaded Congress to phase out the FSA during the war years.

Farmers faced a critical labor shortage during the war as the military forces drained off millions of young men; at the end of hostilities there were 10 percent fewer farm workers than in 1940. Although the labor shortage did not affect Ralph Lee directly, it hurt his wealthier neighbors as farm labor wages increased fourfold during the war because of the scarcity of labor. The Wage Stabilization Board worked hard, successfully in most areas, to hold farm wages below the $2,400 yearly level, which represented a handsome gain for most workers compared to their depression income, but farm wages still lagged far behind industrial wages. Even with wage gains, the shortage was so acute that agrarian congressmen pressured Selective Service to extend draft deferments to farm workers, which it did extensively in 1943 and 1944. Military manpower was essential but so was agricultural production. During the war more women and children worked on farms than ever before and more than fifty thousand workers were imported from Mexico and another fifteen thousand from Caribbean areas such as British Barbados, Jamaica, and the Bahamas.

Finally, by late 1943 and early 1944 enough German and Italian prisoners of war (POWs) were transferred from Europe to America to make it possible to utilize them as farm laborers. The Geneva Convention of 1926 permitted this practice if the POW was willing and the work did not contribute directly to the war effort.

A program was established in Kansas for farmers to obtain POWs if they provided transportation to and from the prison camp, a noon meal, and a horse for a mounted guard. They had to employ a minimum of four men to make it practicable to send a guard and had to pay the workers thirty-five cents per hour; the farmers could work the prisoners a maximum of eight hours per day. A number of Lee's neighbors eagerly took advantage of this opportunity and, nationally, 115,368 POWs were utilized in the farm labor force.

Agricultural historians have accurately labeled the war period as the "second American agricultural revolution." Farmers were now encouraged to plant "from fence row to fence row" and produce all they could. One-fourth of their production was required for the military forces and for Lend-Lease recipients. Although acreage in production in 1945 was 5 percent less than it was in 1932, overall production was much greater between 1941 and 1945 than it was from 1935 to 1939.

Production on these acres increased significantly with the use of fertilizers, which rose from 8.3 million tons in 1939 to 12.5 million tons in 1944. Gains also were registered because the excess capacity for processing food and fibers of the depression years was fully utilized. Finally, good weather during the war years compared to the terrible droughts from 1934 to 1936 helped to raise production. A study by the Bureau of Agricultural Statistics estimated that of the 45 percent increase in crop productivity from 1939 to 1945, 14 percent came from increased use of fertilizers, 14 percent from soil and crop improvements, and 17 percent from good weather conditions.

Labor shortages forced an increased use of tractors, harvesting and haying machinery, and sprayers. In 1939 there were two tractors for every nine farm units; by 1945 this ratio had increased to two for every five units (that is, the number of tractors in 1940 was 1,545,000; by the war's end, there were 2,425,000). Higher prices and supports brought greater agricultural income, permitting farmers to purchase expensive machinery and to make farm and home improvements. Despite wartime shortages of rubber and gasoline, farmers were able to acquire and utilize gasoline-powered equipment to a greater extent than ever before. Most tractors now came equipped with synthetic rubber tires, which made them speedier and far more efficient.

Agricultural income per capita increased 250 percent from 1939 to 1945. Per capita industrial income doubled in the same period. In addition, the OPA helped consumers immensely by holding inflation to 27 percent during the war years. This prosperity permitted farmers to mechanize, to improve homes and outbuildings, to reduce their debts, and to accumulate reserves. Farmers wishing to retire in the prewar period had to sell their farms. In the war years and thereafter, large farms grew larger because of the mechanized ability to farm more acres, and retiring agrarians, now finding renters eager to acquire more acres, could retain possession of their land to reap the benefits of rising land prices.

One of Lee's neighbors, George Hultgren, received an FSA loan in 1940 and saved his dairy farm. Officials told him they doubted, with seven children to raise, that he could pay off his debt in the required forty years. Five years later, as a result of wartime prosperity, he was able to retire the mortgage. Ralph Lee, however, did not fully share in this agrarian affluence because of problems arising from the operation of his service station.

Jim Haun, who was the lessee at the time, decided in late 1942 to join the navy before his draft number was called. The critical labor shortage made it difficult to find another renter so Lee decided to resume management of the service station. Farm conditions were good, but he could make more money selling auto products than he could working on a rented farm; if his station remained idle, he would receive no rent from it. From the fall of 1942 until the spring of 1943 he operated the station while trying to keep up with the winter farm work. Besides caring for the horses, he had to milk and feed seventeen cows and thirty head of stock cattle. He readied the cattle feed before he went to town to work, and Alice and his son fed the livestock before and after school. In 1943 in March, the traditional time of the year for a farm sale, he sold his livestock and machinery by auction and purchased a small acreage on the outskirts of town where he could keep a few milk cows and chickens so Alice would have some pin money.

The service station business at that time was different from when he had built the business more than a decade earlier. The rationing of gasoline and tires had brought about a great change. American forces in World War II were highly mobilized, so these two commodities were vital to the war effort. Japanese forces overran Southeast Asia early in the conflict and by 1942 they had control of 90 percent of America's sources for crude rubber, thus creating an emergency in supplies. The government instituted a crash program of research to develop synthetic rubber.

The most common form of synthetic rubber, Buna-S, was expensive; no factories had been built in the United States to produce it because cheap Asian crude had been available. The government immediately began constructing more than fifty synthetic rubber plants, and as a stopgap measure, on June 12, 1942, President Roosevelt issued a call for a scrap rubber drive. The Lee service station served as the collector for the White City area and 11.5 tons of old tires, raincoats, rubber boots, garden hose, and garter straps were gathered, for which 1 cent per pound was paid, and the government purchased it all for $25 per ton. Profits were donated to charity. To save gasoline, but primarily to conserve tires, a national speed limit of 35 miles per hour was imposed. The synthetic plants were leased to rubber companies on a cost-plus basis. In 1944 the production of Buna-S reached 800,000 tons, which constituted 87 percent of the rubber that civilians consumed in the United States, and the crisis passed.

Gasoline supplies were plentiful early in the war except on the East Coast, in District I as it was labeled, which was supplied primarily by sea-going tankers. German submarines took their toll of these ships before being driven off the coast by the middle of the war. That district, composed of seventeen states and the District of Columbia from South Carolina northward, had gas rationing imposed in mid-1942. For the rest of the nation, gasoline shortages were not common until late 1943 and 1944, but government planners viewed nationwide rationing as a means of conserving vital rubber sources. President Roosevelt waited until after the midterm elections of 1942 before announcing a national plan of rationing, effective January 1, 1943. Later, gas supplies became critical everywhere as increasing amounts of petroleum were devoted to the production of 100 octane aviation fuel, toluene for TNT, and butadiene for synthetic rubber. Gasoline rationing was the greatest sacrifice that civilians made during the war, and there was widespread criticism of the program until they were educated to accept its necessity.

Each automobile was allowed five tires, and new ones could not be purchased until the synthetics became available. Ration cards and windshield stickers were distributed. The holder of an A card received three gallons per week; B cards for workers in essential industries received a supplementary allowance; and the more generous C cards were for doctors. Holders of an X card could get unlimited gallons, and two hundred congressmen immediately requested and received X cards. Truckers were assigned T cards and could buy all the gasoline needed. Wholesale delivery to replenish Lee's supply tanks was not entirely reliable because of the war shortages, so he maintained a ten-gallon hand pump of "regular" gasoline for emergencies.

When he sold gasoline, Lee had to collect stamps as well as money and paste the stamps on special OPA forms. The OPA was placed in charge of this rationing system because it was the only agency at the time with a functioning national network of offices. When he was resupplied, Lee turned in the necessary stamps to the wholesale trucker. This unpopular rationing inevitably gave rise to a black market as criminals counterfeited the stamps and sold them to dealers and individuals in large cities. This fraud was not practiced in small towns like White City, however, as Lee knew his customers well and was aware of how much gasoline they were purchasing each week.

One of Lee's greatest problems was keeping the vehicles of his war workers in operation. The Army Air Forces had built a base at Delavan, twelve miles away, early in the war. The base's primary function was to service heavy bombers and prepare them and their crews for overseas duty. Thirty-one citizens of White City worked there, including eight women who sewed and folded parachutes. This job was not as glamorous as that of Rosie the Riveter but was just as vital to the war effort. Although the workers carpooled, eventually their tires wore out on the sand and gravel roads and new ones were unavailable until synthetic tires made their appearance late in the war. When tires became bald, Lee devised various kinds of liners for them, occasionally by cutting the beads off smaller ones and inserting them as an extra pad between the inner tubes and sharp rocks. Most war workers carried a trunk full of spares, and each evening on their return from work, they dropped off several flats. Late into the evening, Lee dismantled them with hand irons, patched the inner tubes, and reassembled them for pickup early in the morning.

In May 1945, V-E Day was greeted with great enthusiasm, and V-J Day that August brought much celebration. The telephone operator blew the city siren intermittently for a long period of time, the church bells were rung, businesses closed for the day, and thanksgiving services were held in the Christian church. Most veterans came home in a few months but the return of Lee's daughter was delayed.

Ruth Lee had joined the Army Nurse Corps in 1941. She was on duty at Fitzsimmons Army Hospital in Denver when some of the more seriously wounded of Pearl Harbor were flown there for medical attention. Ralph was immensely proud of her as she served in the Fifth Army in North Africa, Sicily, and Italy. She collected five battle stars, and his pride increased with each star as he and the family closely followed the news of these campaigns. Ruth was on occupation duty for more than a year before she returned home on furlough in June 1946. However, her valorous deeds had cost her. While crossing the Apennine Mountains in Italy, she had suffered frostbite on her hands and feet, which affected her heart and circulatory system. As she drove to her new assignment in Chicago following her visit to White City, she died at the wheel and her car went into a ditch before stopping. Her death was a devastating blow to Ralph and his family.

Following the war, Lee decided to try a new occupation. Jim Haun had purchased the town pool hall after his discharge. It was a very popular haunt for the men of the town, and after the war it became a favorite hangout for veterans. As a result of the GI Bill, veterans were paid twenty dollars per week for a maximum of fifty-two weeks while they sought suitable employment. With this increase in business, Haun needed help and offered Lee a job. Lee sold his station to a returning veteran and worked for Haun until late in 1949 when he suffered a debilitating stroke.

Paralyzed on one side of his body, he was forced to retire. For the next several years he suffered intermittent periods of ill health and underwent operations for the repair of old hernias acquired on the farm, a defective gall bladder, and other medical problems. He and his wife celebrated their fiftieth wedding anniversary in April 1964. Ralph died quietly in his sleep two years later on July 5 and was buried in the local cemetery.

Suggested Readings

Walter W. Wilcox, *The Farmer in the Second World War* (Ames, IA, 1947), is the standard account of this topic. Samuel Liss explores the issue of farm labor wages in three essays in *Agricultural History*: "The Concept and Determination of Prevailing Wages in Agriculture during World War II," vol. 24 (January 1950); "Farm Wage Boards under the Cooperative Extension Service during World War II," vol. 27 (July 1953); and "Farm Wage Boards under the Wage Stabilization Program during World War II," vol. 30 (January 1956). Patrick O'Brien, Thomas D. Isern, and R. David Lumly, "Stalag Sunflower," *Kansas History* 6–7 (Autumn 1984), discusses the use of POW labor in Kansas. James A. Maxwell and Margaret N. Balcom, "Gasoline Rationing in the United States,"

Quarterly Journal of Economics 60 (August 1946), examines the rationing issue. Paul M. O'Leary, "Wartime Rationing and Government Planning," *American Political Science Review* 39 (December 1945), written by a former OPA official, discusses how rationing should be administered in the next war. Lee's obituary is in the *White City Register* (Kansas), July 7, 1966.

2

Mary Mihelcich
Iron Miner

Dana Miller

During both the Civil War and World War I, American women took advantage of the opportunities that opened up as millions of men put on uniforms. History repeated itself during World War II. Institutions of higher education (including those in the Ivy League) were suddenly desperate for students. Women discovered professional paths unblocked, even in such male preserves as medicine and the law. Women also obtained or regained access to posts that had been closed to them, such as bank teller, public school teacher (married women had often been banned because of possible pregnancy), and a variety of jobs in industry. Victorian strictures, such as the prewar Illinois ordinance prohibiting women from wearing slacks in public, vanished as Rosie the Riveter picked up her air hammer. By 1943 women made up almost one-third of the American industrial workforce.

The development of two major founts of American wartime production are traced by Dana Miller: the almost limitless high-grade iron ore from the Mesabi Range in northeastern Minnesota and the blue-collar labor of women helping to build the "great arsenal of democracy." Miller shows, through the experiences of Mary Mihelcich in the Iron Range, the problems faced by women when breaking into this physically demanding world.

Dana Miller earned his degrees from Bemidji State College in Minnesota and the University of North Dakota. His research has focused principally on mining in northern Minnesota. He works for the Mineland Reclamation Division of the Iron Range Resources and Rehabilitation Board, Chisholm, Minnesota.

M innesota's Iron Range is located in the northeastern portion of the state, one hundred eighty miles north of the Minneapolis–St. Paul metropolitan area. Its twenty-plus municipalities are situated along U.S. Highway 169 from Coleraine in the southwest to Ely and Babbitt in the northeast, a distance of some one hundred ten miles.

The name Iron Range is not a misnomer. Since the first shipment of iron ore in 1884, from the Soudan Mine, near Tower, more than four billion tons of iron ore have found their way to eastern steel mills. If all four billion tons were loaded on a single train in standard ore cars, the

17

train would be more than 330,000 miles long and stretch nearly four-teen times around the Earth.[1]

The basic method of mining used on the Iron Range has always been the open pit process. Open pit mining consists of removing the overburden—the mixture of sand, gravel, and rock that covers the ore body. The ore is then removed in horizontal layers. Much of the ore mined in this way was known as direct shipping, which because of its high iron content only needed to be loaded into railroad cars for shipment to the mills.

Open pit mining was very labor intensive; many men were needed to mine and load the ore. This type of work, with its long hours and backbreaking dangerous labor, required little in the way of education or language skills. Much of the labor force in the late nineteenth century came from abroad, as the expanding industrial base of the United States at that time demanded more and more workers who did not expect high salaries. Millions of immigrants passed through the ports of Boston and New York on their way to the factories, plants, and mills of America. In this respect the Iron Range was no different from Chicago, New York, and other industrial centers. Tens of thousands of immigrants found their way to northeastern Minnesota and the drudgery of iron ore mining.[2]

From 1890 until the start of World War I, immigrants came to the Iron Range by the boatload to work the mines and log the forests. In 1940 at least fifty separate ethnic groups could be found residing on the range. Most of these people were from the British Isles, northern and southern Europe, and the Slavic regions of eastern Europe. Because of World War I, the flood of immigration slowed to a trickle and never again approached prewar levels.[3]

Over the course of a century, more than four hundred iron ore mines have operated on the Iron Range, the majority of them the property of one corporation, the Oliver Iron Mining Company, a subsidiary of the United States Steel Corporation. The rest of the mines were owned by a number of companies, some with large holdings and many with only one or two mines.[4] The Oliver, due to its size and economic influence on both other companies and the population at large, determined much of the range's business and social lifestyle by its actions and policies.

Much smaller than the Oliver was the Butler Brothers mining company, a family-owned firm that held title to about twenty relatively small properties in 1941. Of these, fourteen had shipped ore during the decade of the 1930s.[5] Patrick and Mary Ann Butler had emigrated to the

United States from Ireland in 1848 and raised eight children, six of them boys. Of these six, five of them would actively participate in the Butler Brothers Company. The sixth, Pierce, went into law and was appointed to the U.S. Supreme Court in 1923 and served there until his death in 1939. The five remaining brothers formed a construction company in 1894 that soon had a number of major projects to its credit, including the Minnesota and North Dakota state capitols and iron ore loading docks in Wisconsin.

The iron ore docks construction led to several contracts on the then-developing Iron Range. In 1902, Butler Brothers stripped the overburden at the Leetonia Mine near Hibbing and then turned the mine over to the Interstate Iron Company for mining. More stripping contracts followed and then, in 1913, Butler Brothers leased several properties in the Nashwauk area and went into the iron ore mining business.[6]

The brothers took an active interest in the mining properties, overseeing operations or talking with the employees about their families and living conditions. The company became known for treating employees fairly and paying a decent wage for a day's work, an anomaly among mining companies.

This paternalism was put to the test during the Great Depression. Much of America's industrial might was based on steel, which is made from iron ore. As the country plunged into the depression, the steel industry buckled and then collapsed, taking the Iron Range with it. In 1929 forty-three million tons of iron ore were shipped from the Mesabi Range to eastern mills. In contrast, only two million tons were required by steelmakers in 1932.[7] Because iron ore mining represented the only industry on the range, the effects were devastating. Men found work when and where they could, sometimes only one or two days per month. Many of the young men and women were forced to leave the area and search for work in the cities.[8] Butler Brothers did what it could, hiring men the company did not really need to strip and stockpile ore for the future, although no one had any idea when the depression would end. Many workers with families who lived in company-owned housing were allowed to stay, paying rent only after everyone was fed and clothed.[9]

Throughout the decade of the 1930s, ore shipments fluctuated like a yo-yo. In 1934, fourteen million tons were mined, forty-six million tons in 1937, and then back to thirteen million in 1938.[10] Workers would find employment for as many as six days per week during some periods and as little as one day per month during others. Many survived by growing vegetable gardens and by hunting and fishing for meat for the table. Often, state game wardens would look the other way when the unemployed took too many fish or shot wild game out of season.[11]

The depression began to subside in the steel industry largely because of the gathering clouds of war in Europe and Asia and the need for American steel to make the implements of conflict for both the United States and European nations. On the Iron Range, many shipments of iron ore came from stockpiles mined during the 1930s, resulting in little increase in employment. In 1939, thirty million tons of iron ore were shipped, and with the stockpiles depleted, mining resumed as never before. The war years' production topped seventy million tons in 1942 and averaged more than sixty million tons from 1940 through 1945.[12]

With the Japanese attack on Pearl Harbor and the U.S. entry into the war, the Iron Range went from no employment to a labor shortage almost overnight. The mines of the Mesabi were opened as quickly as possible. Inactive mines that had filled with millions of gallons of water had to be pumped dry before operations could resume.[13] Butler Brothers called back to work as many of its former employees as could be contacted and hired men with no mining experience as well as those fresh out of the Civilian Conservation Corps.[14] Unfortunately, the federal government not only asked for a much increased production of iron ore but then also drafted many of the men needed to meet that production.[15]

As a result of the National Labor Relations Act of 1935 (the Wagner Act), the federal government put its power behind workers wishing to organize. Subsequent agreements between the Steelworkers Organizing Committee (SWOC) and the mining companies set a framework for hours, wages, and, very important, seniority.[16] One seniority provision was that a union member who was drafted or joined the armed forces maintained and continued to build seniority in the company even though he might be gone for quite some time. Some absences turned out to be for several years. This provision affected many workers who were hired as the depression ended and shortly afterward were inducted into the military.

To keep employees and former employees informed of happenings within the company and to provide a message board for those in the military, the *Butler Miner* began monthly publication in June 1941. It was mailed to all employees and servicemen who had worked for the company. An article in the *Miner* indicated in January 1942 that twenty-five Butler employees were in military service. In May 1945, near the war's end, 276 men were in uniform and 8 more had been killed in action.[17]

Early in the war, before draft quotes were raised, enough manpower was available to meet increased iron ore production, due largely to previous stockpiling, more efficient equipment, and improved ore-handling methods. However, as the United States mobilized, it became difficult to find the manpower to meet schedules. Like many companies, Butler Brothers turned to a large, but largely untapped resource: women.[18]

Prior to World War II women essentially had no place in the business of mining. Nearly all jobs, except for a few clerical positions, were filled by men. Generally, the companies believed that women could not perform the labor-intensive tasks associated with open pit mining. Further, the thought that women could satisfactorily operate heavy equipment such as trucks, shovels, conveyor belts, and the like was anathema. This discrimination against women in mining began to diminish as production quotas grew and the male workforce was called to military service. In early 1943 it became apparent to Butler Brothers that women represented the only available source of labor to maintain production at required levels. The company began to accept applications for employment and hired miners without regard to gender. Women would soon become an important part of the Butler Brothers operations. One such woman was Mary Mihelcich.

Delivered by a midwife in Nashwauk, Minnesota, on February 3, 1922, Mary was the eighth of nine children of Frances and Joe Mihelcich, who had emigrated from Croatia, a part of the Austro-Hungarian empire, in 1906. Joe found relatively constant employment during the 1920s, but when the depression hit, the family was forced to move to different communities in the area to find work. On many occasions, Joe left the family in Nashwauk and searched for work in distant towns.

The Mihelcichs, desperately poor like most other immigrants who depended on mining for a livelihood, scratched their way through the 1930s living a hand-to-mouth existence. At best, Joe would get three to six days of work per month and the strain of not providing for his family led to a bout with alcohol; it was a bout he lost. All this made a bad situation for the Mihelcich family even worse. When Mary was in the ninth grade in 1937, she quit school "because I didn't have no clothes to wear and no money. So I quit . . . to go to work and help my mother out . . . 'cause we lived on relief for years and years."

Mary cleaned houses for those few who could afford it, earning about ten cents per hour for a few hours each week. When the opportunity arose, she also picked up a job in the local café, washing dishes and doing janitorial work. A Works Progress Administration (WPA) project in Nashwauk provided nearly two years of employment at eighty dollars per month, and when that ended she got a job in the school laundry until 1943.

Mary and her friend Ann Shebly learned that Butler Brothers was hiring women to work in the mines around Nashwauk:

> I and my friend Ann went in there and her and a couple of other girls got called but they didn't call me. Well, my brother used to work for Butler's. And he [got a bad reputation], but they kept him because he was one of the best workers they had. Finally though, Butler had had enough and one of the bosses came and said, "I'm sorry, Nicky. We've kept you and kept you because you work more than two, three other fellas, but you're done now." So . . . then when I went to sign up, of course, they recognized my brother's name right away. So they didn't bother calling me. So I jumped on my bike, [go] over there, and I tell them, "I want to see this fella [the personnel officer] about a job." [The secretary] says, "I'm sorry, [he's] not here." And I says, "That's alright, I haven't got anything to do, so I'll just sit here in front of the place and sleep here and maybe someone will come along and they'll go get me a sandwich." She looks at me, gets beet red in the face, and says, "Just a minute." She goes in the back and out comes [a superintendent]. He says, "Can I help you, Mary?" I said, "Ya, I want to know. I think we [Ann and I] was the first two girls to come out here. And you hired three girls and you haven't called me. And you know why! Because of my brother! That isn't fair. You give me a chance to show you what I can do, and if you're not satisfied with my work—fire me!" So, in a day or two he calls me with work.

When Mary reported, the company assigned her to the Galbraith group of open pit mines, just northeast of Nashwauk. Large (by 1930s standards) electric shovels scooped the soft ore from the pit and loaded it into trucks capable of carrying about fifteen tons per load. The trucks would haul the ore to a surface-level stockpile or dump the load where it could be moved by conveyor belt to rail cars for shipment, usually to Superior, Wisconsin, or Duluth, Minnesota. Large ore-carrying boats then transported the ore to steel mills along the lower Great Lakes. Of course, as more and more ore was mined, the pit became deeper and consequently the ore became more difficult and expensive to transport to the surface.

At this point, Butler Brothers made use of several novel solutions to mine all the ore that was available. The two most favored were the barney car and the conveyor belt. The barney car was a small ore car on a rail system powered by an electric motor, which raised the ore to a higher level of the mine to trucks or a conveyor belt. Mary recalled, "I worked on . . . the barney car. We had a steep incline so they put this [track] in there and they had an operator on top that pulled the levers and [it was] like the bottom of a box car. It had a chain on it and it went down in the bottom and it had a little box and I would have to push a button [for it to go to the top]. A man at the top unloaded it. And I worked on the [conveyor] belt line too."

Mary Mihelcich (*left*) and Ann Shebly with mine buildings in the background. *Courtesy of Mary Mihelcich*

The conveyor belt systems used by Butler Brothers were, in some cases, as long as five hundred feet. Mary would walk along the length of the belt, "and it was our job if the truck dumped any rocks or anything [fell] on the runway . . . to go and pick 'em up. When they dumped that day, they let me stay there, because I was such a good worker. So, I'd . . . take the broom and sweep the whole place down. One of [the] truck drivers says, 'One of these days, Mary, we're going to get you a mop and pail. We want it washed out!' "

For the most part, being a conveyor belt attendant was a boring job. At the same time, a conveyor belt is a very dangerous piece of equipment to work near. "So I used to get bored and I'd get a broom and I'd sweep underneath the belt, you know. The guys used to tease me, just to pass time, and it was a little dusty and they says, 'Are you nuts?' And I says, 'I gotta do something. I just can't stand around.' When the foreman found out I was using a broom, he says, 'Mary, you don't do that! The broom could get caught, and up you go with the belt.' And we never had safety hats." In those days, the company encouraged, but did not require, its employees to wear safety glasses and boots. Few did so.

Mary received a lesson in the dangerous nature of conveyor belts near the end of the ore season. "I remember that one time I was up on top and that was in September. Colder than heck. So I sit close to the machinery [because] it gave off heat. . . . [Once] I fell asleep. I don't know what woke me up, [but] I moved over to the side, and I bet it wasn't even five minutes and I heard a BANG against the thing in the middle. I look up and . . . the belt had split in half and hit the back plate. I could have been a goner if I hadn't moved."

In the mining industry, shift work is the norm. Once machinery is operating, it is rarely shut down, necessitating round-the-clock schedules. Butler Brothers employees worked eight-hour shifts and rotated between days (7 A.M.–3 P.M.), afternoons (3 P.M.–11 P.M.), and nights (11 P.M.–7 A.M.) on a regular basis. It is interesting that even without a full complement of workers, overtime was seldom available. Mary said that most of her overtime came as a result of working the shift following hers because the person scheduled did not show up. This proved to be a rare occurrence, however, because everyone needed the money.

Until the advent of taconite iron ore production in the 1950s, the iron ore industry on the Iron Range was annually affected by the harsh Minnesota winters. With freezing temperatures beginning in October and November, washing plants could no longer operate and equipment shut down for even a short period would freeze up. Also, the main method of transporting iron ore (by boat on Lake Superior) was not possible because the lake froze enough to close the inland harbors and prevent the ore boats from operating. Although some men were employed throughout the winter in stripping operations and some stockpiled ore for the next ore season, these jobs were given strictly on a seniority basis. The rest of the workers were laid off. Of course, management personnel and others such as those in clerical and accounting positions continued to work, but they were not covered by the union contracts and thus were exempt from seniority requirements. Mary, with only three years of employment, never got the chance to work through the winter.[19] To help make it to the next ore season, Mary saved what money she could, and the state of Minnesota provided a small amount of unemployment compensation.

Mary lived at home with her mother throughout the war. Rationing was in effect and some items were hard to obtain, but the family got by better than they had during the depression. "My [sister's] husband went into the service and she lived with us for about a year, so we got enough [ration] stamps. You were only allowed [to buy] one pack of cigarettes in each place. So, dumb Mary used to go to every joint [bar] in Nashwauk to buy a package of cigarettes to send to my brother overseas. Well, he comes back from the war, he says, 'Heck, I had a good buddy and he never smoked so he would go buy carton after carton and he never let me pay for the cigarettes.' I says, 'And you couldn't tell me that! I'm embarrassed, begging cigarettes for you.'"

In the small towns of the Iron Range, Mary found that the nightlife and other entertainment, except for the movies, left a lot to be desired. "We went to the Roadway [a bar in neighboring Calumet]. And Ann's sister worked at a place in Bovey." Most of the time, they had to hitchhike to other towns. "There's a reason why we bummed [a ride], because back then who had cars? Maybe there was ten to fifteen cars in town [owned by] young guys, ya know. And they took you out once or twice and that was enough. Come across, ya know. [If you don't] 'we ain't gonna spend money on you.' So I told the girls, 'I don't know about you, if I have to go out myself, I'll go out there and bum.' So I never dated." Mary's friends changed often during the war. "Because girls would get married, and I'd have different friends. So there was about three or four changes before they all got married on me."[20]

For the most part, the war was always an item of conversation, especially when any of the local boys were killed or wounded. But with each passing year, it ceased to be the only concern. There was a resoluteness to finish the job of destroying the Axis powers, but it was made within the framework of a tough existence for those working in the mines. Those on the Iron Range home front seemed to realize that the best way to help the war effort was not to indulge in rabid patriotism, but to do the jobs assigned to them and get by on what was available.[21] Ironically, for Mary Mihelcich, the war years, with all of their restrictions, layoffs, rationing, and other annoyances, were an improvement over the depression period. At least she had a job and some money.

After the 1945 iron ore season and the end of the war, Mary was laid off by Butler Brothers. That fall and winter many of the men returned from the service and reported back for work. Under union rules, they maintained their positions on the seniority roster and were called back based on their time of service with Butler Brothers, for which their military service was considered as time actually worked for the company. Mary found herself well down the list, with many World War II veterans in front of her. As a result of a slowdown in the iron ore industry following the war and the sale of Butler Brothers to the M. A. Hanna Company in 1948, she did not work again at Butler Brothers.[22] Her three years of wartime employment did not qualify her for a pension.

Mary Mihelcich has lived a tough life but has taken it all with the stoicism for which Iron Range residents are known. Mary married in 1953 and had five children. Although her husband died at age fifty-eight of cancer, she carried on, raising the children, living in her own home, and making her own way. Now in her mid-seventies, she remains as feisty, independent, and honest as she was in her younger years. She is in many ways typical of the Iron Rangers who "wo-manned" the home front and supplied the support and the iron ore to win World War II.

Notes

1. D. N. Skillings, *Minnesota Mining Directory for 1995* (Duluth, MN, 1995), 44–58.

2. Dana Miller, "Immigration, Naturalization, Americanization: A View on the Establishment of a Cultural Identity on Minnesota's Mesabi Range," paper delivered at the Missouri Valley History Conference, Omaha, Nebraska, March 1988.

3. John Syrjamaki, "Mesabi Communities: A Study of Their Development" (Ph.D. diss., Princeton University, 1940), chap. 1.

4. Skillings, *Minnesota Mining Directory for 1995*, 44–58.

5. J. J. Craig, *Mining Directory of Minnesota 1941* (Minneapolis, MN, 1941), 180.

6. *Butler Miner* (Cooley, MN), May 1944, 2–18.

7. J. J. Craig, *Mining Directory of Minnesota 1933* (Minneapolis, MN, 1933), 196.

8. Dana Miller, *The Iron Range Resources and Rehabilitation Board: The First Fifty Years* (Eveleth, MN, 1991), 1–5.

9. Craig, *Mining Directory of Minnesota 1941*, 202.

10. John Peil (Minnesota conservation officer), conversation with author, 1965.

11. H. H. Wade, *Mining Directory of Minnesota 1950* (Minneapolis, MN, 1950), 222.

12. *Skillings Mining Review* (Duluth, MN), various issues, 1941–43.

13. Milan Grozdanich (former Butler Brothers employee), tape-recorded interview with author, August 10, 1998.

14. Ibid.

15. Bert Andreas (former Butler Brothers executive), interview with author, August 5, 1998.

16. *Butler Miner*, February 1942, 12; May 1945, 11.

17. Mary Mihelcich (former Butler Brothers employee), interview with author, July 25, 1998. For the purposes of this article, Mary's maiden name has been used.

18. *Butler Miner*, April 1944, 10.

19. Andreas, interview.

20. Mihelcich, interview.

21. *Butler Miner*, March 1944, 10.

22. Mihelcich, interview.

Suggested Readings

The author has studied Iron Range history for more than three decades. There is no single volume that provides a comprehensive history of the area, but there are a number of monographs on ethnicity, immigration, radicalism, and other topics. Many published works about the region are of a corporate or economic nature and are limited in scope to a single company, such as Butler Brothers, and were generally aided in some way by the company itself. Additionally, iron ore mining companies exhibited an almost xenophobic fear of any kind of publicity. In many instances, records were destroyed when the company ceased doing business on the Iron Range or were closed to any kind of historical inquiry. For historians, much of the record of company-employee interaction must be gathered through oral histories. Although oral histories are admittedly imperfect, in some cases they represent the only viable means of providing that record.

Blum, John M. *V Was for Victory: Politics and American Culture during World War II*. New York, 1976.

Hoopes, Roy. *Americans Remember: The Home Front*. New York, 1977.

Lingeman, Richard. *Don't You Know There's a War On?* New York, 1970.

Terkel, Studs. *"The Good War": An Oral History of World War Two*. New York, 1985.

3

William H. Hastie
The Freedom to Serve

C. Alvin Hughes

The war not only opened new opportunities for women but it also accelerated the efforts of black Americans to achieve social, political, and economic equality. The Roosevelt administration, often because of heavy prodding by the president's wife, Eleanor, moved cautiously to help black Americans with the Fair Employment Practices Commission. Pessimistic analysts predicted that the Democratic Party was spelling its doom by eroding its base in the segregationist "solid South." In fact, this courting of black Americans proved to be a long-term source of strength to the Democrats as blacks moving to Los Angeles, Detroit, and New York City exercised the ballot. In retrospect, World War II largely solidified the transfer of black allegiance from the Republican Party of Abraham Lincoln to the Democratic Party of Franklin D. Roosevelt.

Black Americans also sought the opportunity to fight for their country. At the beginning of the war, small numbers of blacks served in segregated regiments in the army; others waited on tables in the navy as mess attendants. However, no blacks flew for the Army Air Corps and none wore the Marine Corps uniform. To rectify this situation, William H. Hastie, a member of the so-called Black Brain Trust, joined the Roosevelt administration to grapple with challenges confronting black Americans. Hastie faced rough sledding, as Alvin Hughes reveals.

Professor C. Alvin Hughes earned his doctorate at Ohio University; his principal field of research and publication is African American history. Since 1977, he has taught at Austin Peay State University in Clarksville, Tennessee. Among his publications is "Hate Only Hate, Fear Only Cowardice: William Pickens, a Philosopher of Activism," *The Griot* (1999).

As the countries of Europe and Asia moved toward war, the United States began to emerge from the throes of an economic downswing of seemingly unending proportions. The African American population, which traditionally experienced the "last hired, first fired" syndrome, seized the opportunity, made possible by the high demand for manpower in the military and in the defense plants, to expand its role in national defense. To gain better political leverage, African American voters began to make the great shift from the Republican Party to the Democratic Party and to the administration of Franklin D. Roosevelt. Scholar-activists such as William H. Hastie and the other members of what was referred to as the Black Brain Trust decided to use the end of the Great Depression and the economic opportunities created by the war to catapult the African American agenda to a higher national level. They demanded that the United States do the right thing and allow its African American citizens the freedom to serve the nation at home and abroad in its hour of greatest need. The Black Brain Trust decided that there would be no "close the ranks" pledges during World War II as there were during World War I, but full speed ahead for "victory at home and abroad." The African American press picked up the theme and published it widely as the Double-V Campaign.

In 1940, as the United States prepared for war, it was not clear what roles African Americans were to play in this major event. In fact, their very status as citizens was not well established in the mind or customs of the majority population. This lack of clarity regarding their status placed African Americans in a precarious situation. Most of them understood that the Fourteenth Amendment to the U.S. Constitution stated very explicitly that "all persons born . . . in the United States . . . are citizens of the United States" and as such had all the privileges and opportunities, and responsibilities and obligations, to utilize their talents for national defense as well as for the general welfare of the nation.[1] However, in 1896 the Supreme Court had sanctioned in *Plessy v. Ferguson* the principle of "separate but equal," which implied that during this national crisis African Americans were expected to do their equal part but separate from others in fighting for the same cause: freedom and democracy.

This principle of "separate but equal," or doing your part under separate and unequal conditions, did not sit well with the "new Negro," the scholar-activists who believed in "the system" and in the principle of democracy. How can victims of an unjust system fight for the freedom of others under a totalitarian regime without questioning their own system and the limitations it placed upon them? The U.S. involvement in World War II provided another venue for African Americans to continue their struggle to remove "separate but equal" from the legal language and daily practice in American life.

The Double-V Campaign, as it was conceived, required deliberate action on two fronts. The military needed manpower to fill its ranks, and African Americans made themselves available in numbers far beyond the ability of the established Negro units in the armed services to accommodate them. This dilemma challenged the War Department— either stop accepting African American inductees or rapidly increase the number of segregated units to place them in. The Black Brain Trust, however, suggested that African American inductees be allowed to serve in the same units with other inductees, thereby challenging the principle of "separate but equal" in the military service. The second part of

William Hastie, appointed as civilian aide to the secretary of war, 1940–1943. *Courtesy of Moorland-Spingarn Research Center, Howard University, Washington, DC*

the Double-V Campaign demanded that discrimination be ended in defense plants so that African American civilians could get jobs and work to produce war matériel in a variety of industries in a cooperative and integrated environment.

The Black Brain Trust included such public intellectuals as Walter White of the National Association for the Advancement of Colored People (NAACP); Mary McLeod Bethune, president of Bethune-Cookman College; Robert C. Weaver, a Harvard-trained economist; Eugene K. Jones, executive secretary of the National Urban League; and others who served as "Negro advisers" in federal agencies during the New Deal and war era. As a member of the trust, William H. Hastie, dean of Howard University Law School, was appointed civilian aide to Secretary of War Henry Stimson. Hastie brought his years of experience as a civil rights lawyer and as an expert on the Fourteenth Amendment to the War Department to challenge the wall of segregation that hindered America's ability to prepare for the war and to use all of its resources, especially its manpower, efficiently.[2]

William H. Hastie was born in 1904 into the privileged class of the black community in an integrated section of Knoxville, Tennessee. Hastie's father was a businessman, a pharmacist, and a graduate of Howard University in Washington, DC, but he earned a living mostly as a clerk in the U.S. Pension Office. Hastie's mother, Roberta Childs-Hastie, was a professional career woman with degrees from Fisk University in Nashville, Tennessee, and Talladega College in Talladega, Alabama; however, she gave up her career to tutor her son so he could take his place among the best and the brightest. As William's tutor, Roberta Hastie had a great influence upon her son, whom she groomed to be an example of what others could be if they were given the proper education and training. Described as a "race woman, she was a live-wire. Civil Rights–minded. Very strong character,"[3] Roberta Hastie was a good model for W. E. B. Du Bois's concept of the talented tenth and their obligation to lead the race by example. Young Willie grew up under the watchful eye of two parents who instilled in him the need to aim high.[4]

A change in his father's employment allowed the Hastie family to move from Knoxville to Washington, DC, which meant that Willie had access to one of the best high schools in the city, Paul Lawrence Dunbar High, which produced a series of famous alumni, including Charles Drew, Montague Cobb, Adelaide Cromwell Hill, and Robert C. Weaver. Dunbar High created new stars, not Uncle Toms, who were expected to "do well in school, go to college, and enter a profession."[5] Dunbar High not only had the best and brightest teachers but also parents who insisted that their children toe the line. Hastie graduated in 1921 as valedictorian of his class, with a strong sense of the need to be militant against both discrimination and racial indignity.[6]

From Dunbar High, Hastie went off to Amherst College along with two of his classmates, Montague Cobb and George Winston Harry. While at Amherst, Hastie and the other African American students experienced, firsthand, racism at work through the practices of ostracism and exclusion in social gatherings and in extracurricular activities. In spite of these obvious distractions, Hastie excelled in both scholarship and in athletics, earning a Phi Beta Kappa key and several other honors. He won academic awards in several areas: the Walker Prize in Mathematics; the Porter Prize Admission Contest for Latin, English, and Mathematics; the Addison Brown Scholarship for best scholar for three years; the Woods Prize for excellence in culture and faithfulness to duty as a man and scholar; and several other awards in German, Greek, and philosophy. He was valedictorian of his college class as well.[7]

After Amherst, Hastie took a position at the prestigious Bordentown Manual Training School for Negro youth in New Jersey—the Tuskegee of the North. It tended to be more Du Boisian in that it hoped to develop men who worked as carpenters rather than simply being carpenters without manhood virtues or the desire for full citizenship rights. Du Bois argued that the object of all true education was not to make men carpenters; it was to make carpenters men. Bordentown was a leadership training school for middle-class Negro students, a black Forest Hills for the tennis club set. Hastie spent two years teaching at Bordentown before beginning studies at Harvard Law School. From 1927 to 1930, Hastie labored at Harvard Law preparing for "the battles" that were to come.[8] He became the editor of the *Harvard Law Review*, joining a cousin, Charles Houston, as the second African American editor. Houston, Hastie, and their pupil, Thurgood Marshall of Howard University Law School, would join together later to chip away at the wall of segregation that they considered an affront to the Fourteenth Amendment.

During the 1930s and 1940s, Hastie applied his expertise as a scholar, lawyer, and later a judge to uproot the doctrine of "separate but equal" and to move the nation one step closer to becoming "one nation under God with liberty and justice for all." The economic turnabout in the early 1930s forced attention in another direction. Hastie represented the NAACP in a joint effort with dozens of other African American organizations to open up jobs in the private sector in industry and in government-sponsored work programs during the 1930s. The organizations formed the Joint Committee on National Recovery, which in 1935 became a part of the mammoth National Negro Congress. As the National Negro Congress sought to open opportunities for people to work, the NAACP shifted its focus to the campaign for equalization.

The NAACP decided to launch an attack against the 1896 *Plessy* decision by insisting that the principle of "separate but equal" be implemented. The group demanded that in areas of the country that had no black educational institutions (there were, for example, no graduate schools in the South), African Americans should be allowed to attend white schools. Where black schools did exist, the facilities of those schools and the salaries of their faculty and supervisors should be equal to white schools to comply with the Supreme Court's 1896 decision. Pursuing cases first in North Carolina, then Maryland and Virginia, NAACP lawyers Marshall, Hastie, and others challenged the system that perpetuated inequality; they finally won cases in Maryland and Virginia. Although these legal victories were historic, Hastie thought that the real problem was not equalization but segregation, whereas others such as Du Bois argued that segregation was a problem only if it discriminated unfairly, "not just because it segregates."[9] When the United States entered World War II, these issues carried over into the area of defense preparation and military manpower procurement. Could the principle of "separate but equal" be effective in national mobilization or would it limit the opportunities of African Americans in the war effort?

The coming of World War II and the politics of reelection for a third term for Franklin D. Roosevelt were essential elements in the challenge against segregation and discrimination at the national level. Although many African Americans had switched from the Republican Party to the Democratic Party during the depression, President Roosevelt needed their support more acutely in the 1940 election because many conservative Democrats, especially southerners, were fed up with New Dealism. This political situation plus the arrogance of Steve Early, the president's press secretary, in the famous kicking incident, called for immediate damage control in the African American community.[10] James Sloan, a black New York City policeman on crowd-control duty at Madison Square Garden where the president was speaking, did not recognize Early and blocked his entrance to the presidential train. In his frustration with the policeman or in his haste to avoid missing the train, Early kicked the policeman in the groin. This incident, widely covered in the black press, was bound to cause defections of blacks from the Roosevelt camp. Roosevelt's African American political advisers suggested that the president make some high, visible appointments of African Americans to ensure their continued support in the upcoming election.

Roosevelt concurred and promoted Col. Benjamin O. Davis as the first African American general in the U.S. Army. The president also made two civilian appointments—Col. Campbell Johnson as assistant to General Lewis Hershey of the Selective Service, and William H. Hastie as civilian aide to Secretary of War Henry L. Stimson. The politics of reelection and the irresponsible behavior of Steve Early had opened the doors for inside agitation and for inside accommodation. As a general, Davis did all he could to minimize the difficulties faced by African American soldiers, whereas Hastie, as civilian aide to the secretary of war, sought to highlight the problems of African American soldiers and argued for the need to end discrimination and ultimately segregation in the armed forces.

Prior to 1940 the War Department followed the "well-established principle that the races should not be mixed within organizations—it is necessary to set up specific units to which colored personnel may be assigned."[11] Rear Adm. Adolphus Andrews, chief of the Bureau of Navigation, reported to the NAACP in 1937 that the navy had been considering enlisting colored sailors for some time. But after the navy experimented with some Filipinos and Samoans and deemed that test a failure, it concluded there was "no reason to believe a Negro experiment would be otherwise."[12] The Air Corps had no colored units so it did not accept applications from African Americans as flying cadets. In August 1940 the War Department declared its policy was "not to intermingle colored and white enlisted personnel in the same regimental organization."[13] Secretary of War Stimson and Assistant Secretary of War Robert P. Patterson believed that "unity can be destroyed by attempting to establish a program which is contrary to the War Department's plan. . . . Experience has proved the undesirability of mixing white and colored personnel in the same unit, and the War Department is convinced of the undesirability of changing this policy at the present time."[14] Finally on this matter, Col. E. R. Householder of the Adjutant General's Office reported to a conference of Negro editors that the "Army cannot change civilian ideas on the Negro. The Army is not a sociological laboratory. The Army's job is to train soldiers. To address itself to racial problems would be to endanger efficiency and morale."[15] The War Department's position on this issue of race was clear-cut: white and colored soldiers could not work together in the same units; so says society, so says the military. William H. Hastie believed otherwise and assumed the responsibility of moving the War Department in a new direction.

Hastie accepted his new position as civilian aide to the secretary of war with some reluctance. After all, by 1940 he was a well-established leader in the fight for integration and was entering a department where the official practice was segregation. Hastie wanted it to be made clear that he was not entering this position as an appeaser or as an apologist for the discriminatory practices of the War Department, nor was he becoming one of those Negro leaders whom W. E. B. Du Bois described as useless window dressers whose advice no one had any intention of following.[16]

Hastie, along with other African American leaders involved in the equalization-segregation-integration debate, had made his position clear: "(1) segregation was morally wrong since it embodied an undemocratic doctrine of racial inferiority, (2) segregation denied full military opportunities to black soldiers . . . inferior status . . . destroyed their esprit de corps, and (3) segregation was an unnecessary luxury."[17] As to his obligation to the War Department, Hastie was to "develop plans for the effective use of black troops/civilian (manpower), organizing black units in all branches of the service, investigating discriminatory complaints, working with the Selective Service Committee and other agencies concerned with blacks in the Armed Forces."[18] Although Hastie's position and concerns differed from those of the War Department, Thurgood Marshall advised him to take the job and use it to attack discrimination in the armed forces.[19] Perhaps something could be done "to minimize discrimination despite the segregation patterns and to prevent segregation from spreading, especially to new kinds of units and to training schools."[20]

The official guidelines under which Hastie worked were not the War Department's practice of segregation but the principles found in the Selective Training and Service Act of September 16, 1940 (which established the Selective Service System), and the statements from the White House generally advocating a system of fairness. The Selective Service Act proved to be both a help and a hindrance. It called for the training of all males between the ages of twenty-one and thirty-five for one year of military service. Section 3(A) of the Selective Service Act provided that "within the limits of the quota [generally 10 percent] . . . any person regardless of race or color . . . shall be afforded an opportunity to volunteer for induction," and Section 4A(a) of the act stated:

"In the selection and training of men . . . in the interpretation and execution of the provisions of this Act, there shall be no discrimination against any person on account of race or color."[21] However, the part of the act that proved to be a hindrance to Hastie and his goal allowed "the armed forces to retain the final say over the eligibility of any man to serve. This meant that the armed forces could use their eligibility standards to control the 'proper' proportion of blacks to be inducted."[22] In addition, the Selective Service Act did not address the problem of segregation in active-duty units at all and Secretary of War Stimson and Secretary of the Navy Frank Knox made it very clear that there would be no social experimentation in the armed forces.[23]

Statements from the White House were more encouraging to Hastie. On October 9, 1940, President Roosevelt announced that "Negroes would serve in the Armed Forces in proportion to their percentage of the general population."[24] Also, according to the White House, "it is the policy of the War Department that the services of the Negroes will be utilized on a fair and equitable basis."[25] Although the language of the White House was less than severe, the intent was that the fair and equitable treatment of Negro troops was to be within the context of a segregated armed forces. Negro troops were to be trained and assigned to Negro units. "The policy of the War Department is not to intermingle colored and white enlisted personnel in the same regimental organization [nor . . . to make changes which] would produce situations destructive to morale and detrimental to the preparation for national defense."[26]

It was quite clear from the beginning of his tenure as civilian aide to the secretary of war that Hastie's purpose in accepting the post was in direct conflict with official policy. Hastie said, "I am assuming this post in the hope that I will be able to work effectively toward the integration of the Negro into the Army and to facilitate his placement, training, and promotion."[27] To ensure that he was in line with the sentiment of other African American leaders, Hastie met with the Black Brain Trust to confirm their position on this matter and to develop a common strategy to achieve their end: a fully integrated armed forces. Not only did the Black Brain Trust go on record in support of integrating the armed forces, but so did many other organizations, such as the National Urban League, the Citizens' Nonpartisan Committee for Equal Rights in National Defense, the National Negro Congress, and, of course, the NAACP. However, conservative Negroes supported the War Department's stance and called upon African Americans to put the war first and do as was done in World War I: close ranks until afterward, and then resume the drive for victory at home. Hastie's task became even more challenging when General Davis came out against changes in the military, and the NAACP began to flip-flop on the issue of segregation in regard to training black airmen at the all-black Tuskegee Airfield.

During the three years (1940–43) that Hastie served as the civilian aide in the War Department, he approached the issues from a scholarly stance. He spent months studying the army's policies and drafting briefs and memos; he attempted to solicit from them greater freedom for Negroes to serve the nation without hindrances. Failure to lift restrictions on Negro troops, Hastie asserted, slowed down military preparedness and thus prolonged the war. Military needs demanded full participation of all citizens to bring a quick and victorious end to the war. Not only must discrimination end and segregation be lifted but the physical and verbal abuse of Negro soldiers by both military officers and the civilian population around the bases must also cease. Hastie did succeed in a small way in getting the secretary of war to issue a directive, over the objections of General Davis, to cease the practice of using any racial epithet "deemed insulting to a racial group" by military superiors.[28]

Hastie pushed the enlistment of more African Americans by getting the armed forces to advertise in Negro newspapers, by admitting blacks to new training schools in the Army Air Forces, by forcing the navy to allow African Americans to serve in positions other than messboy, and by opening the Marine Corps to black enlistees. The two great obstacles that Hastie could not overcome were the "southern culture" of the military and the decentralization of policy implementation. In other words, the military was controlled by southern racial mores and the political concept of nullification. The armed forces would not allow any practice that violated local customs or standards; if the local communities where the Negro troops were based were segregated, then so must be the armed forces. The practice of leaving the decision to the local Selective Service boards kept many blacks out of the military; and even if they were inducted, then it was still left to the armed services to decide if and when they would serve. Even though the White House issued statements on equity and fairness, those statements only applied if no one in the army and no local civilians were offended in any way. Local Selective Service boards could overlook Negroes; and furthermore, white officers who did not want to serve with Negro inductees could complain to their superiors or to their congressmen to avoid Negro units.

Hastie's persistent complaints on the behalf of Negro troops about personal assaults, verbal insults, exclusion from training slots, and separation of donated Negro blood from white blood shut doors in the Army Air Forces and Marines, and his suggestion that integrating the troops was the best solution to ending prejudice and brutality against black servicemen created a hostile environment for him in the War Department.[29] Army Chief of Staff Gen. George C. Marshall admitted that something needed to be done, but "experiments with the Army in the solution of social problems are fraught with danger to efficiency, discipline, and morale."[30] The army tried for toughness, making any sexual contact between blacks and whites during wartime a felony punishable by death. Gen. Dwight D. Eisenhower reportedly suggested that blacks in the Women's Army Corps should be used as companions for black male soldiers. These ideas were vehemently denounced by Hastie as excessive and as a misuse of black women in the armed forces.[31]

As an aide to the secretary of war, Hastie did not think it was appropriate for him to use his position or membership in the Black Brain Trust to go over his boss and appeal directly to the commander in chief to get some help for the African American soldiers. However, Hastie did have the support of the NAACP and the black press, which constantly published grievances expressed by the black soldiers and also printed details about numerous racial incidents as evidence that action was needed. Hastie concluded that although Secretary of War Stimson was a good man and a patriot, he "simply did not understand racism."[32] Stimson and the members of the committee, in turn, felt that Hastie was too much of an inside agitator and began avoiding him and ceased inviting him to attend the department's Advisory Committee on Negro Troop Policy. Hastie realized that he had become an insider who was really outside. He could continue his memo campaign or use his office to show his color, but Hastie decided to return to his old position as dean of Howard University Law School.

Phillip McGuire, a historian who has published widely on Hastie and World War II, concluded: "Hastie's failure as civilian aide can be attributed to his inability—in spite of the overwhelming moral and empirical evidence—to convince the War Department and the military's top brass that the injustices of racial discrimination and segregation retarded rather than improved the efficiency of the armed services."[33] Hastie simply felt "he could do more for black troops as a private citizen since the War Department was ignoring his recommendations and avoiding his counsel."[34]

Hastie's resignation, effective at the end of January 1943, created another opportunity for the black press to highlight the grievances faced by the African American troops both in and out of uniform. The principal complaints included no blacks in the Pentagon, only two morale officers on duty, no black athletic program comparable to that for white officers, no black photographers in the Signal Corps, blacks used only as ground crews in aviation, refusal to use black trained meteorologists, transferral of liberal white officers from black posts, assaults upon black troops in uniform, Negro-hating officers assigned as leaders, and blacks in southern camps as the victims of attacks ranging from beatings to murders.[35]

About a week after his resignation, Hastie issued an explanatory statement. He listed the immediate cause of his resignation as the discriminatory policy being developed by the Army Air Forces. He believed that the Army Air Forces simply did not want any blacks to serve, especially as flyers. He charged that the Army Air Forces, believing that race controlled a man's capacity and aptitudes, had no intention of training blacks as flyers and rejected those who qualified for other posts. Furthermore, there was no program to protect black soldiers from civilians who interfered as they were carrying out their duties in uniform or who harassed them when they were out of uniform.[36]

Hastie's open letter to the press did not go unnoticed by the War Department, which then expanded the program to train black flyers, established two new squadrons, and promised to replace Hastie but with a man of a more "southern background." The War Department felt that "a southerner who is accustomed to discrimination and segregation in all its most vicious forms, would have no quarrels with Army policy and practice where Negroes are involved. A good buffer and front man seems to be desired."[37] Several southern black college presidents were candidates, but eventually Hastie's assistant, Truman K. Gibson, was named as his replacement. Gibson, a Chicago lawyer, was a more moderate voice for the War Department.

Ironically, the War Department did not (as expected by some in the African American press or because it had been already denounced by that group), select a successor to Hastie with a more "southern background." The southern culture that Hastie confronted in the War Department and that hindered his performance was not the traditional racial attitude associated with southern life or customs; it was the southern conservative political ideology of local control, or the ability of local draft boards, community officials, and individuals in military units exercising the power to nullify national policy that called for fairness for all enlistees in the armed forces. Hastie could not convince the War Department that to allow such local power not only denied the African American soldiers the opportunity to compete but also slowed down national military preparedness and threatened the security of the United States. Hastie's real problem was that his agenda, the Black Brain Trust agenda, was inconsistent with military policy. Hastie was not content to work *for* the War Department; he worked *in* the War Department for the elimination of discrimination by trying to force it to open up or loosen its policies and allow the other Americans the freedom to serve.

Although Hastie left his post as civilian aide to the secretary of war somewhat frustrated, he had helped plant the seed that gave birth to a unified U.S. armed forces that overthrew the old rule of having a white army, a black army, and a women's service corps. As the transition took place from Hastie to Gibson, the turn of events in the war itself influenced the future role of African Americans in the armed forces. The new civilian aide did serve on the Advisory Committee on Negro Troop Policy, headed by John J. McCloy, assistant secretary of war in charge of the department's racial policy, which completely shunned Hastie and weighed heavily in his decision to resign. Bernard C. Nalty argued that, by the summer of 1943, because of Hastie's resignation, the black 99th Fighter Squadron joined with the white 33rd Fighter Group and participated in the North African campaign against the German air force. Unfortunately, Col. William W. Momyer, commander of the 33rd Fighter Group, gave the black aviators a very negative assessment. According to Momyer, the African American flyers were "not of the fighting caliber of any squadron in the Group. They failed to display the aggressiveness and desire for combat that are necessary to a first-class fighting organization."[38] Momyer's superior, Brig. Gen. Edwin J. House, went even further and denounced the entire Tuskegee experiment as a failure. This negative report from the field, augmented with the many reports of individual assaults and riots at various camps, forced Assistant Secretary of War McCloy to consider recommending that the department's policy on racial segregation be modified.[39]

Although Gibson, the new civilian aide, did not "believe that racial attitudes which have been firmly entrenched over a period of years can be changed in a short time by any general statement,"[40] it is important to note that the resignation of Hastie, followed by the negative reports on the performance of the black aviators and the political impact that it had in America, greatly influenced the move toward improved racial relations, even though the official policy of segregation remained in place. As in civilian life, before the nation was willing to move to integration, the armed forces first tried fairness through equalization. Army Chief of Staff Marshall began the process by calling for "even-handed discipline" to improve race relations on and off post and for "adequate facilities and accommodations" for African American troops.[41]

Hastie's recommendation that integration was best for the War Department eventually prevailed although Hastie moved on and continued the civil rights struggle in a different forum. After reviewing studies such as the Gillem report (1946), which recommended ending discrimination and segregation for African American military officers, the Civil Rights Commission's report (1947), which recommended ending discrimination and segregation in civilian life, and the Advisory Commission on Universal Military Training's report (1948), which proposed the same for military life, President Harry Truman took the radical step in 1948 and issued Executive Order 9981, establishing "equality of treatment and opportunity for all persons in the armed services, without regard to race, color, religion, or national origins."[42] It was a difficult fight, but at last national interest nullified local power and customs and allowed all persons the freedom to serve.

After his resignation from the War Department, Hastie returned to Howard University Law School as dean and resumed his role assisting Thurgood Marshall and the NAACP with legal cases involving racial discrimination. Hastie was especially concerned with the problems of lynching, disfranchisement, and segregation. He joined the antilynching crusade, which ultimately failed to get Congress to pass legislation against lynching. However, Marshall, with Hastie's assistance, won legal victories by getting the U.S. Supreme Court to declare white primaries in the South unconstitutional in the famous *Smith v. Allwright* case (1944) and to end legal segregation on buses involved in interstate commerce (*Morgan v. Virginia*, 1946). These two cases laid a foundation for the voter education and registration drives of the 1960s and the Freedom Rides in 1947 and 1961. After the Morgan decision, Secretary of the Interior Harold L. Ickes nominated Hastie to be governor of the Virgin Islands, and in 1949 President Truman nominated him to serve on the U.S. Court of Appeals for the Third Circuit in Pennsylvania. Hastie, who served in both these positions with distinction, died in April 1976, having fought a good fight "in the bittersweet war against bigotry."[43]

Notes

1. "Constitution of the United States of America," in Paul S. Boyer et al., *The Enduring Vision* (Boston: Houghton Mifflin, 1998), Appendix A-12.

2. John Hope Franklin, *From Slavery to Freedom: A History of African Americans*, 7th ed. (New York: McGraw-Hill, 1994), 392–93.

3. Gilbert Ware, *William Hastie: Grace under Pressure* (New York: Oxford University Press, 1988), 4.

4. Ibid., 5.

5. Ibid., 9.

6. Ibid., 11.

7. Ibid., 19.

8. Ibid., 33.

9. Ibid., 71.

10. Ibid., 97–98.

11. Roy Wilkins, "The Old Army Game," *Crisis 52* (May 1945): 130.

12. Ibid.

13. Ibid.

14. Ibid.

15. Ibid., 131.

16. Phillip McGuire, *He, Too, Spoke for Democracy: Judge Hastie, World War II, and the Black Soldier* (New York: Greenwood Press, 1988), 12.

17. Ibid., 8.

18. Ibid., 12; Phillip McGuire, "Desegregation of the Armed Forces: Black Leadership, Protest, and World War II," *Journal of Negro History* 68, no. 2 (1983): 149.

19. Ware, *William Hastie*, 97–98.

20. Ibid.

21. George Q. Flynn, "Selective Service and American Blacks during World War II," *Journal of Negro History* 66, no. 1 (1984): 14.

22. Ibid., 15.

23. Ibid.

24. Ibid., 18.

25. "The White House Jim Crow Plan," *Crisis* 47 (November 1940): 350.

26. Ibid.

27. Phillip McGuire, "Judge Hastie, World War II, and Racism," *Journal of Negro History* 4 (October 1977): 353.

28. McGuire, *He, Too, Spoke for Democracy*, 57.

29. Ware, *William Hastie*, 98.

30. Ibid., 99.

31. Ibid., 100, 106.

32. Ibid., 122.

33. McGuire, *He, Too, Spoke for Democracy*, 98.

34. McGuire, "Judge Hastie, World War II, and Racism," 357.

35. "Expect Gibson to follow Hastie Exit," *Chicago Defender*, January 30, 1943.

36. "Why I Resigned," *Chicago Defender*, February 6, 1943.

37. Ibid.

38. Bernard C. Nalty, *Strength for the Fight: A History of Black Americans in the Military* (New York: Free Press, 1986), 151.

39. Ibid., 156.

40. Ibid.

41. Ibid.

42. McGuire, *He, Too, Spoke for Democracy*, 105.

43. Ware, *William Hastie*, 241.

Suggested Readings

Dalfiume, Richard M. *Desegregation of the U.S. Armed Forces: Fighting on Two Fronts*. Columbia, MO, 1969.

Foner, Jack D. *Blacks and the Military in American History*. New York, 1974.

Franklin, John Hope. *From Slavery to Freedom: A History of African Americans*. 7th ed. New York, 1994.

MacGregor, Morris J., Jr. *Integration of the Armed Forces, 1940–1965*. Washington, DC, 1981.

McGuire, Phillip. *He, Too, Spoke for Democracy: Judge Hastie, World War II, and the Black Soldier*. New York, 1988.

McNeil, Genna Rae. *Groundwork: Charles Hamilton Houston and the Struggle for Civil Rights*. Philadelphia, 1983.

Nalty, Bernard C. *Strength for the Fight: A History of Black Americans in the Military*. New York, 1986.

Stillman, Richard J., II. *Integration of the Negro in the U.S. Armed Forces*. New York, 1968.

Ware, Gilbert. *William Hastie: Grace under Pressure*. New York, 1988.

4

The Hara Family
The Story of a Nisei Couple

Thomas Hara

Not all ethnic minorities in the United States enjoyed enhanced opportunities during the conflict. In one of the grimmer episodes in American history, Japanese Americans living on the West Coast were evicted from their homes and placed in internment camps in desolate areas.

Given the hard feelings engendered by the Pearl Harbor attack, some isolated injustices against Japanese Americans might have been expected, although not condoned. Harder to explain were the actions of the top army officer on the West Coast, Lt. Gen. John DeWitt. Although the times called for a cool head and a reasoned outlook, DeWitt stoked the fires of hysteria with pronouncements such as "A Jap's a Jap. It makes no difference whether he's an American or not." When, three months after Pearl Harbor, not one charge of sabotage had been brought against Japanese Americans, DeWitt still thought that there was a great likelihood that such an act would occur.

As irrational as DeWitt's pronouncements appear today, even more difficult to understand was the stance taken by the U.S. government against some of its citizens solely because of their ancestral background. The order for the evacuation of Japanese Americans was signed by President Roosevelt, endorsed by Congress, and upheld by the Supreme Court. Many of them were allowed only forty-eight hours to dispose of their homes and belongings. Ultimately, 112,000 Japanese Americans, of whom two-thirds were U.S. citizens, were dispossessed; the government never filed charges against them.

Ironies abound in this sad affair. Japanese Americans in Hawaii, who made up a much larger proportion of the population than in California, remained in their homes and at their work because the U.S. Navy needed their help in repairing damaged warships at the Pearl Harbor base. At the same time, the U.S. Army recruited volunteers from the internment camps; 33,000 Japanese Americans responded. By the end of the war, one Nisei formation, the 442d Regimental Combat Team (which was made up of second-generation Japanese Americans), had so distinguished itself in combat that it was one of the most decorated regiments in the history of the U.S. Army. The unit paid a heavy price, taking more than 100 percent casualties during the Italian campaign (with replacements filling in for those soldiers killed or wounded).

Among those who suffered in the darkest single chapter of America's World War II record were members of the Hara family. Thomas Hara, a graduate of Austin Peay State University in Clarksville, Tennessee, persuaded his parents, Rose and Benji, to record their story. Thomas Hara served in the U.S. Army as both an enlisted man and an officer. He currently works as a munitions disposal expert for UXB International.

Until recently, one of the least publicized episodes in American history was the forced removal and detention of more than 110,000 Japanese American citizens who lived on the West Coast at the outbreak of World War II. This is not one of the greatest moments in the American past, and many who were victimized by that experience would not talk about their years as prisoners of their own government. Unfairly stigmatized by accusations of disloyalty by virtue of their physical appearance, they could not find the voice within themselves to tell others what they had experienced. For Rose and Benji Hara this silence lasted for more than forty years. This chapter is not, of course, a definitive history of the Japanese American internment. Taken from Rose and Benji's written and spoken accounts, it presents in human, personal, and ethical terms the experience of two American citizens.

The Japanese attack on the U.S. naval base at Pearl Harbor on December 7, 1941, triggered a series of events on the West Coast of the United States that culminated in one of the most extraordinary episodes in the history of this country—the establishment of relocation camps in America for the express purpose of interning American citizens. On February 17, 1942, President Franklin D. Roosevelt signed Executive Order 9066, which made Japanese Americans on the West Coast subject to military edict. Executive Order 9066 also appointed Lt. Gen. John L. DeWitt commander of the relocation. Lieutenant General DeWitt and California State Attorney General Earl Warren (later Chief Justice of the U.S. Supreme Court) went on record as backing a policy of mass exclusion. DeWitt stated: "The very fact that no sabotage has taken place to date is a disturbing and confirming indication that such action will be taken."[1] Warren supported DeWitt's argument before a congressional committee in February 1942, saying that to believe the absence of sabotage by the Japanese population was proof of loyalty was "simply to live in a fool's paradise." Warren saw the absence of sabotage to that point as an "ominous sign" that "the fifth column activities that we are to get are timed just like Pearl Harbor was timed."[2]

DeWitt also testified before a congressional committee: "A Jap's a Jap. They are a dangerous element. . . . There is no way to determine their loyalty. . . . You can't change him by giving him a piece of paper."[3] Thus, under the guise of military necessity, American citizens were herded into relocation camps. Eugene V. Rostow described the situation: "One hundred thousand persons were sent to concentration camps on a record which wouldn't support a conviction for stealing a dog."[4]

Ten relocation camps were erected in remote areas in the country's interior. These were not the death camps of Nazi Europe, but they were characterized by barbed-wire fences, guard towers, searchlights, and armed military guards. The relocation camps were specifically built to imprison civilians, none of whom was ever charged with any crime. Eventually, the camps housed men, women, children, infants, the elderly, and even the infirm.

Most of the incarcerated, some 77,000 out of 120,000, were U.S. citizens, born and raised in this country.[5] These second-generation Japanese Americans were known as Nisei, a subset of whom were known as Kibei: Nisei who had returned to Japan for schooling. Others were resident aliens, known as Issei. These people were first-generation immigrants who had come to the United States more than fifty years earlier. However, unlike their European counterparts, the Issei were denied the rights to become naturalized citizens by federal immigration laws.

The government's exclusion policy was based on an incredible notion that this particular group of people, because of their ancestry, had to be regarded as inherently disloyal to the United States. They were presumed to be a racial nest of spies and saboteurs because of their physical appearance. They had no individual recourse at all.

The internment of the Japanese Americans was an episode unparalleled in the history of the United States. A group of American citizens and their alien parents became the victims of a racist policy that ignored all the protections of individual rights that are intrinsic to the principles of our constitutional government. However, in that time of national crisis, panic, emotion, greed, and political expediency prevailed, and the Constitution was grossly violated. All three branches of our government failed the trust and mission given to them by assuming a policy that included prejudices and racist overtones. The exclusion and internment of Japanese Americans during World War II was an injustice felt at the deepest personal level by those who experienced it, and it is only now that some of those who lived through those times have recovered and are strong and courageous enough to be silent no more.

Representative of the human costs of the relocation was the experience of approximately five hundred fishing families who lived and worked on Terminal Island in Los Angeles Harbor, near a navy installation. On February 14, 1942, by authority of the president and the attorney general, the navy posted signs on the island ordering the Japanese to evacuate by March 14. However, on February 25, only eleven days later, the navy posted a second notice that superseded the first, ordering the Japanese Americans to evacuate by February 27. That notice gave those on Terminal Island only forty-eight hours to leave their homes. The navy made no provision for heads of families already incarcerated or for bank accounts that were frozen. Church groups, particularly the Quakers, tried to get the navy to extend the deadline with no success.

The chaos that resulted is unimaginable. The scene on Terminal Island on February 26, 1942, the day before the deadline, was described as follows:

> The narrow streets between the little shacks were jammed with trucks and milling women and children. Secondhand dealers, "descending like wolves to prey on the helpless," flocked in to take the things people could not carry with them. They were reported to be giving a nickel on the dollar. A Nisei volunteer wrote later, "The women cried awful. . . . Some of them smashed their stuff, broke it up, right before the buyers' eyes because they offered such ridiculous prices . . . the beautiful wedding tea sets, saved for better homes, lying smashed to pieces on the floors of cottages."[6]

Benji and Rose Hara were two residents of Terminal Island who were relocated. In 1985, while working on my undergraduate degree at Austin Peay State University in Clarksville, Tennessee, I persuaded my parents to record their experiences during World War II. What follows is in their own words.

Rose's Story

My name is Rose Hara. I was born Fusako Ikeda in the town of Fort Lupton, Colorado. My parents' family name was Ikeda. After both my parents died during the World War I flu epidemic, I was adopted by the Kawagishi family of Denver, Colorado, when I was an infant. My adopted parents owned a barbershop and pool hall.

As was the custom of many alien Japanese parents in those days, my stepsister and I, when I was seven, were sent to live with my grandparents in a small, provincial village in the southern part of the main island of Japan. After finishing grammar school, I attended a girls' school from which I graduated in 1935 and returned to the United States.

Two other sisters and two brothers were also sent to Japan after I was. They remained in Japan and married there. They did not return to the United States until after World War II. After I spent a short period [of time] in Denver, Colorado, I returned to California and lived on Terminal Island. I worked in the fish canneries until December 1941. On September 27, 1940, I married Benji Hara, who was a radio operator on a tuna boat.

After Pearl Harbor, Benji was held in the San Diego jail without charges for three weeks. When the Federal Bureau of Investigation (FBI) came to Terminal Island on February 25, 1942, we didn't know what to think. We were so young, we didn't realize what was going on. We were so confused and afraid. They took all the Issei and Kibei men away and put guards on the drawbridge so no one could leave or enter the island. My father was one of those who were taken. He was imprisoned in Bismarck, North Dakota (in a prisoner of war camp), for a year before he was moved to a relocation camp.

Some newspapers started saying we were spies and accused us of all sorts of ridiculous things. Then they started demanding that we all be moved away from the coast. In California, most of those accusations and demands were made by the Hearst newspapers. The navy arrived and tacked up the first evacuation poster. We were told the island had been condemned and we had thirty days to vacate. We packed up a few of our household goods and sent them to relatives in Colorado. We intended to follow, but then we began to hear that other people had been beaten up on the road and we were afraid to make the trip. Benji had been out of work for quite awhile too, so we really didn't have any money to travel that far and there wasn't anyplace else for us to go.

About two weeks before the day we were supposed to leave our home, the government issued a new evacuation notice that said we had to get off the island in two days. It was just terrible. People came over from the mainland in trucks, buying our things for little or nothing because they knew we had to get rid of them or leave them behind. They were buying stoves and sofas for $5 or $10. We could take only what we could carry in one duffel bag. We had no choice but to take what we could get, however pitiful it was. We didn't know what was going to happen to us. Many people ended up leaving most of their belongings behind to be looted. Some people, in frustration, smashed their things because they were offered such ridiculous prices. We lived in several places under restriction and curfew after leaving Terminal Island. One of those places was the basement of the Quaker church. We slept on cots they had set up for us.

The Hara family (*left to right*): Minoru Hara (Benji's brother and a Pacific theater veteran in the Military Intelligence Service), Rose Hara, and Benji Hara. Photo taken in the Bronx, New York, c. 1967. *Courtesy of the Hara family*

In 1942 we were sent to an internment camp in Poston, Arizona. We traveled to Poston by train. The blinds were drawn over the train windows all the way to Arizona, so we couldn't see where we were going. There was a whole list of things we weren't allowed to take, like cameras, scissors, or a kitchen knife. Benji had his typewriter in the bottom of the duffel bag and they even took that away. The Quakers were able to find the typewriter, and later when it had been declassified as a security risk, they sent it to him.

Poston was a big concentration camp in the middle of the desert. There were rows after rows of army barracks and armed guards in towers. A tag— bearing our camp identification number—was tied to each person's coat. Each of us quickly memorized our number because it became like our name.

We were given mattress covers and told to fill them with straw. We shared a small barracks room that had no furniture with other people. Army cots were provided for our straw-filled mattress covers. The showers, bathrooms, and mess halls were located far away from our barracks, which was really hard on some families, especially those with little children and the elderly.

The first summer was terrible. Dust storms would blow up out of nowhere. It was awful if you got caught in one because you couldn't see the next barracks. The sand would blow into the barracks through the cracks between the floorboards. At first, the barracks had double roofs, but eventually the top layer of shingles blew off during the dust storms.

Because it was so hot in the daytime, we would wet down the floorboards and the edges of the spreads that covered our cots. Then we would crawl under the cots and lie there until about 2 P.M. After that, it was so hot, it didn't matter where you were. Many of the old people, especially those from northern California, died during those first six months.

We organized ourselves into blocks and elected our own government. We had to organize because the federal government hadn't provided any educational facilities for the children. Benji took a job teaching algebra.

Every day in the winter the children filled lard buckets with charcoal that the old people had made from mesquite, which grew in the desert. The charcoal provided the only heat we had that first winter, and the cold in the winter was as bad as the heat in the summer. By the second winter, we had enough handmade adobe bricks to build a proper school building.

Poston was a horrible place when we arrived there, but we made it beautiful. We made furniture out of scraps of wood. We covered the walls with paintings and partitioned the barracks to give privacy to families. We planted Japanese gardens and built gateways and pools. By the next summer, with all the grass and plants, we found that the dust storms didn't come through as often.

On February 9, 1943, my first son, Lawrence, was born in Poston by caesarean section in the makeshift camp hospital. There was no doctor. In late 1943, Benji was allowed to leave camp to look for a job in the east. Because I was Kibei, I was blacklisted and more suspect, so I remained in camp with our son.

About a year later, I was able to join my husband, who had found a job in Long Island City, New York, as a radio engineer. The government paid my train fare only to Cleveland, Ohio; from Cleveland to New York City I paid my own way. In New York City, we lived in a "railroad flat," a common housing facility during the war. It had one bedroom and community kitchen and bath facilities. It was in the Columbia

University area. When Columbia bought the apartment building for student housing, we moved to a two-bedroom apartment in the City College area. We lived there until we moved to Florida in 1971.

On June 25, 1951, our second son was born in New York City. Benji read a lot of American history in those days, so we named our son Thomas after Thomas Jefferson and Thomas Paine. Both our sons have college educations. Larry is a biochemist for General Foods Corporation and has a master's degree. Tom, a captain in the U.S. Army, is an Airborne, Ranger, and Special Forces soldier. In spite of everything that happened to us, my husband and I were able to make a good living, and our sons were able to get college educations, become good citizens, and contribute to our country.

I often wonder if students are taught of the wartime internment of Japanese Americans. Although time has passed, I still wonder why we were prisoners in our own country. We were American citizens by birth and upbringing. We committed no crime, and yet we were dislocated from our homes and livelihoods and were herded into relocation camps. I wonder if people know that our civil rights were violated.

Despite what has happened to us, I still think that America is a good country. Where else would we have been able to do so well?

Benji's Story

My name is Benji Hara. My father, an immigrant who arrived in this country in 1898, worked with maintenance gangs on the tracks of the Santa Fe Railroad in California. As was common among the early immigrants, a marriage was arranged for him. My mother, a "picture bride," came to the United States in 1914 to marry him. At the time of my birth in 1915 in San Diego, California, my father was employed as a house servant in the home of a bank president. Between the time of his arrival in the United States and his employment in San Diego, he had worked as a railroad gang member, strawberry farmer, and pool hall owner. He had managed to attend a language school and learned to speak, write, and read English. He was one of the few in his circle of friends that took advantage of this opportunity.

I was about three years old when my father decided to enter into the fishing business and moved to East San Pedro, a manmade island in Los Angeles Harbor. This fishing town later was named Terminal Island. My father became a commercial fisherman when the industry was in its infancy. I remember seeing the bright blue arcs of the radio-telegraph transmitting station visible through an open door as we went by a fenced area of a World War I wireless station. Perhaps this fascinating sight and a story in a Horatio Alger book my father had given me, *Mark Mason's Victory, or the Story of a Telegraph Boy*, were subconscious influences in my becoming involved in radio and electronics as my profession.

My early education was obtained at the East San Pedro grammar school. In later years, there were several hundred children born of immigrant parents attending this school. Because most of these parents did not attend American schools, they were not well versed in the English language; therefore, the children became bilingual to some degree. My mother never learned to speak English and I never mastered the Japanese language, so communication with her was limited to everyday casual conversations pertaining to things in and around the home. My father did speak and write English, so communication with him was easier. He was the one who gave me spelling lessons so I excelled in that subject in grammar school.

When I graduated from high school in 1934, I was given a job as a crew member on my father's fishing boat. I remember the cold, miserable winter nights hauling the net for sardine. I decided fishing was not what I wanted to do for a living, and I quit the job after one year. I had made enough money to enroll in a technical school in Los Angeles to study radio engineering. In 1937, I graduated from technical school, but there were no engineering job opportunities for Orientals, so I took a job as a radio operator on a tuna clipper, maintaining Morse code communication between ships and shore stations. The tuna fishing grounds covered the offshore areas of Mexico, Central America, and down to the Galapagos Islands on the equator and as far west as 400 miles to the outlying islands and reefs in the Pacific Ocean. The tuna catch was sold by contract to the various canneries in San Diego and Los Angeles. I worked on three different tuna clippers between 1937 and December 1941. The last trip lasted ninety-one days and unfortunately, we arrived in San Diego the day after Pearl Harbor, December 8, 1941. Our boat crew consisted of resident alien Japanese and Japanese Americans born in the United States. When we heard the news on the radio, I anticipated that we would have some problems because of it, but I never dreamed of the hardships and indignities that we were to experience.

Upon our arrival at San Diego harbor, sailors from a navy patrol boat boarded our tuna clipper. Several of the patrol crew carried submachine guns. Our boat was searched from stem to stern and one rifle and one shotgun, which we used for shooting sharks, and all kitchen knives and scissors used for mending nets were confiscated. Crew members were herded to the bow deck at the point of the machine guns. An armed guard was stationed in the engine room to watch the engineer. I was on the bridge with the fishing captain with another guard watching us. We were ordered to proceed to the cannery dock. Customs and immigration authorities boarded us there. We were told that everyone was to be taken to the Immigration Station to check on our status. I remained on the boat with the engineer until we could hire another engineer to take care of the refrigeration machine for the frozen tuna in the hold of the boat. All other crew members were taken away.

That evening, after we were able to hire an outside engineer, the boat's engineer and I started to pack our little ditty bag with toilet articles and a change of underwear since we thought it would be at least an overnight stay. The agent said, "Oh, you're going to be out right away and you won't need that," so we did not take them. The only thing I took was my adrenaline chloride vaporizer for inhalation to alleviate my asthmatic condition, which always troubled me when I returned from the warm southern climate to the cooler California weather. I thought we were going to the Immigration Station but when we got out of the car, we found ourselves in front of the county jail.

We entered and were put into a holding tank to await processing. After a mug shot and several sets of my fingerprints were taken, I was led through a door, told to pick up two blankets from a pile on the floor, and was led up two flights of open stairwell. It was about 10 P.M. by this time. On every landing, there was a large solid steel door, and never having been in a jail before, I wondered what a commercial refrigerator might be used for in a jail! I did not know that each of these doors was an entrance to cellblocks. Upon a signal from the guard who led me up the stairs, the electrically controlled door opened and a regular inmate trustee let me in. Thus, I was "thrown" into the third-floor cell block of the San Diego County Jail for being a citizen of Japanese ancestry. The floor of the cell was full of sleeping men. They were other alien Japanese and Japanese Americans possibly from other boats and the city of San Diego. After the first night of sleeping on the concrete floor, my asthmatic condition got worse and on the following day I had to convince the jail authorities to give me a bunk in one of the cells.

During the following weeks, other alien Japanese fishermen were brought into the cell block. None of my shipmates was in the same cell block, and the only person I knew was Captain Takahashi, a tuna boat skipper. Eventually, all the alien Japanese were removed from the jail and (we were to learn later) were taken to another facility in the Los Angeles area and subsequently sent to POW camps in Montana and North Dakota. During this incarceration period, we were not allowed to contact anyone on the outside. A series of questioning sessions began, and those of us remaining were called singly on certain days to report to the main downstairs office. During these sessions, which were conducted by the FBI, agents asked us questions pertaining to birthplace, schools attended, who we knew, and so on. After several of these sessions my records seemed to consist of written information several inches thick.

Daily life in the cell was very boring. Everyone was issued a tin cup and a tablespoon, which we carried hooked to our belts; if we laid them down, they were stolen and hammered into a souvenir. Meals consisted of four slices of bread and coffee for breakfast, no lunch, and supper consisting of, if I remember correctly, an entree, vegetable, and bread and coffee. Any money that we had when we were first brought into the jail was held in the office but later could be used to order cornflakes, sugar, and milk to supplement the furnished food. A radio and a hot plate were available in the cell block. Each of us saved two slices of our breakfast bread and with the sugar and milk we were able to order, we made a sort of porridge on the hot plate with an empty gallon can. We ate this porridge for lunch.

After I had spent three weeks in jail, my name was called on the public address system for what I thought was going to be another session of questioning by the FBI. When I got downstairs to the office, an FBI agent said, "You're okay, you can go." I asked if I was going to get any documents showing that I had been investigated and released. The agent replied, "No, we don't give out anything like that." He then asked if I had any way of getting back home. I replied that I could call my wife and have someone drive down to pick me up. The agent said that I had better do that because if I tried to take a bus or train, someone would try to turn me back in. So after three weeks of incarceration in the San Diego County Jail without any charges against me, I was released.

As I stepped out of the front entrance, a convoy of trucks filled with GIs passed by. When the GIs who saw me yelled, "There's a Jap!" I immediately scooted back into the jail building. After they had gone by, I walked to our ship's broker about a mile away and called home. I walked back to the jail building and waited many hours for my wife, who hadn't seen me for 120 days, to come and get me.

I arrived home about three days before New Year's Day 1942 to find that my father-in-law had been taken away. He was eventually interned in a POW camp in North Dakota. No specific information regarding the status of aliens and citizens of Japanese ancestry was furnished to us; we only knew what was published in the newspapers. According to one report, California would be divided into a military and nonmilitary zone, and we would all have to move away from the coastal military zone. Another rumor was that we were to be relocated to detention camps. As we were nervously waiting for the next step, a mass raid was made on all the homes of Terminal Island in February 1942. The men were either FBI or deputized FBI agents and the homes were searched without warrants. During this raid, all components of my amateur radio station equipment were confiscated after they asked me what the components were. I was not given a receipt.

The next news we received was that we would be allowed to travel inland to relocate to other states. I decided we would go to Denver where my wife's relatives lived, so we shipped some clothing and bedroom articles there. Rumors of all kinds were floating around. When we heard that some people who had moved inland were getting beaten up, we became afraid and canceled our trip to Denver, so we stayed on Terminal Island.

One night we were startled by the sound of heavy guns. We ran out and saw beams of searchlights scanning the skies while the guns were being fired from military bases in Long Beach and San Pedro. We did not see any target picked up by the searchlights, which were scanning haphazardly across the sky. The next day, the newspapers reported that an unidentified aircraft was flying over the area. The navy immediately announced that all persons of Japanese ancestry must leave their homes within forty-eight hours. We and other people who were sympathetic to our problem believed that the incident on the previous night had been staged to justify an immediate move.

At the time, we were living in a cottage rented from one of the canneries. My household consisted of my wife, my wife's sister, and my brother. The Quaker Society had established a hostel in Los Angeles for families that had nowhere else to go. We stayed at the hostel until President Roosevelt's Executive Order 9066 was issued on February 19, 1942. The order required that all persons of Japanese ancestry must report and register for evacuation to government internment camps, which we later learned had been built secretly in the early months of the war. People evacuated from Terminal Island were scheduled to be sent to a camp in Manzanar, California, in the desert. Having previously heard of the desert dust storms, I became apprehensive about how the climate would affect my asthma, so I requested to be sent to an internment camp in a nondesert area.

We were sent to Poston, Arizona. With one suitcase and a duffel bag per person, we were taken by railroad from Los Angeles through the Mojave Desert and into Parker Dam, Arizona. After a bus trip of five or ten miles south, we reached the internment camp of Poston I. Poston was the only camp that contained more than one section. Poston I, II, and III were each one mile apart. The three camps eventually housed 20,000 persons. My cousin was one of the early volunteers to go into this camp to make final preparations for receiving the thousands of internees. When we reached the camp, we were assigned to a room in one of the barracks and each of us was given a mattress cover, which we had to fill with hay to use as bedding. Army cots were provided for each person in the household group. We were assigned a room with another family, a widowed mother with two young daughters. My cousin was waiting for us. With a garden hose attached to the single faucet located at one end of each barracks, he hosed down all the sand and dust that had accumulated on the edges of each rafter and the floor. Water on the floor was no problem since the floorboards had quarter-inch gaps between each board, and the hot weather quickly dried out the boards.

After the dust and commotion and confusion of the first few days had subsided, we began to try to adjust to our new circumstances. We held block meetings during the first weeks to select a manager and volunteer cooks. One room in each barracks was assigned as the block manager's office where all complaints, requests, and other matters were handled. One barracks in each block contained the cooking facilities and the mess hall with tables and benches.

At many block meetings, complaints were aired about the food. Initially, the government published a list of daily menus, but the supplies required were not available to the cooks. Months afterward, it was discovered that the food supplies shipped into the camps were being pilfered by the Caucasian supply managers and sold to the outside black market. Later, many of the fresh vegetables we ate were grown in the camps by internee farmers who had come from the Imperial Valley and San Joaquin Valley. Our fish diet consisted of barrels of salted cod from the East Coast, which was an unfamiliar fish to West Coast Japanese and not too appetizing, especially when salted. Meat consisted mostly of frankfurters. For breakfast we had toast and apple butter. Although not always appetizing, the food was nourishing, if you ate it!

My next problem was how to make our living quarters more comfortable. The only furniture supplied were an army cot and the straw-filled mattress. We stored our clothing and bedding in the suitcase and duffel bag we had brought. The scrap lumber left over after the barracks were built became the source of wood for the construction of stools and benches for our rooms.

When summer came, the daytime temperature was over 100 degrees in the shade most of the time. Everyone began to build desert coolers, which consisted of a screen made with excelsior or woodshavings, as the outside part of a housing containing a large 16-inch fan blade and motor. The screen was kept moist by a water supply that dripped along the top edge of the screen. The internal fan pulled in the outside air through the wet screen and lowered the air temperature. Because there was no running water in the rooms, the water was held in a wooden box above the screen. The box was filled at regular intervals with buckets of water from the faucet located at one end of the barracks. In my younger days, I had watched my fisherman father build many wooden rowboats and skiffs; now this knowledge came in handy, for I had learned how to make leakproof wooden boxes for the desert coolers. The fan blade and motor were ordered from Denver through the mail from the Montgomery Ward catalog. That company must have had a booming business filling orders from the many camps located in the desert. The government provided an allowance of four dollars per month for clothing; and with the accumulation of several months of allotments, we purchased whatever became necessary.

Before we made the desert coolers, we tried to stay cool by wetting down the entire floor and the overhanging sides of the bedspread on our cots. Then we crawled under the cot. Any breeze that came up through the spaces in the wet floorboards and the open door and windows provided some cooling. But early in the afternoon, this technique did not work because the temperature was too high. Some people dug deep holes in the sandy ground under the crawl space of the barracks and tried to keep cool. A stop was put to this practice because of the possibility of cave-ins.

Because of the summer heat, the barracks in our camp were built with double roofs. The top roof was about one foot above the lower one with open air space in between. During dust storms, many of the top roofs were torn off by the wind, and repairs were delayed for weeks. An approaching dust storm could be seen before it hit camp, and whatever one was doing outside at the time was stopped and everyone ran for the shelter of the barracks. The dust and sand became so heavy during these storms that adjacent barracks became blotted from view. Then the dust came up through the gaps between the floorboards and covered everything in the room. Fortunately, these desert storms did not cause me to have asthma attacks. I may have overcome them and become cured by then. Cleaning up after every dust storm became a standard chore. To protect our clothing from these dust storms, we obtained portable closets from Montgomery Ward.

Seven thousand people now lived in Poston, and facilities and services for a town of this size became necessary: rubbish collection, road maintenance, building maintenance, teachers, and administrative office workers. The government wages for this work were from twelve dollars per month to sixteen dollars per month.

In Poston, accreditation for the school system that was established in camp was obtained from the California Board of Education. The volunteer teachers were mostly professionals who were interned. I was accepted as a volunteer teacher. I taught high school algebra and was an assistant teacher of electricity. Grammar school and high school classes began in the fall of 1942. One or two rooms in a barracks on certain blocks were allocated as classrooms. One school building was constructed entirely of adobe bricks handmade by a volunteer corps of workers.

We had no direct outside news except through newspapers, which were occasionally available in the sparsely stocked canteen. Radios were prohibited in camp. Because of my amateur radio interests and my commercial radio operator's experience, I was proficient in Morse code. Since some of my electrical students showed interest in ham radio, I started a class in Morse code. The audio tone oscillator was made from salvaged pieces of a broken car radio. The first day of class caused quite a commotion because the sound of Morse code coming out of the speaker carried across the firebreak to the administration building. Soon a Jeep carrying the camp manager and two armed MPs came racing to the classroom wanting to know what I was doing. I explained the activity and assured them that it was not an actual on-the-air radio transmission. They were satisfied with my explanation, and my students and I had great fun during subsequent classes.

In my plans to be "marketable" when I was released, I obtained civil service ratings as a radio instructor in the Air Corps and a radio instructor in the Signal Corps. But as soon as those services found that I was an internee, I could not get an appointment.

Sometime during 1943 the government announced plans for relocating internees from the camps to the Midwest or the East Coast. I decided to try to get work in the field of my interest: radio. I made inquiries to the War Relocation Authority (WRA) office in Philadelphia. I knew that Philco was in Philadelphia and RCA was in nearby Camden, New Jersey, so I applied for relocation just for myself. My plan was to have my wife and first son, who had been born in the camp, follow me later. My request was approved and I was given tickets to Philadelphia and fifty dollars in cash. At this point, I did not have any savings and all my possessions were in household furniture, most of which we had lost prior to internment. So on Columbus Day, October 13, 1943, I "set sail" out into the world.

The relocation group consisted of one trainload of Japanese Americans, most of whom were going to either Chicago or New York. I was the only one going to Philadelphia. When I arrived in Philadelphia, I reported to the WRA office. Many families that were sympathetic to our plight offered temporary housing to relocated internees. I became a guest with a family in the Chestnut Hill area in north Philadelphia.

When I started to look for a job, I found that it was impossible to get work in electronics because the entire industry was engaged in classified wartime production. A couple of weeks later, I was offered a temporary three-hour-per-day job as gardener in the western suburbs of Philadelphia in Wallingford, near Swarthmore College. I was given room and board in exchange for my work. The owner of the house was a member of the Quaker Society and he was in charge of the establishment of the hostel for the relocatees around the country.

After finishing my chores every day, I rode the suburban train into the city seeking work without success. In the evenings, to pass the time, I attended lectures given by visiting professors at Swarthmore College. Eventually, I decided to move back to the city and rented a room in a home owned by a Quaker family close to Temple University. They were most gracious and kind.

After trying practically every electrical and electronic plant, including broadcast stations, without success, I finally found a warehouse job with the Nicholson File Company, which made all kinds of files from fingernail files to large 18-inch machine files. I was given the job of packing prepackaged files into wooden crates, and later I replaced the shipping clerk when he was drafted. After a couple of weeks they offered to train me to do office work but I thanked them and declined. I was planning to return to the internment camp and try to relocate in the Chicago area, this time with my family.

In March 1944 I decided that since I was so close to New York, I would see the city before going back to Arizona. On the day of my visit to New York City, I reported to the WRA office and was told that an electronics company, Radio Engineering Labs (REL), in Long Island City was looking for workers. I went to the plant and was immediately given a job. The president of the company sent me to a building where they were manufacturing LORAN systems, which were classified secret at the time. The engineer in charge asked me if I had a navy clearance. Of course, it was not possible for me to get such a clearance. I returned to the main plant and was assigned to test unclassified equipment made for the Signal Corps. I tested the units on a go/no-go basis per test procedure but was not allowed to see any schematic diagrams. After a week or so, the foreman decided I was trustworthy, and he gave me the schematics for the modules I was testing. Having the schematic made it possible for me to make repairs on defective units on the test line rather than sending them to the repair department. Later I was promoted to final inspector of overall equipment. When the production of this Signal Corps equipment was completed, I worked as a technician on portable backpack radio equipment made for the Marine Corps.

About four months after I started at REL, my wife received permission to join me with our son. Because my wife was a Kibei (a U.S. citizen educated in Japan), the government funded transportation only from Arizona to Cleveland, Ohio. I had to pay the transportation from there to New York City. By this time, my draft status had changed from 4-F to 1-A; during the internment, we were disfranchised citizens. Now my employer at REL said that I could apply for draft exemption because I was in a war industry. How ironic!

When the war ended, I was promoted to a position in the lab and my practical education in FM technology began. I participated in the design of the first postwar commercial FM receiver, early FM broadcast, and point-to-point transmitter links. I also designed some modulator equipment and installed the first experimental FM stereo transmitter in New York City. Later I became a specialty designer for all the FM Tropospheric Scatter system radios produced by REL. Equipment was furnished by REL to a chain of stations starting in the Aleutians, across

Alaska, the Canadian Arctic Circle to Greenland, and then to Iceland and England. The chain of stations continued through Spain, Italy, and Greece and terminated in Turkey. This was a U.S. Air Force and NATO communication system. By this time the company was sold and became a part of a holding company, Dynamics Corporation of America. I worked for REL for twenty-seven years in New York and moved with the company to Florida in 1971 when Dynamics decided to combine REL and another division in Florida. I retired from REL in April 1985, after forty-one years of employment. I still do some consulting work for the company.

My life has not been a Horatio Alger rag-to-riches story but I have been fortunate to have made a living in the profession of my choice. My sons have grown to become good citizens who contribute their talents to industry and our country. I hope their lives will become even better in the years to come.

I have been a member of the U.S. Power Squadron and have contributed whatever I could as an instructor. Since 1971 I have been a member of the U.S. Coast Guard Auxiliary and have held both elected and appointed offices in the Delray Beach–Boynton Beach Flotilla. My contribution includes serving as instructor in the Public Education Safe Boating Courses.

Regarding the evacuation and internment of Japanese Americans, legal scholars, organizations, churches, newspapers, and many other groups have expressed their opinions on the gross violations of our constitutional rights and the injustices we suffered. These findings have been recorded in volumes of publications of all kinds. The congressional committee formed to study the evacuation and internment has recommended compensation on a per-person basis and a governmental public apology. A majority of the members of Congress and the administration have not yet supported the redress bills reintroduced each year. The committee report recommends compensation to all living former internees. A large percentage of the internees are now deceased, and if each succeeding Congress delays long enough, we shall all be dead and payments will not be made. As for me, I am waiting for a public apology from my government, which may never come.

In spite of everything that happened to us, I was able to make a good living and provide for a college education for both of my sons. I'm grateful to my country for that opportunity. Heck, I've even forgotten my tag number.

Postscript

In 1992, Benji and Rose Hara received the following note:

> The White House
> Washington, D.C.
>
> A monetary sum and words cannot restore lost years or erase painful memories; neither can they fully convey our Nation's resolve to rectify injustice and to uphold the rights of individuals. We can never fully right the wrongs of the past. But we can take a clear stand for justice and recognize that serious injustices were done to Japanese Americans during World War II.
>
> In enacting a law calling for restitution and offering a sincere apology, your fellow Americans have, in a very real sense, renewed their traditional commitment to the ideals of freedom, equality, and justice. You and your family have our best wishes for the future.
>
> Sincerely,
> s/George Bush
> President of the United States
> October 1990

This letter came with the Haras' $20,000 restitution payments. Their payments went into a trust fund for their grandchildren. Their older son, Lawrence, received the same note and his payment in 1993. (Reparations were issued to internees according to age, which accounts for the time lapse.)

Benji Hara was seventy-nine years old when he died on December 24, 1994. At the time of Benji's death, Lawrence was a biochemist for General Foods Corporation. I was preparing to retire from the U.S. Army after twenty years of service. Both of us had master's degrees and were married. Lawrence has two sons who knew Benji as Grandpa.

Benji served more than twenty years in the Coast Guard Auxiliary during his retirement. In the auxiliary, he showed his love of the sea by donating not only his time but also his experience in electronics. The Coast Guard Auxiliary buried Benji's ashes at sea, where he "set sail" again into the world. In 1995 the Boynton Beach, Florida, Coast Guard Auxiliary radio room was named in his memory.

Rose Hara lives in Florida but is preparing to move back to California to be with her sisters. She is grandmother to Lawrence's two sons and daughter. Rose Hara still has Benji's Horatio Alger book.

Notes

1. John Tateishi, *And Justice for All* (New York: Random House, 1984), xv.
2. Ibid., xv–xvi; Bill Hosokawa, *Nisei: The Quiet Americans* (New York: William Morrow, 1969), 288–89.
3. Hosokawa, *Nisei*, 260.
4. Michi Weglyn, *Years of Infamy* (New York: William Morrow, 1976), 53.
5. Tateishi, *And Justice for All*, xiii. Although 110,000 people were involved in the West Coast evacuation, 120,000 ethnic Japanese eventually came under the War Relocation Authority's custody. This number included 1,275 institutionalized individuals transferred to the centers; 1,118 citizens and aliens evacuated from Hawaii; 219 voluntary residents; and 5,981 who were born in the camps. WRA Statistic Section.
6. Audrie Girdner and Anne Loftis, *The Great Betrayal* (New York: Macmillan, 1969), 101. After the war my parents received some reparation for all their possessions lost or taken during relocation. They settled for ten cents on the dollar, which was about all that any of the internees got.

Suggested Readings

Bosworth, Allan R. *America's Concentration Camps*. New York, 1968.
Brimmer, Larry D. *Voices from the Camps: Japanese Americans during World War II*. Danbury, CT, 1994.
Crost, Lyn. *Honor by Fire: Japanese Americans at War in Europe and the Pacific*. Novato, CA, 1996.
Daniels, Roger. *Concentration Camps: North American Japanese in the United States and Canada during World War II*. Melbourne, FL, 1993.
Grodzins, Morton. *Americans Betrayed: Politics and the Japanese Evacuation*. Chicago, 1949.
Hosokawa, Bill. *Nisei: The Quiet Americans*. New York, 1969.
Sone, Monica. *Nisei Daughter*. Boston, 1953.
Weglyn, Michi. *Years of Infamy*. New York, 1976.

5

Harold D. Lehman
A Conscientious Objector's Story

Harold D. Lehman

If Japanese Americans suffered for their ancestry, those with pacifist convictions also paid a price. Although outright refusal to serve in the armed forces was relatively rare, the government did imprison fourteen thousand Americans for draft evasion, less than 0.04 percent of all registrants. Of this total, four thousand were Jehovah's Witnesses.

Some conscientious objectors satisfied themselves and their country by filling noncombatant roles in uniform, most notably as medics. Widely praised for valor under fire, corpsmen carried no weapons and wore distinctive Red Cross armbands. In the European theater, the enemy generally respected these markings. In the Pacific, because the Japanese usually directed heavy fire against them, medics quickly discarded such insignia.

Conscientious objectors from traditionally pacifist groups such as the Amish, Mennonites, and Quakers generally chose public service under a special provision of the 1940 draft act. These people did work of national importance with the Civilian Public Service program.

Harold D. Lehman, a Mennonite from Virginia, describes his wartime experience working with the National Park Service, the mentally ill, and retarded children. After the war, Lehman went on to earn advanced education degrees from Pennsylvania State University in State College and the University of Virginia in Charlottesville. In a forty-five-year career, he taught at the elementary, secondary, and university levels. He has written several books, including *Called to Teach Adults* (1981). His four sons are all college professors.

As a young boy, sitting by my father in the college chapel, I gave rapt attention to the elderly man's public lecture: "Reminiscences of the Civil War." Peter S. Hartman, age eighty-six, had a vivid recall of that conflict and its effect on the Mennonite community in the Shenandoah Valley of Virginia. Young men in his church, because of their peace convictions, went into hiding when ordered into the Confederate army. Seventy-two Brethren and Mennonite men who were trying to flee across West Virginia to the Union side were captured and later incarcerated in the infamous Libby Prison in Richmond.

Hartman recalled that soldiers from both sides came to his family farm near Harrisonburg and confiscated horses, hogs, and sheep, leaving only some chickens and four milk cows. Because the Shenandoah Valley was known as "the granary of the Confederacy," the Union army burned most of the barns and mills in the immediate area. When Gen. Philip Henry Sheridan made his destructive raid through the valley in 1864, young Hartman, then of draft age, accepted the Union general's offer of safe conduct to the North. He hired to a farmer in Pennsylvania until the war was over and was among the thousands who viewed President Abraham Lincoln's body lying in state at Harrisburg on its final journey to Springfield, Illinois.[1]

A few years later, as a teenager, I heard a local Mennonite minister talk about his experiences as a conscientious objector (CO) during World War I. Aldine Brenneman and his brother had been inducted into the U.S. Army at Camp Lee, Virginia. When they refused to put on their uniforms and drill, the Brennemans were repeatedly questioned, counseled, cajoled, and threatened. They were assigned to the remount station to care for the horses and mules and were later imprisoned in the guardhouse with only a blanket. They slept on the cold concrete floor for twenty-six days during winter weather.

Aldine Brenneman served time in a detention camp, was arrested six times for refusing work orders, faced the Board of Inquiry, and was frequently harassed by junior officers. After serving for seven months as cook for the CO contingent in Camp Lee, he was furloughed to a farm. His discharge paper, dated February 6, 1919, carried these notes: "Physical condition—good, Character—good, but is not recommended for reenlistment."[2]

Such accounts of conscientious objectors had a strong influence on me. The stories reinforced the social and religious upbringing that I had received through the Anabaptist-Mennonite tradition. The Mennonites and the Amish are the spiritual heirs of the Anabaptist movement, a radical wing of the Protestant Reformation dating back to the sixteenth century in Europe. Nonparticipation in warfare, sometimes referred to as nonresistance, has been a cardinal doctrine among the three historic peace churches: Mennonite, Church of the Brethren, and Quaker. Within this context I did not give serious consideration to any possibility other than registering as a conscientious objector when I was subject to the draft during World War II. This decision led to my being assigned to the Civilian Public Service program from October 1942 to June 1946.

The Civilian Public Service Program

By the mid-1930s world events seemed to portend war in Europe and in the Far East. Consequently, leaders of the peace churches began to search for ways through which COs might be permitted some form of alternate service to military duty. Many still remembered the hostility and persecution faced by COs who served directly under the military in World War I. It was hoped that future wartime experiences of drafted COs might not only express their aversion to war but would also provide a positive expression of peace and an opportunity for humanitarian service.

The original reading of the Burke-Wadsworth draft bill in 1940 would have exempted as conscientious objectors from military service only members of those sects whose creed or principles forbid their members to participate in war in any form. The bill would have required COs to perform noncombatant work that the U.S. president decided was suitable. Such service was to be under the supervision of the military. These stipulations, which were of great concern to representatives of the peace churches, led to intense negotiations with congressional and military leaders.

The final wording of the Selective Training and Service Act broadened CO recognition from sectarian membership to include those who by reason of religious training or belief had become conscientious objectors. The law directed that COs could be assigned to work of national importance under civilian direction. Two less favorable stipulations were that local draft boards were to determine classification and that the program was to be run by the Selective Service System (SSS).

As a compromise between church and state, the Civilian Public Service (CPS) program accommodated reasonably well the peace convictions of the church and the concerns of a warring nation about this troublesome minority of draftees. CPS base camps were set up in former Civilian Conservation Corps (CCC) facilities, most of which were located in isolated rural or forested areas. The work under civilian direction was supervised by federal agencies such as the U.S. Forest Service, the Soil Conservation Service, and the National Park Service. Beginning in 1942, detached service was available for CPS volunteers to work in state mental hospitals alongside employees. The SSS paid the transportation costs to camp and had ultimate supervision over the program through the regulation of work hours and the conditions of absence, furloughs, and service discharges. The cooperating churches financed the day-to-day cost of maintaining the men in the camps and had responsibility for their nonwork hours.

The twelve thousand men in CPS during World War II were a diverse group. Fifty-eight percent came from the historic peace churches. The other 42 percent represented more than two hundred religious and nonreligious groups. In addition, six thousand COs served time in prison for their refusal to be drafted or for noncooperation with the CPS system. The third option for drafted COs was the I-A-O position (drafted into the military with noncombatant status). During World War II, thirty thousand men registered with the I-A-O classification and served as medics, office clerks, and cooks and in other noncombatant positions.[3]

Registration to Induction

When the Japanese struck at Pearl Harbor, I was a senior at Bridgewater College, Virginia. Although Bridgewater was a Brethren college, only a minority of the faculty and students supported the pacifist stand. On December 8, 1941, when the U.S. Congress voted for war, twenty male students in the college immediately signed up for officer reserve training. Girlfriends wept because the men shortly would be off to war. It was a day of mixed emotions on campus.

On February 16, 1942, I registered with the SSS and requested Form 47 to apply for CO status. It was possible to ask church advisers to help fill out the form, and I chose Pastor Aldine Brenneman. The questions on Form 47 were designed to reveal the sincerity of the registrant's position. One important item stood out: "Describe a situation in your life when you demonstrated a nonresistant or peaceful action." I described a minor auto accident in which a town council member ran a stop sign on entering an intersection from a side street. My front bumper caught his rear fender and bumper, causing minimal damage to his vehicle. He demanded that I pay for the damage to his car because he was the experienced driver. I was the novice even though I had the right of way. The policeman on the scene, in deference to the councilman, suggested that I pay for his repairs, which I eventually did.

The decisions of local boards across the country varied in response to those who applied for CO status via Form 47. Some boards deferred COs for farm work. Other boards that had few CO applicants were reluctant to give them IV-E classifications, and those men were forced to appeal. Like most of the Brethren and Mennonite men in Rockingham County, Virginia, who requested CO status, I was eventually classified IV-E as a conscientious objector available for civilian work that contributed to the national interest.

My local board seemed to be capricious in its decisions. After I had graduated from college in the spring I had taken a temporary job with a local hatchery. The owner and operator of the hatchery was a Mennonite. Both he and I were classified IV-E. There were two other employees. One requested and received an I-A-O classification and was subsequently drafted into the U.S. Army as a noncombatant. The other young man, not a Mennonite, was classified I-A but was deferred during the entire war to run the hatchery for the owner, who was serving in the Civilian Public Service for three and one-half years.

In the months preceding my induction on October 27, 1942, I do not recall any hostile treatment except an occasional taunt of "slacker" or "yellow belly." During that time, I served as an air-raid warden in our village, visiting homes and asking for blackout cooperation during air-raid drills. Several of us covered the village on bicycles, checking whether lights were extinguished or hidden from view. We were trained to recognize enemy airplane silhouettes and to watch for them. I regarded this service as one I could conscientiously do.

Because the community had a sizeable Mennonite and Brethren population, we were not pressured to buy war bonds or to participate in scrap collections. It was recognized that our churches generously donated money to support the CPS camps and also shared food and clothing with the CPS base camps and those overseas through denominational agencies. Like everyone else in the community we were issued ration coupons for sugar and gasoline.

The first Mennonite CPS camp, Number 4, near Grottoes, Virginia, was opened on May 22, 1941. The work projects at Grottoes were directed by the Soil Conservation Service. The proximity of this camp, just twenty miles from my home, meant that I was somewhat acquainted with a typical CPS base camp. I had visited the camp several times, and men from the camp frequently came to our community for a weekend religious service or social event.

According to the policy of the SSS, the original induction into CPS had to be at a base camp at least two hundred miles from where the draftee had registered. Before induction each draftee was given a physical examination by a designated medical doctor. In my case the examination was quite perfunctory: height, weight, and eye chart. The doctor made it clear that his interest was in sending young men off to camp, not in issuing medical deferments.

My greeting from the President of the United States, Order to Report for Work of National Importance, was mailed by the Local Board of Rockingham County, Virginia, on October 12, 1942. It read:

> Having submitted yourself to a Local Board composed of your neighbors and having been classified under the provision of the Selective Training and Service Act of 1940 as a conscientious objector to both combatant and non-combatant military service (IV-E) you have been assigned to work of national importance under civilian direction. You have been assigned to the Galax Camp located at Galax, Virginia.

Furthermore, I was directed to report to the local board at 8:00 A.M. on October 27. The order was signed by a member of the local board and then cosigned by the director of CPS Camp Number 39 at Galax after my arrival in camp that evening.

CPS Camp Number 39, Galax, Virginia

On the morning of October 27, with travel and meal vouchers in hand, I said good-bye to my family and girlfriend and boarded the Greyhound bus for Galax. Six Mennonite young men were in the group; three were married and three single. One of the men was my former boss at the hatchery. Our moods were mixed: a hint of adventure, sadness at leaving loved ones, uncertainty as to when we could come home, anxieties about the restricted life we were about to enter. The optimist in our group was quite sure that we would be home by Christmas (1942). We reached the Galax bus station that evening and were taken in a canvas-covered truck to the former Galax CCC camp, a set of barracks and outbuildings on the top of the Blue Ridge Mountains, several miles north of the state line with North Carolina.

Our group and two similar contingents from Ohio and Pennsylvania, twenty men in all, were the pioneer inductees at the Galax CPS camp. The previous occupants in the CCC camp had obviously vacated the barracks in a hurry. We spent the first week cleaning up the buildings and grounds. Within weeks a full contingent of 150 men had arrived, along with the Mennonite camp staff of director, assistant director, nurse, and dietitian.

At CPS Camp Number 39 we worked along a newly constructed segment of the Blue Ridge Parkway, a scenic highway that eventually joined the Shenandoah and Great Smoky Mountains National Parks, a distance of 485 miles. The camp was one of several located along the Blue Ridge Parkway and Skyline Drive. The project work at Galax included grading highway banks, building culverts, seeding roadsides, maintaining forests, and fighting forest fires when necessary. The park rangers were reasonable men to work for, were safety conscious, and provided variety in the manual jobs assigned to us. I liked the outdoor work but was glad to be transferred for some weeks to the National Park Service (NPS) office at the camp where I monitored the short-wave radio, communicating and transmitting messages among park rangers on patrol and with other NPS offices within a radius of 100 miles. At other times I operated a small tractor to clear brush that had fallen during an ice storm.

The Mennonite staff at the camp directed the educational and religious programs for the off-duty hours. Classes were offered in first aid, typing, Mennonite history, peace and nonresistance, and choral singing. The park rangers gave instruction on fire-fighting, which was put to use during an extensive forest fire in the spring. Religious services were held on Sunday; frequently, visiting ministers spoke. We had limited facilities for basketball and volleyball in an abandoned church building nearby. There was a small camp library.

Generally the morale was good at the Galax base camp, although there were times of boredom when we were confined to the barracks during winter storms. The camp population was diverse: various branches of Mennonites and Amish plus a minority of men from nonpeace church backgrounds. Weekend leaves or extended furloughs were tightly regulated by the SSS policies, just as they were for the military. We were discouraged from going into the town of Galax because the SSS wanted to keep COs "out of sight, out of mind." Incidentally the local prejudices against us had less to do with our being COs than with the perceived notion that we were all "damn Yankees."

The most pervasive morale factor at Galax was the nature of our work. During wartime there was practically no recreational travel along the Blue Ridge Parkway. In terms of "work of national importance," ours hardly qualified as a wartime necessity. In May 1943 the Galax CPS camp was closed and the entire camp population moved to Three Rivers, California, also under the NPS. I, however, missed that transfer because I volunteered for a unit in the mental health field.

Work in a Mental Hospital

As early as 1942 there was a growing interest among many CPS men for more direct involvement in some form of social welfare. At first the SSS resisted the idea because of fears of adverse public reaction if men were brought out of the isolation of base camps. But the wartime need for attendants in many areas was acute. Many low-paid hospital employees were leaving for better paying jobs or were drafted. So by mid-1942 approval had been granted for the establishment of CPS units in mental institutions. By the end of the war some three thousand COs fulfilled their commitment to work of national importance in sixty-five of the nation's public mental hospitals and state training schools for the retarded. The CPS experience triggered a major change in the care of America's mentally ill—but that's another story.

In February 1943 the Mennonite CPS office in Akron, Pennsylvania, informed me of a new unit to be opened at the Training School at Vineland, New Jersey. It was to be a small unit of twelve men, each a college graduate with a minimum of two years' teaching experience. I just qualified on both counts, having taught in Virginia public schools for two years with a Normal Certificate prior to finishing college. The Akron office also sent a copy of an article published in the *Survey Graphic* written by Dorothy Canfield and entitled "Thoughts at Vineland."[4] After reading her article about this school, which was famous for its programs and research with mentally handicapped children, I immediately applied for a transfer.

There was only one hitch. For some technical reason, probably because the Vineland Training School (VTS) was a private institution, I had to transfer there by way of the state mental hospital at Greystone Park, New Jersey. Furthermore, there was no definite word as to when the Vineland unit would open. Even though I arrived a day early at Greystone according to my transfer orders, I was immediately suited up in "whites" and assigned to duty on a medical-surgical ward for men. Without any orientation or training I had to learn the routine expected of hospital attendants on the job. Thanks to the supervisor and student nurses I was soon changing soiled bedsheets, feeding and bathing patients, using restraining techniques if necessary, and transporting patients to the barber or for electric shock treatment. The two working shifts at that time were from seven to seven. I was on the day shift. My brief experience at Greystone Park was a traumatic one: I observed a patient die on my first afternoon on duty. I had great respect for the

CPS men and their wives who worked for months or even years in this kind of service.[5]

One evening, after a week of duty at Greystone, three of us who had signed up for the VTS were told to pack our clothes and report to South

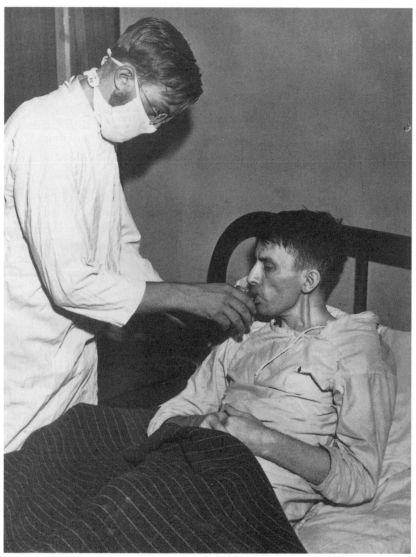

A CPS orderly assists a patient by giving him medicine at the Cleveland State Mental Hospital, Ohio, c. 1945. *Courtesy of the Mennonite Central Committee Photograph Collection, Archives of the Mennonite Church, Goshen, Indiana*

Jersey the following day. We drove by car to Vineland and thus inaugurated CPS Unit Number 92 on March 27, 1943.

Transfer to Vineland, New Jersey

The Vineland Training School was one of the few private institutions to obtain a CPS unit. The story was told that Pearl Buck, Dorothy Canfield, and Eleanor Roosevelt gained an audience with the president in the Oval Office to request that a CPS unit be placed at Vineland. Pearl Buck had a special interest in the request. Her only birthchild, Carol, was mentally retarded. Buck had donated a cottage to the VTS in which Carol, by then an adult, lived with other women her age. Dorothy Canfield (later Fisher) was a noted columnist whose article on Vineland would gain national coverage in *Survey Graphic*. With Eleanor, the three successfully lobbied President Roosevelt to authorize CPS Unit Number 92.

From the early decades of the twentieth century, the VTS had been a leading research center on mental retardation. Prior to World War I the Binet-Simon Intelligence Test had been brought to the school from France, translated, and adapted for use in the United States. The Vineland form of the Binet-Simon test was later revised by Lewis Terman at Stanford University, becoming the well-known Stanford-Binet Intelligence Test. Other important research on the Kallikak family studied the inherited and environmental causes of mental retardation. Research Director Dr. Edgar A. Doll devised the Vineland Social Maturity Scale, a measure to indicate a child's "social quotient."

The VTS had been established as a residential school for the mentally retarded in 1888. By World War II, 900 children of both sexes were enrolled on two campuses, one in town and one on a nearby farm. The term "children" was used broadly for all the residents, who ranged from two-year-olds to the aged. The institution had complete facilities in which many of the older children performed routine tasks. There was a laundry, a shoe repair facility, a truck farm, a cannery, a greenhouse, an orchard, a print shop, and a machine shop; many worked as housekeepers or kitchen help. The VTS was called "The Village of Happiness" and its institutional motto was "Happiness first, all else follows." With considerable integrity, these aphorisms set the operational ethos for the institution.

The VTS promised to be a stimulating setting for a CPS unit. Unfortunately, not all of the positions to which the CPS men were assigned measured up to the qualifications that the institution had specified. One man with a master's degree in music and college teaching experience spent several years as night watchman. Another was assigned to shoveling coal in the boiler house, another to grounds maintenance. It was one of those men who on a frustrating day revised the Vineland motto to "Let us find happiness in our work, lest we never find it."

In the early months at Vineland most of us served as relief houseparents, taking over a cottage of perhaps twenty children while the regular houseparents were on a weekend or vacation break. Being in a number of cottages with boys of different ages gave me a variety of experiences. In a cottage of schoolchildren, I was responsible for getting them up in the morning and dressed for school, supervising their meal times in the dining hall, taking care of them after school, putting them to bed, and supervising the bedtime prayers. For the other children, I had much the same responsibility except that they had work assignments instead of school. In the few cottages with severely handicapped children, the responsibility was considerably more involved because they needed care around the clock.

Goshen Relief Training Unit

I had just settled into the routine at Vineland when another transfer opportunity appeared. The Mennonite CPS office and the Mennonite colleges were opening a summer Relief Training Unit at Goshen College in Indiana for CPS college graduates who were willing to commit themselves to at least twelve months of relief service overseas following the cessation of hostilities. I wrestled long and hard with this decision before volunteering. On June 14, 1943, eighty-one CPS men enrolled at Goshen College for an intensive program of relief training. The summer program was as rigorous as similar college programs for navy or army officers. Over the next ten weeks we had fifteen semester hours of course work in philosophy and the history of Mennonite relief, community health and nutrition, area and country studies, Mennonite heritage, and physical fitness. In addition, there were thirty minutes of calisthenics before breakfast, two hours of conditioning and athletics each afternoon, and two hours of working for the college each day. I was on the dishwashing crew for the whole summer.

Hopes for immediate overseas relief work were dashed at the end of the summer with the passing of the Starnes Amendment, which was attached to the Military Appropriations Bill in the U.S. Congress. Among other things, the amendment specified that COs could not be released to colleges for relief training programs. Furthermore, no federal appropriations could be used to send COs outside the United States and its territories and possessions during the war. It was, however, possible to continue relief training in selected CPS camps or units. At the end of the summer each of us was given the option of continuing such training at a Gulfport, Mississippi, unit or returning to the camp or unit from which we had come. I chose to return to Vineland.

Return to the Vineland CPS Unit

When I returned to Vineland in late August 1943, the Training School was willing to use some of us as teachers in the day school. I was offered that assignment and subsequently taught for the next three school terms until June 1946. Although I was not trained in special education I had two years of teaching elementary school under my belt. Teaching was my chosen career, and I felt this assignment was a fortunate turn of events.

Approximately three hundred children were enrolled in the school under the capable leadership of Alice B. Nash, a noted educator. The full-time enrollees in school ranged in ages from six to twenty. The level of academic work they were able to handle varied from kindergarten to approximately fourth grade, although no formal grade levels were used. Rather, children were grouped in small classes, never exceeding twelve, according to their ability. At weekly faculty meetings, decisions were made periodically as to the best class placement for the children.

The regular teaching load was six forty-minute classes per day. The ages of the boys in the six classes I had varied from ten to the upper age limit. The objective was to carry each child as far as he or she could go with emphasis on reading, writing, and number skills. My classes were in those three areas, plus physical education. Rote learning methods worked best. Neither class assignments nor tests were used. Except for the perennial discipline problems I found it to be an interesting, but not very challenging, job. And yet there were times of individual progress and achievement that made it rewarding. My summer months were filled with a variety of assignments: supervising boys in garden chores, picking cherries and peaches, serving as night watchman, assisting in Boy Scout troop activities, and officiating at athletic events—field day, softball games, and swimming.

In November 1944 our unit leader transferred to another CPS location, and I was asked by the Mennonite director of hospital units to take on his responsibilities. My teaching load was adjusted to give me two afternoons per week for the administrative and clerical work of the unit. I met each week with the institution's superintendent, C. Emerson Nash, who was technically the camp director of Unit Number 92. I handled the requests for leaves, furloughs, transfers, and releases, and I kept the financial records. We held a meeting each Tuesday evening with a varied program: educational, social, religious, or unit concerns.

Women against the Good War[6]

Of immediate import to me was my marriage to Ruth M. Krady on December 30, 1944. In October 1942 when I was inducted we had a tentative understanding that we would get married after the war. But with the uncertain duration of the conflict, that intention was subject to revision. Ruth had a previous connection with the CPS program. She had served as a secretary in the Mennonite Central Committee's CPS office in Akron, Pennsylvania, from January 1941 to August 1942. In the early months of the war the office was small, so she held a variety of positions: receptionist, typist, stenographer, and file clerk. She set up files for the men as they were inducted into all the camps, beginning with the original Mennonite camp at Grottoes.

Ruth joined me at Vineland shortly after New Year 1945. CPS wives were welcome at the Training School as long as the couple had no children. If a baby was born, mother and child had to live off-campus. Three of the CPS wives at Vineland were teachers; one was secretary to the school principal, Mrs. Nash. Ruth was employed as secretary to the purchasing agent. Her boss, an older single woman, was responsible for distributing vegetables and fruits brought in from the farm to the various kitchens on the grounds. Her department also ordered and disbursed all the products the institution needed to buy. Ruth's work included keeping inventory records, working with the boys who delivered the foodstuffs and goods across the campus, and on Saturday afternoons helping to wait on the children in the store. This was the time and place when the children with good behavior records for the previous week could purchase candy and personal items. Ruth worked longer hours than I did and incidentally made a higher salary. When we left the Training School, one of Ruth's associates said that she would miss her and her good work.

Although the administration at the VTS was generally grateful for the labor that the CPS men and wives supplied for the institution, a few employees made it clear that we were not appreciated. Older women, in particular, who may have had a son or nephew in the military were understandably anti-CPS. Because I was the unit leader and a teacher, Ruth and I ate in the top staff dining hall. The seating arrangement at round tables was permanent. Two women department heads at our table constantly made snide remarks about the CPS program and certain people within the unit. There was little we could do except to let the remarks roll off without comment. In a few cases employees influenced older children against the COs, but most of the children sensed the motivations that brought us to Vineland and respected those in the CPS for their presence and quality of service.

Ruth vividly remembers V-J Day. She accompanied a carload of CPS members who drove into central Philadelphia to walk the streets and celebrate the end of the war. On the way home the group had a sober conversation about the use of the atomic bomb on Japanese cities and how it might influence future peace initiatives in the world.

During World War II some two thousand women voluntarily joined the CPS program. They were nurses, dietitians, and matrons in base camps; some were single women who volunteered for mental hospital service; some were wives who joined their husbands in hospital units; some were spouses who moved near the base camps where their husbands were stationed. The women attendants on female wards in mental hospitals were doing the same kind of heroic duty as the CPS men during this era of severe staff shortages. Despite cultural hostility and discriminating policies, the CO women of World War II sought to demonstrate their humanitarian convictions by taking part in CPS work.

Civilian Public Service Postscripts

Within months after V-J Day and the conclusion of the war, CPS men were eligible for release. Discharges were regulated by the SSS on a point system, with the length of service receiving the priority. By the end of June 1946 all the CPS men were gone from the Training School. My official discharge, which I was able to sign for myself as unit leader, came on April 8. My wife and I decided to stay until mid-June to finish out the school term. For those two months I was paid a regular teacher's salary.

It is important to note that men in CPS received no salary regardless of length of service. For personal needs, each of us was given a monthly token of between five or fifteen dollars, depending upon the base camp or unit in which we were located. There were rumors that someday we might get a share of the monies paid to the federal government by the agencies and institutions for whom we worked. The final word was that the accumulated amount had been absorbed at some point into the general fund of the U.S. Treasury. CPS men who left dependents at home often suffered serious need because the government provided no financial support for their families. In most cases the home church came to the aid of the family.

CPS veterans did not receive benefits through the GI Bill of Rights or from any other program that serves military veterans. In some communities the Mennonite Church helped former CPS men to go to college by giving them tuition grants. The Mennonite Church with a constituency of 120,000 at that time gave direct support for their CPS camps in cash and gifts in kind of $3.387 million. In lieu of war bonds, Mennonites subscribed more than $4.9 million for government civilian bonds during World War II.[7]

The generally favorable response that the public gave to CPS during World War II recognized several aspects of the program. Civilian work of national importance was performed across the nation in 151 camps and units. CPS was made possible through the generous support of the historic peace churches and at minimal cost to the government. Finally, the CPS men worked for the duration without salary or subsequent veterans' benefits. On several occasions I had conversations with military personnel about the CPS program and what I was doing during the war as a civilian. The clincher in their minds was invariably the no-pay proviso. In fact, it brought out some generous responses: a shared lunch, a proposal to buy a meal for me, and an offer of several dollars. Incidentally, my stereotypes regarding military personnel were revised also.

In the waning months of our CPS service at Vineland the unit decided to produce a summary report evaluating our experiences. Over the three years the unit had maintained a constant strength of from twelve to sixteen men, plus a number of wives working as paid employees. Our collective experience had introduced us into every department within the institution. We felt confident that our observations and evaluations might benefit the Training School and ultimately contribute to the welfare and happiness of the children.

Although our nine-page report was done in good faith, it was quite critical of what we felt was an inflexible institutional bureaucracy. Our report reflected both the idealism and the frustrations we shared as a group of young professionals. Fortuitously, the VTS had a change of top administrator just as our unit was leaving in June 1946. The new superintendent welcomed me into his office and accepted our report as one piece of orientation to his new position. He invited me back in ten years to see what progress had been made. Ten years later I returned for a visit. Not much had changed.

My reentry into civilian life, at least back into my home community, took a detour for the summer of 1946 because I enrolled in graduate studies. In the fall my wife and I returned home to Harrisonburg. I had accepted a position at Eastern Mennonite School (now University) as an instructor in English and physical education. Because my parental home, church, and community supported the CO position, I was welcomed back as a CPS veteran. At the same time I knew that some CPS men would find reentry difficult because they did not have a background of support. Some would face personal rejection and job discrimination because of their service record as a CO.

In reality, I was the one who had to adjust upon reentry. For the war years I was out of the sheltered Mennonite community. My experiences had revealed a far wider world. I had learned to accept and appreciate persons from other branches of the Mennonite Church and a number of other religious groups and pacifist persuasions. I had participated in a variety of work opportunities from the crest of the Blue Ridge Mountains to a huge mental hospital to a private school for disadvantaged children. My tasks had provided the stimulation of relief studies and the responsibility of unit leadership. I had developed a new respect for our government, which recognized and accommodated the range of convictions for nonparticipation in war and the desire to contribute some form of humanitarian service during the "good war."

According to Albert Keim, "CPS was not an ideal program. But in the brutal world of the 1940s the twelve thousand CPS men stand out as an astounding anomaly. . . . Their real significance lies not in their work or the nature of their organizational arrangements. It lies in what they represented and in their refusal to participate in the madness that was World War II."[8]

Notes

1. Peter S. Hartman, with Harry Anthony Brunk, *Reminiscences of the Civil War* (Lancaster, PA: Eastern Mennonite Associated Libraries and Archives, 1964).

2. Fred Miller, "Aldine Brenneman's Account of Experiences at Camp Lee, VA, during World War I," 1963. Unpublished paper in possession of author's daughter, Merma B. Shank, Harrisonburg, Virginia.

3. Among the books written on Civilian Public Service in World War II are Melvin Gingerich, *Service for Peace* (Scottdale, PA: Herald Press, 1949); Albert N. Keim, *The CPS Story* (Intercourse, PA: Good Books, 1990); and *Mennonite Encyclopedia*, 5 vols. (1955), *s.v.* "Civilian Public Service," 1: 604–11.

4. Dorothy Canfield, "Thoughts at Vineland," *Survey Graphic* (February 1943): 50–54.

5. Among the books written on service in mental hospitals as part of Civilian Public Service is Alex Saroyan, *The Turning Point* (Scottdale, PA: Herald Press, 1994).

6. Title taken from Rachel Waltner Goossen, *Women against the Good War* (Chapel Hill: University of North Carolina Press, 1997). The term "good war" was linked to Studs Terkel's 1984 acclaimed book of that name.

7. Gingerich, *Service for Peace*, 342.

8. Keim, *The CPS Story*, 101.

Suggested Readings

Anderson, Richard C. *Peace Was in Their Hearts*. Watsonville, CA, 1994.

Gingerich, Melvin. *Service for Peace*. Scottdale, PA, 1949.

Goossen, Rachel Waltner. *Women against the Good War*. Chapel Hill, NC, 1997.

Keim, Albert N. *The CPS Story*. Intercourse, PA, 1990.

Saroyan, Alex. *The Turning Point*. Scottdale, PA, 1994.

6

John Wayne
The Man and His Hero

John C. Lindeman and William J. Woolley

Most Americans never saw a shot fired in anger. Indeed, civilians during World War II knew less about conditions in the war zones than their great-grandparents had learned about combat in the Civil War. To keep the enemy from gaining valuable intelligence and to shape public opinion at home, the U.S. government and armed forces instituted tight controls over the press and private communications. All mail to and from the war zones was censored—a monumental job in itself. The press labored under tight constraints as to what it could publish. For instance, not until the middle of 1943 did a photograph appear of Americans killed in combat—and the release of that shot was so touchy that presidential approval was required. Americans in uniform were forbidden by regulation from keeping diaries.

Such tight controls, while burdensome, often made good sense. A famous wartime poster cautioned, "Loose lips sink ships." This warning was not mere hyperbole. A Kentucky congressman incautiously revealed in 1943 that American submarines were escaping Japanese destroyer attacks by diving to greater depths than the Japanese thought possible. The unfortunate slip was published by at least one newspaper. Japanese intelligence noted the story; the Japanese navy made the requisite adjustments; and the U.S. Navy lost, by one estimate, eight submarines (each with a crew of ninety) that might otherwise have survived. In wartime, the public did not need to know everything.

But the public naturally hungered for information about their relatives and fellow citizens fighting in far-flung corners of the globe. With television barely an embryo, most Americans got their news from the radio, magazines, newspapers, and newsreels shown along with feature films in movie theaters. To produce the newsreels, filmmakers sent photographers to the war fronts. Their best work retains an immediacy striking even today.

Still, many Americans gained their impressions of combat from Hollywood dramatizations. The film industry was certainly supportive of the war effort and churned out hundreds of movies. Although some of these were fluff, other films made a serious effort at portraying the grim realities of combat. But no matter how honest an effort, the medium was handicapped by inherent restrictions. Given the realities of warfare, movies could not, by their very nature, impart to an audience many of the most striking features of modern combat. Filmmakers found it impossible to portray the long stretches of everyday boredom or the vastness of large-scale operations, the stifling heat or wet cold, the repulsive smells of rotting vegetation and flesh, the noise and concussion of artillery fire, and the horror of seeing comrades hideously mangled.

Representing many of these contradictions—and bringing with him some new ones—was one of the most famous actors in Hollywood, John Wayne. Already a major star in Westerns before the war, Wayne made six war movies but never saw combat himself. The film star's story is told by John C. Lindeman and William J. Woolley. Lindeman specialized in American film history at Ripon College in Wisconsin. Woolley, a historian with advanced degrees from Indiana University, has been on the faculty of Ripon College for almost three decades. He is the author of "George S. Patton Jr. and the Concept of Mechanized Warfare," *Parameters* 15, no. 3 (Autumn 1985); reprinted in Lloyd J. Mathews and Dale E. Brown, eds., *The Parameters of War* (1987).

During World War II, John Wayne became one of the top movie stars in America both in terms of fan support and the commercial success of his films. Yet the John Wayne that Americans knew was not the actor himself, but the screen hero he and his studio had created. By 1939 that hero had developed a persona that had become predictably consistent from film to film and had become recognized and popular with American audiences. In the films John Wayne made between 1939 and 1945, both war movies and Westerns, that hero raised and dealt with issues about the war that concerned Americans most; those films thus reflected and articulated those concerns while at the same time they interpreted the war in a way that led Americans to feel they better understood it and the role they were to play in it. Hence, any study of the role of John Wayne during World War II must necessarily focus on two lives: that of Wayne himself and that of his film hero.

Wayne's hero was created, in part, by Wayne himself in response to long-felt psychic needs generated by an unstable childhood and adolescence. Wayne was born on May 26, 1907, in tiny Winterset, Iowa, and given the name Marion Robert Morrison. His early life was transient and insecure. Due to his father's inability to make or manage money, the family was often in debt and repeatedly forced to move. Young Marion, understandably, constantly felt like a social outsider. This sense of instability and isolation was aggravated by a chaotic home life. Marion's parents, Clyde and Molly, had a stormy marriage. Clyde was friendly and well liked but improvident. Molly, however, was shrewd and forceful and soon dominated the family. She also came to identify Marion with her hapless husband and even renamed him Marion

Mitchell after Clyde's father (Robert was her father's name and she didn't think Marion was living up to her father). Afterward, young Marion increasingly became the target of Molly's anger at her husband and frustration with her marriage.

His childhood experience left Marion far more consumed by the desire for acceptance than most young males and led him to focus much of his attention and energy on reconstructing his identity and self-image along lines he thought would make him popular. He began with his name, which he hated because he thought it sounded girlish. He tried several nicknames, but rejected them as well until some people began calling him "Little Duke" after his constant companion, the family's giant Airedale, Duke. Marion liked the masculine sound of "Duke" and quickly promoted it as his name and the basis around which he began to reconstruct his new and more popular identity.

His efforts paid off in high school where Duke Morrison became extremely popular. His good looks and athletic abilities helped, but his success was due chiefly to his frenetic efforts to be a leader in everything that counted in the community. In high school he excelled in both his studies and football, winning respect from student peers and teachers. He was also an active member of the Boy Scouts, YMCA, De Molay, the debate team, the school newspaper, dance committees, and the student council; in addition, he was president and salutatorian of his graduating class.

Because his family had finally settled in California, Duke entered the University of Southern California (USC) in 1925, intending to use his looks, intellect, athletic abilities, and energy to establish himself as the ideal American male in college as he had in high school. And he was successful, at least initially. Even as a freshman he starred in football, won academic awards, led the debate team, and pledged the most popular fraternity on campus. He also met Josephine ("Josie") Saenz, who later became his first wife.

However, even though he seemed to be an unqualified social success at USC, Duke increasingly thought he was not really part of the life and community. He was uninterested in that portion of his studies aimed at a career in law, which his parents had picked as the road to financial and social security. And he did not feel genuinely comfortable among his fraternity brothers. Most of them were "rich kids" while Duke was a "scholarship boy." Duke felt this social stigma with increasing keenness because he was not accepted by Josie's parents, either. They were members of the Hispanic elite in southern California and were acutely conscious of the social differences between themselves and the Morrisons, a working-class family headed for divorce. Moreover, Duke's social skills were largely in the area of drinking beer with buddies; once again he was the uncomfortable outsider in the polite society of the Saenz family.

Through this period, Duke began to see a growing contradiction in his life. Although his goal had been acceptance for himself for what he was, he had achieved his popularity only through role-playing, trying to be someone he was not. The class distinctions he had seen in his fraternity and in the Saenz family made the contradiction painfully obvious. He could try to fit into the Saenz family by putting on his polite face while with them, just as he put on his happy face for his wealthy fraternity brothers and his serious face in his meaningless classes. But these new roles seemed so artificial he began to sense he was denying himself.

At that moment, Hollywood came to his rescue. Through his football coach, Duke found summer work at Fox Studios. Although the job was no more than manual labor, it introduced Duke to Hollywood. And he loved it. Like others, he was captivated by dreams of big checks, unlimited opportunities, and public adulation. However, what Duke liked most about Hollywood was that it seemed to be a place where parents and social origins counted for little so that one could separate role-playing from real life and be accepted for who one was. So although Duke returned to USC in the fall of 1926, he did not stay long. A broken collarbone terminated his football career and scholarship. Efforts to work his way through school in pursuit of a law degree soon appeared to be as hopeless as they were meaningless, and by spring Duke was back doing manual labor at Fox Studios.

Once there, it was not long before his good looks were noticed by producers and directors. One of the first to discover him was the famous director, John Ford. Although Ford did not offer him a role in a film for ten years, the two men soon formed a close father-son mentoring relationship. Another director and Ford contemporary, Raoul Walsh, saw Duke moving furniture, and after a brief screen test, he cast him as the lead in the Western, *The Big Trail*. While shooting the film, the producer objected that the name "Duke Morrison" did not sound really American. A Revolutionary War buff suggested "Anthony Wayne" as a screen name, but "Anthony" was rejected as too Italian. "John," however, seemed American enough, and with that Duke Morrison became John Wayne.

The Big Trail, released in 1929, was a disaster as a film, but it gave Wayne a name, exposure, and an identification with Westerns. Unfortunately, it did so at a time when the popularity of the Western was in sharp decline. Moreover, much of the failure of *The Big Trail* was blamed on Wayne's inability to act. As the depression settled in on America, Wayne began his Hollywood career typecast as a second-rate Western actor, an identification that stayed with him for a decade.

During the 1930s, Wayne built his career on Saturday matinee Westerns. They were cheap products, often shot in as few as six days, and Wayne made nearly sixty of them. With the Western out of favor in urban America, he was in Hollywood purgatory; but Wayne was happy there. He took advantage of his time to learn acting from the great, but aging, stars of the silent film era. He also began to build an impressive fan base. Although released nationally, his films were most popular in the rural South and West where the idealization of the West as the last area still dominated by simple values, family bonding, and opportunities for growth and action proved as attractive to younger and older males as it did to Wayne. Boys and farmers in southern and western towns for the weekend would crowd theaters to see John Wayne movies. Even the predictability of Wayne's films proved attractive. Audiences knew that Wayne would be the good guy, that he would always beat the bad guy, and that he would always get the girl—and they loved it.

Most important, the Western was where Wayne felt comfortable. The frontier West, as idealized by Hollywood, seemed to offer both wide territory for individual exploits and small communities based on a personal, family atmosphere. There a man would be judged for his accomplishments, not his family name. There a man could find his place without the need to move from town to town to escape creditors. There traditional gender roles were well established—no domineering women usurped the role of head of the household. In short, Hollywood's Western fantasy seemed to allow Wayne to play hero roles that were no longer artificial but represented the person he thought he was and wanted to be. Wayne played the role well because he believed in it; and by 1939, he was king of the matinee Western.

At that moment, John Ford offered Wayne the part of the Ringo Kid in his new blockbuster Western, *Stagecoach*, which became the vehicle that got Wayne out of matinee Westerns and into top-grade feature films. *Stagecoach* was a critical and commercial success, signaling that Westerns were back in favor. It also allowed Wayne to be seen by audiences for whom he was a fresh face. And although the Ringo Kid was basically the same kind of hero Wayne had played for years in matinee Westerns, the values of simplicity, integrity, and masculinity were appealing to these new audiences as well.

Stagecoach was followed in 1940 by another major Western, *Dark Command*, with Wayne in the leading role. It, too, was a critical and financial success, emerging as one of the top-grossing films for Republic Pictures that year. It also proved that Wayne was more than just a one-hit wonder dependent on John Ford. Instead, Wayne demonstrated that he had the acting ability and fan base to carry a top film on his own. Wayne and Republic Pictures then went on to produce seven more films in 1940 and 1941, many of them hits, which indicated that as America entered World War II, John Wayne was rapidly becoming one of the nation's top stars.

America's entry into the war posed a major dilemma for Wayne. Many well-known Hollywood figures joined the services. Wayne wanted to enlist also but was hesitant to leave his career just as it was beginning to flourish. He was also concerned about money. Like his father, Wayne cared little about money, often spending it as fast as he earned it. But he was also painfully aware of how financial failure had destroyed his father's self-confidence and his parents' marriage and was reluctant to risk the loss of his earning power. As a result, it was not difficult for Wayne and his studio to decide that since a man nearing thirty-five would be of little use in combat, it would be in the nation's best interest if he continued his career in Hollywood. Studio lawyers then took charge of securing a deferment. Wayne initially consoled his conscience with the idea that he would seek deferment only for a year or two until he got his career firmly established, but he spent the entire war in Hollywood.

In terms of his career, Wayne's decision to avoid service in the armed forces during the war was a good one. The momentum and upward movement of his career that began in 1939 continued and accelerated during the war years. He released dozens of films, and with each one his star status in the country grew. He could pack theaters not only with his big productions but with lesser ones also. Republic Pictures even took to rereleasing some of his old matinee Westerns, which also played to full theaters.

And as his status as a star grew, Wayne's power in Hollywood grew as well. He was now able to take increasing control of his career. He felt free to turn down projects and to choose the directors with whom he would work. Cecil B. de Mille had to make a major personal effort to talk Wayne into appearing in his film, *Reap the Wild Wind*, a part Wayne would have begged to get just a few years before. Wayne also grew more confident and even arrogant on the set. He offered advice, whether solicited or not, to actors and directors. By the time the war ended, few doubted John Wayne's status as a star or his power. And the momentum he built during the war continued afterward. In 1946 he produced his first film, in 1949 he was nominated for his first Oscar, and in 1950 he was declared to be Hollywood's most popular star.

In terms of his private life, however, the decision to avoid service was disastrous. In the 1930s, Wayne had been credible in playing his hero in Westerns because he believed in that hero and wished more than anything to be able to be a moral paragon like him. During the war, his personal life moved increasingly in the other direction. And as it did, Wayne became more and more edgy and despondent and sought release in an all-consuming work schedule, in the company of his few remaining friends, and in alcohol.

The first casualty in all this was his marriage, although by the beginning of the war, Wayne had already decided that his relationship with Josie, whom he had married in 1933, was finished. For years he had been growing increasingly tired of what he thought was the social pretense in his life with Josie. To suit her they were always entertaining members of the social set. Given his exhausting work schedule, with ten- and twelve-hour days at the studio, Wayne had little energy left to put on a tuxedo and engage in polite chatter with people with whom he had nothing in common. Moreover, Josie was becoming increasingly religious and active in her church. She sought the company of priests until Wayne thought that the house was constantly filled with them. He began to feel he was suffocating and losing his freedom.

In 1941, while relaxing in Mexico, Wayne met a young prostitute named Esperanza Baur (called Chata). Although they were only together for a few days, she made a great impression on him. He saw her as a young and innocent free spirit, symbolizing the values in life he saw as most important. With Chata he felt he would be able to regain control of his life and be the person he wanted to be. He kept in touch with her after he left Mexico. Finally, in 1943, he separated from Josie and invited Chata to Hollywood. Despite the desperate pleas of friends, the separation became permanent and the Waynes were divorced in late 1944.

Wayne and Republic Pictures came through the divorce relatively unscathed. At the time, this move was remarkable for a man who had made his career playing the moral hero; but Wayne's fans did not seem to care what he did with his private life as long as the hero he portrayed remained constant. His friends, however, were scandalized by the idea that Wayne would give up the elegant, personable, and deeply moral Josie for a former prostitute. He was criticized heavily, especially by his mentor, John Ford, and his children all but ended their relationship with him. At the same time, his illusion that he would find freedom and a moral rebirth with Chata soon died. Their eventual marriage was a disaster due, in part, to the increasing remorse Wayne felt about his divorce from Josie and the moral failure it represented to him.

As his marriage to Josie had deteriorated, Wayne turned more and more to his studio friends for his social life and personal support. During the middle and late 1930s, John Ford had brought a small group of film people (Wayne, Ward Bond, Henry Fonda, and others) into a special circle that amounted to an extended, masculine family. The men took trips to Mexico for fishing, drinking, playing cards, and other activities associated with male bonding. For Wayne, who had never had a stable family life and who had always seen himself as the outsider, this new family became an almost indispensable base of support, especially under the growing pressure and tension incurred by his rising career.

The war, however, broke up this circle. As a naval reservist, Ford was called immediately to active duty. Fonda and most others enlisted soon afterward, so that only Bond and Wayne remained. Wayne had known Bond since USC days, and as the war absorbed his friends and his relations with Josie deteriorated, he began to lean more and more heavily on Bond. Although Bond remained supportive during the war, the relationship was not altogether a healthy one for Wayne, who was deeply concerned with issues of moral behavior. He was bedeviled by his increasing failure to live up to the standards he set for himself; moral issues, however, meant little to Bond. His carefree attitude gave Wayne some momentary escape from his growing sense of guilt, but only at a cost of deepening that sense of guilt later.

Wayne also felt as anxious and as guilty about his failure to enlist in the armed services as he did about his role in the failure of his marriage. His anxiety in this regard came from two sources. The first was his draft status. The III-A "family member" deferral Wayne had gotten in 1942 had to be periodically renewed. Although the lawyers at Republic Pictures were able to win renewed deferrals even after his divorce by claiming II-A status by virtue of his being employed by a "vital industry," the thought of being drafted continued to haunt Wayne. The other source of anxiety was a growing sense of guilt about not serving. Ford chastised him repeatedly about this, as did other friends who were in the service. Several times he nearly enlisted, and on one occasion he seemed so close to doing so that Herbert Yates, president of Republic Pictures, threatened to sue him for breach of contract. Given Wayne's status in Hollywood, it is likely that Yates's threats were only a bluff, but they are indicative of the emotional strain that the issue created for Wayne.

Wayne responded to these anxieties in two ways. He noticeably distanced himself from the war and war efforts. Although he made a few appearances in support of bond drives and at United Service Organizations (USO) rallies, he never threw himself into this work the way stars such as Bob Hope and Bing Crosby did. Instead, he put all of his time and effort into his films in an attempt to validate the idea that they represented a meaningful contribution to the war effort. Wayne's other response to his anxieties was to drink more and more heavily. Much of the drinking was done with Bond as a way to preserve the sense of community he had enjoyed with Ford's extended family. Although Wayne never became an alcoholic, his drinking bouts with Bond became more frequent, longer in duration, and more notorious as the war went on.

Although he became one of Hollywood's top stars during the war, he had little personal connection with it. He made only six war films and engaged in little other direct war work. Nevertheless, Wayne's films were critical in helping the American public formulate and express an understanding and a view of the war. The person who made them so, however, was not so much Wayne himself as the hero he portrayed.

Wayne's rise to national stardom was not the result of superior acting ability. If acting ability is measured by the variety of roles an actor can play, Wayne was no more than barely competent. For decades, he played only one role: his hero. However, what Americans loved was not Wayne's acting but his hero. They went to John Wayne movies to see the hero they knew Wayne would portray do the things they knew he would do, and they were never disappointed.

The Wayne hero was constructed by Hollywood studio writers and remodeled by Wayne to fit his own outlooks and needs. Working for market-oriented studios, film writers had learned by the 1930s the kinds of heroes Americans wanted. And no one knew this better than the writers of and actors in the matinee Westerns. The Western, after all, was a film genre based on heroes and heroism. The writers for these Westerns had no illusions that they were creating art. They knew they were writing for a mass market so that formulas that drew popular public reactions in one film were soon copied in others. By the mid-1930s, the contours of the American hero most likely to appeal to the public were well known to both writers and actors.

For Wayne, however, the heroes he played were more than just fictional characters to whom he must give credible life. For him, the Western hero was a man who came from nowhere but who made himself respected by demonstrating his high degree of moral integrity, superior abilities, and secure sense of his own individual identity. He was also a real man who dominated women rather than let himself be dominated by them. In short, the Western hero John Wayne played was the man John Wayne wanted to be. Although Wayne may not have been a good actor, his deep personal investment in and near identification with his hero endowed his portrayal of that hero with an intensity and integrity that gave the role a sense of genuineness and credibility few other actors could achieve.

The Wayne hero, as defined in 1939, was made up of several distinct characteristics, some of which were in conflict with each other; but the conflict tended to enhance the image of the hero, giving him a greater sense of both complexity and accessibility. Because the Western was an action film, the hero was a man of tough, physical action. In Hollywood's West, values were clearly defined and ambiguity rarely present so that decisiveness and moral conviction were easily attained and expressed in direct action. The Western was also an American genre and the hero was clearly American, expressing and defending the nation's values. Indeed, Wayne's films suggested that it was his hero's very commitment to these values that gave him the inner strength to win in any conflict.

At the same time, the Hollywood West was a preindustrial society and the Wayne hero was distinctly preindustrial and even anticapitalist in outlook, eschewing materialism and gain in favor of proper and self-less moral action. Moreover, he often acted alone, being wary of working within organized or corporate groups. In contrast, the villains in Wayne Westerns were clearly materialist in goals and often worked in groups.

The Wayne hero was also an individualist who struggled to be accepted for what he was. He was often a stranger who entered a community. Yet he was also a communitarian, expressing and defending the ideals and values of the community including selfless devotion to the good of the whole. Finally, the Wayne hero was an unabashed chauvinist who dominated women and taught them that their proper place was in the home.

However, because the Wayne hero was partially the product of film writers who were highly sensitive to changes in American public opinion, he did not remain static. Certain features of the hero's character and personality, such as honesty of expression, a readiness to engage in violent physical activity, and a chauvinistic attitude toward women, remained constant, allowing him to continue to be recognized and accepted from film to film. Other aspects of his character, however, including values and outlooks, changed as public opinion and Wayne's own outlooks changed during the war, giving the hero a virtual life of his own as he developed with the society he reflected.

The interaction between Wayne's hero and the war began with *Dark Command* in 1940. The Wayne hero in this film was Bob Seton, who rode into Lawrence, Kansas, on the eve of the Civil War. His obvious strength of character made him so well liked and respected he was elected sheriff. Thereafter, Seton was dragged into increasing violence and possible participation in the coming Civil War. When the Quantrill gang burned Lawrence late in the film, Seton reluctantly concluded that fighting in the coming war might be unavoidable; he consoled himself with the hope that it would lead to a better and happier world.

At a time when Americans were wrestling with the issue of possible participation in the war raging in Europe, Seton was a natural vehicle for depicting that portion of American opinion moving reluctantly toward that conclusion. He was otherwise still the classic Wayne hero of the late 1930s: the plain-speaking outsider imbued with basic American moral values who became an insider within his new community by espousing and defending it in violent and physical action. His opposition to the Quantrill gang showed him also to be an individual in conflict with materialistic corporate structures.

America's entry into World War II had a major impact on the Wayne hero as public concern shifted from whether to enter the war to why America was in the war and what being at war meant to its citizens. This shift can be seen in changes in the hero in Wayne's first war film, *Flying Tigers*, released in 1942. In *Flying Tigers*, Wayne played Jim "Pappy" Gordon, the commander of a Flying Tiger squadron in China on the eve of the war. In the film, Gordon retained many of Bob Seton's familiar qualities. He was a stranger who entered a community and, in fighting for it and the ideals in which he believed, won the adulation of his fellow pilots and the Chinese people. He was also a scrappy warrior whose idealism made him impervious to enemy fire and victorious even when outnumbered. Moreover, he loved a submissive woman who confined her activities to taking care of orphan children. And finally, he entered the conflict reluctantly in the hope that victory would lead to a better world.

Flying Tiger leader Jim "Pappy" Gordon, played by John Wayne, with his new fighter ace, Woody Jason, played by John Carroll, in *Flying Tigers. Courtesy of the Wisconsin Center for Film and Theater Research, Film and Photo Archive, Madison, Wisconsin*

What changed was the attitude toward individuality. The idea that Gordon and his pilots seem to take on the Japanese empire single-handedly caught the spirit of the Wayne hero as the lone individual against the corporation. However, the key idea in the story was the need to subordinate individualism to teamwork and idealistic globalism. Woody, a crack pilot, is converted from self-centered materialism to an altruistic globalism for which he finally sacrificed his life. In addition, while Gordon and his pilots acted like individual heroes in the air, they were still clearly part of a corporate organization.

The idealistic vision of World War II as a selfless American moral crusade did not last long. As the material and human cost of the war became more obvious, especially as American forces took on more and more of the combat load, disillusionment set in and the war itself became the enemy. Winning the war was seen as the way to end it, not the means to create a better and happier postwar society. Indeed, as race riots erupted in the North and West and labor unrest grew, Americans began to grow increasingly apprehensive about the impact of the war on the social fabric.

Wayne's hero soon reflected these changes, as can be seen in *Fighting Seabees*, made in 1943. In the film, Wayne played "Wedge" Donovan, the owner of a construction company contracted to build bases for the navy on Pacific islands. Over navy objections that fighting called for training, Donovan armed his men to allow them to defend themselves from Japanese attacks. Their first brush with the Japanese, however, was a disaster, which led Donovan to allow his men to get the training that transformed them into the Seabees.

"Wedge" Donovan retained many of the qualities that characterized Bob Seton and Jim Gordon. He was an outsider coming to redeem a troubled land. His integrity and concern for his men earned him their affection and respect. He was combative and forceful. And he remained a dominating chauvinist. In this case, the love interest was an aggressive and sharp-mouthed news reporter who learned from Donovan the joys of returning to traditional womanhood. And as in *Flying Tigers*, the main issue in the story was the suppression of individualism in favor of teamwork within the confines of a corporate organization. The fact that fighting on their own turned out to be disastrous for Donovan's men made it clear that it was only by working within organizations like the navy that Americans could win the war. The spontaneous individualism of the earlier Wayne hero was now out of date and dangerous.

Finally, the optimistic moral idealism that had characterized both Bob Seton and Jim Gordon began to disappear. The war was portrayed less as a struggle between good and evil and more as a contest between competing corporate groups. The Japanese were no longer evil; they were just the other team. The Americans' victory was due to superior organization, training, and leadership rather than any inherent moral goodness. Finally, neither Donovan nor anyone else seemed to feel that the war would lead to a better world. Donovan continued to exhibit a few good moral traits, including Bob Seton's honesty and simplicity of character, and he cared about his men, but otherwise he was to be admired as representative of the superior leadership of American military and capitalist corporativism.

The disillusionment with a moral and idealistic vision of the war escalated in 1944 and 1945. Wayne's hero reflected this attitude, losing not only his remaining optimism but even some of his integrity. This disillusionment is best seen in *They Were Expendable*, released in 1945. In the film, Wayne plays Lt. Rusty Ryan, who commanded a squadron of PT boats in the Philippines at the outbreak of the war. Although the men on the boats were heroic in sinking a heavy cruiser, the squadron was gradually chewed to pieces until even Ryan's boat was forced ashore and destroyed; the crew had to walk to Manila. In Manila, Ryan and several of his officers boarded the last plane out of the city, abandoning the crew to be killed or captured by the Japanese.

The Wayne hero was still recognizable in this film, but only barely so. Ryan was a courageous warrior who came from outside to fight, but many other elements changed. The issue of individualism, so central to *Flying Tigers* and *Fighting Seabees*, almost disappeared in *They Were Expendable*. The PT boats may have represented the "little guy" in a struggle against the "big guys," but it was also clear that however heroic such individualism might seem, it was suicidal in a world at war.

The moral and idealistic vision of the war also disappeared. The Japanese were not pictured as human beings; they appeared only on death-dealing cruisers or in airplanes. And they were not depicted as evil but as a dangerous force like the war itself. Ryan and his men no longer fought for a cause, as they did in 1942 in *Flying Tigers*, or even to end the war, as they did in 1943 in *Fighting Seabees*. They fought only to survive. The society they were defending abandoned them, presumably because, as the title of the film angrily suggests, they were "expendable." Finally, the Wayne hero was no longer a clear representative of the ideal moral values of his society. He was still brave in combat, but although Donovan died to save his men in *Fighting Seabees*, Ryan abandoned his.

To be sure, this erosion of the moral integrity of the Wayne hero by 1945 reflected Wayne's sense of his own moral decay. This sense was aggravated in *They Were Expendable* because his old mentor, John Ford, directed the film. Ford was merciless, castigating Wayne on every failure and insisting on the abandonment scene as a reminder to the star that he had abandoned his country by avoiding military service. But the film also represented America's own discouragement and disillusionment with the war as seen in other contemporary war films such as *A Walk in the Sun* and *Lifeboat*.

For both Wayne and his hero, World War II did not end in 1945. He continued to make films about the war for several decades. Indeed, Wayne's hero came to be seen as the personification of the modern

American fighting man, and Wayne's films about World War II became the war for later generations. And in these films, such as *Sands of Iwo Jima* (1949), *The Wings of Eagles* (1957), and *In Harm's Way* (1965), the Wayne hero continued to change. As the nation moved further from the war, the hero began to revert to the moral icon seen in Wayne's 1942 films. As he did so, Wayne and his hero became major contributors to the growing memory of World War II as the "good war."

Yet, for Wayne, World War II was not a "good war." His goal in the late 1930s had been to become the moral hero he portrayed. During the war he rose to be one of the leading stars in America, but he did not become his hero. Instead, the war demonstrated that he could never live up to the moral standard set by his hero. For Wayne, the war became a "good war" only by an act of mental reconstruction in which his hero played a major role.

It is likely that the same was true for much of the American public. While they lived through it, World War II seemed like anything but a "good war." It was only through later reconstruction of memory that the "good war" began to emerge. It was a false memory but a comforting one, and John Wayne and his hero were part of it.

Suggested Readings

Davis, Ronald L. *Duke: The Life and Image of John Wayne*. Norman, OK, 1998.
Doherty, Thomas. *Projections of War: Hollywood, American Culture, and World War II*. New York, 1993.
Koppes, Clayton R., and Gregory D. Black. *Hollywood Goes to War*. New York, 1987.
Roberts, Randy, and James S. Olson. *John Wayne: American*. New York, 1995.
Sklar, Robert. *Movie-Made America*. Rev. ed. New York, 1994.
Wayne, Aissa, and Steve Delsohn. *John Wayne, My Father*. New York, 1994.

II

The Government

7

Henry Morgenthau Jr.
American Statesman and
German American Jew

Dewey A. Browder

Although virtually everyone participated in the war effort, Jewish Americans had a special interest in seeing Nazi Germany defeated. The fanatical anti-Semitism of the German leadership was well known, and Nazi atrocities against German citizens of Jewish background were all too evident before the war in racist legislation, the burgeoning concentration camps, and vicious pogroms. Once the conflict was under way, the German leadership extended its racist policies to the ultimate by aiming through the Final Solution at nothing less than the physical extermination of all Jews. Other groups considered "subhuman," such as Gypsies and homosexuals, were also targeted.

Beginning in the summer of 1941, and accelerating thereafter, the Nazi regime began murdering hapless victims by the thousands. Villainy on this scale could hardly be kept secret, but when news leaked to the Allies, their wartime reaction was curiously muted. Historians have since asked if the British and American governments could have taken more effective measures to hamper the genocidal policies of the Nazis and to assist their victims.

A look at one of the Jewish leaders in the Roosevelt administration shows the complexity of the situation. Initially, Henry Morgenthau Jr. was slow to act, but as the enormity of the Nazi atrocities became more evident, Morgenthau advanced a plan to punish Germany and to prevent that country from ever again threatening world peace. In this shift, Morgenthau echoed the sentiments of his chief, Franklin D. Roosevelt, who had long felt that the Germans were to blame for World War I. As the advancing Allied armies revealed to the world the horrors of the concentration camps, the president wrote to Morgenthau: "We must be tough with Germany, and I mean all the German people, not just the Nazis."

Dewey A. Browder has published widely on German American relations. His most recent book is *Americans in Post–World War II Germany: Teachers, Tinkers, Neighbors, and Nuisances* (1998). While serving as an officer in the U.S. Army, Browder earned a Ph.D. in history from Louisiana State University in Baton Rouge. Currently, he is a faculty member at Austin Peay State University in Clarksville, Tennessee.

Henry Morgenthau Jr., U.S. secretary of the Treasury (1934–45), was one of the most important men in America during World War II. His influence went far beyond the oversight of the nation's economy, the rightful purview of his position. He also intervened significantly into the business of both the State and War Departments. Such influence often caused considerable chagrin in these two departments, but frequently Morgenthau acted at the behest of President Franklin Roosevelt, who sought the secretary's advice and gave him this extended reach.

Henry Morgenthau Jr. was born on May 11, 1891, to a well-to-do German Jewish family in New York City. His father had emigrated from Mannheim, Germany, in 1865 and become successful in real estate investments. As a child, Henry Jr. learned to help others. His parents supported a number of charities, and he came to believe that the purpose of the good life was to assist those who needed help. His parents exposed him to music and culture. They offered him excellent educational opportunities; however, he was more inclined toward physical outdoor activities than intellectual pursuits. At Phillips Exeter Academy he usually earned Cs or lower. He first studied architecture and then agriculture at Cornell, but he never graduated. Agriculture proved to be very appealing, and he firmly believed that land is the source of prosperity. In 1913 he took a major step with that belief in mind: he purchased several hundred acres of farmland in Dutchess County in the Hudson Valley. That farm would remain his true home until his death in 1967. In the beginning, the main product was fruit since much of the land was covered by orchards, but Morgenthau had diversity in mind. He quickly added beef cattle to the farm, and after World War I, he started raising potatoes, cabbages, squash, rye, corn, and dairy cattle. He and his wife, Elinor, took to the country life and helped supervise rural schools, fairs, and a mobile library. They set up a visiting nurses' service for Dutchess County, and they worked with the Grange and the local dairymen's cooperative. Morgenthau undertook to publish a farm paper, the *American Agriculturist*, which offered the latest scientific farming techniques as well as cooking and housekeeping tips.

One of Morgenthau's neighbors was Franklin Delano Roosevelt, who lived at nearby Hyde Park. Morgenthau and Roosevelt first met in 1915, and Roosevelt tried to convince Morgenthau to campaign for sheriff. In 1920, Roosevelt ran for vice president on the Democratic Party's ticket. Morgenthau worked for Roosevelt during the campaign, and the two men grew closer socially and politically. In 1928, Roosevelt ran for and won the office of governor of New York. Morgenthau then served as chairman of Roosevelt's Agricultural Advisory Commission and made the new governor the farmer's friend by pushing legislation that provided tax relief to farmers, expanded rural schools, and funded agricultural research projects. After Roosevelt was reelected in 1930, he appointed Morgenthau to the post of conservation commissioner. In this position, Morgenthau demonstrated administrative and managerial skills that encouraged Roosevelt to take him to Washington after capturing the presidency in 1932. Roosevelt appointed Morgenthau successively to be chairman of the Federal Farm Board, governor of the Federal Farm Credit Administration, undersecretary of the Treasury, and finally, secretary of the Treasury. Thus, Henry Morgenthau Jr. and Franklin Delano Roosevelt took their friendship and complementary abilities and interests to Washington.[1]

It was this relationship that gave Morgenthau greater access to the president than any of his fellow cabinet members. Roosevelt knew him, trusted him, and relied upon him. And Secretary Morgenthau was not a shrinking violet. He willingly thrust himself and his department into crisis-management situations when he thought others were too slow to act or when he simply thought he knew best.

Secretary Morgenthau's time in office paralleled very closely the era of the Third Reich (1933–45), and since Nazi Germany presented America with its greatest challenge to that point in the twentieth century, the versatile Morgenthau proved to be one of Nazi Germany's most formidable opponents off the battlefield. Indeed, this second-generation German American Jew helped arm America's allies around the world by his firm support for the Lend-Lease program. However, he did not always put his considerable weight behind moral causes that cried out for support. The best example of this reticence was his unwillingness to take a strong, timely position on the American reaction to the Holocaust as a whole or even the Final Solution specifically. He was instrumental in starting the War Refugee Board, but by the time of its creation, January 1944, most of the damage had been done by the Nazis in their genocidal assault on European Jewry.

Morgenthau seemed to be everywhere in Roosevelt's administration, especially once the war started. But in spite of his many contributions to the war effort, Henry Morgenthau Jr. is best remembered for the Morgenthau Plan, which he proposed in September 1944 for the reorganization, control, and punishment of postwar Germany. Through this plan, the secretary of the Treasury clearly attempted to frame national

Henry Morgenthau Jr. *Courtesy of Franklin D. Roosevelt Library, Hyde Park, New York*

and international policy in an area beyond his usual scope of responsibility. The Morgenthau Plan was never implemented, but it embodied a spirit of righteous vengeance that survived in some instances for a brief period in the postwar era; and because of it, his name has long been associated by some Germans with their postwar hardships.

Material Assistance to the Allies

When World War II erupted in Europe in 1939, the United States was a likely source for the supplies Britain and France needed to resist the Nazi juggernaut. In November of that same year, President Roosevelt authorized the "cash-and-carry" export of arms to belligerents. France, however, soon fell to the Germans, while Britain ran out of funds. Hitler had to be stopped, and in early 1941, Roosevelt instructed Secretary of the Treasury Morgenthau to prepare a bill that would give the president authority to help any nation he judged deserving. Once approved, this bill constituted the Lend-Lease Act. Ultimately, Lend-Lease aid totaled $50 billion, of which $31.4 billion went to the British Commonwealth, $11 billion to the USSR, and $3 billion to France and its possessions. The remainder went to thirty-five other nations, including China.

The United States extended material assistance in other ways as well, but Lend-Lease was the principal means of providing American help to those nations Roosevelt thought were fighting democracy's war. Britain clearly enjoyed a privileged status as the primary recipient. The USSR, in contrast, received much less aid. Morgenthau welcomed the Soviets as an ally against Germany, but he was wary of the long-term foreign policy implications.[2] However, Morgenthau had been instrumental in arranging logistics support to America's allies even before the advent of the Lend-Lease program. For example, in 1938 and 1939, when the French came looking for military aircraft to bolster their defenses, Secretary Morgenthau arranged for the French to buy the P-40, an advanced plane he described as the "best plane in the world." When President Roosevelt and the army general staff proved reluctant, Morgenthau offered the convincing argument: "Think about it again. . . . If your theory [is] that England and France are our first line of defense, then if you want them to be our first line, let's either give them good stuff or tell them to go home, but don't give them some stuff which the minute it goes up in the air it will be shot down. No sense in selling them that which is out of date."[3]

The Treasury Department got the task of arranging the sales to the French because Morgenthau was interested in expanding American industry and because the War Department had proved to be uncooperative. Of equal importance was the fact that Roosevelt viewed the Treasury's Procurement Division as the best prepared agency to handle the French request.[4]

In 1945, Morgenthau assessed the larger logistics support program: "I think the Air Corps got at least one full year's headstart due to the fact that airplane factories, engine factories, had been working on Allied orders, and all this was done from this office. . . . The idea of Lend-Lease was sort of born there that day [in reference to the meeting with President Roosevelt and Secretary Morgenthau in early 1941] . . . and there was no question that the Treasury wrote the Lend-Lease Bill and got it through the House and Senate. . . . Certainly we have raised the money [$450 billion] that the war has cost."[5] Morgenthau later stated in his diaries that he was driven by two purposes throughout the war: (1) the winning of the war; and (2) the idea that aid should be extended in volume in accordance with the military importance of the nation's allies and the efficiency with which the recipients could employ the equipment and supplies provided to them.[6]

The Jews and the War Refugee Board

From the very beginning, Morgenthau had found the Nazis' racial doctrine abhorrent, but it was not until December 1943 that he took decisive action to counter those racial policies. Indeed, Morgenthau was fully occupied with winning the war until the end was in sight, and then his interests turned to the postwar occupation and settlement of Germany, because he found that a "renascent Germany constituted the single greatest potential threat to peace in Europe."[7]

Only very briefly did he make a focused effort to save the Jews from the Nazi terror. John Morton Blum, who compiled Morgenthau's diaries, believes this was Morgenthau's "signal wartime success . . . in nurturing [a] humanitarian purpose in American foreign policy." The principal instrument for this humanitarian aid was the War Refugee Board, which Roosevelt established in January 1944 at the behest of Secretary Morgenthau and John Pehle, the man destined to become its executive director. To prompt President Roosevelt, Morgenthau had prepared and then showed to the president a draft of an implementing executive order. The board, according to the proposal, was to be composed of the secretaries of Treasury, State, and War. Roosevelt was dubious and directed Morgenthau to discuss the matter with Undersecretary of State Edward R. Stettinius. Morgenthau convinced Stettinius of the necessity for such a board, and with concurrence from Stettinius, Roosevelt established it on January 22, 1944.[8]

Morgenthau wanted to provide relief to all who were persecuted by the Nazis. He always contended that he sought to make America a place of refuge because he was the secretary of the Treasury of the United States and not because of his religion. But Morgenthau was, after all, Jewish, and the Jews were the special target of the Nazis' genocidal policies. Morgenthau knew all too well about genocide. He had spent time in Turkey during World War I, where his father had been the U.S. ambassador. While visiting his father in Turkey, Morgenthau became aware of the Turkish attempts to annihilate the Armenians, and he carried those memories into World War II. His views of the current situation were also colored by his ideas about Germany as a nation. Believing Germany responsible for World War I, he disapproved of German manners, and he despised Prussian autocracy, which he thought prevailed in the country as a whole.[9]

The War Refugee Board would come to the aid of the Jews of Europe, but other victims of persecution were to be rescued as well. Roosevelt charged the board with the responsibility for cooperating with interested American and international agencies; to utilize the facilities of the Treasury, War, and State Departments in furnishing aid to Axis victims; and "to attempt to forestall the plot of the Nazis to exterminate Jews and other minorities." At the same time, Roosevelt told the Bureau of the Budget to furnish the board with $1 million for start-up administrative purposes. Furthermore, Roosevelt stated that he expected the other members of the United Nations to cooperate in this important task.[10]

The establishment of the War Refugee Board was a welcome and important step in the rescue of Nazi victims. It was, however, too little, too late. Roosevelt knew of the mass murders as early as 1942, and the War Refugee Board should have been set up at that time. Beyond the fact that America was tardy with its help, Roosevelt's stated commitment to come to the aid of the Jews of Europe proved to be little more than lip service to a noble cause. The board, as pointed out by David S. Wyman, author of "The Abandonment of the Jews," "received little power, almost no cooperation from Roosevelt or his administration and grossly inadequate government funding" (90 percent of the board's funds came from contributions by Jewish organizations).[11]

The effectiveness of the board was also diminished by apparent anti-Semitism within the State Department. Assistant Secretary of State Breckenridge Long was frequently named in such accusations. He denied he was anti-Semitic, but Morgenthau did not hesitate to raise the issue with President Roosevelt and other senior State Department officials. In another instance, one Foreign Service officer complained, "That Jew Morgenthau and his Jewish assistants like DuBois are trying to take over this place." Observers realized that Josiah DuBois Jr., an assistant to the secretary of the Treasury, was not Jewish.[12]

Anti-Semitism was not the only domestic impediment to the War Refugee Board. The government simply was not united in its approach to the victims of Nazi policies. Indeed, the War Refugee Board had to contend with the inconsistencies of a national policy that advocated the rescue of the victims while simultaneously denying these same victims a place inside U.S. borders. Another major irony was that more than one hundred thousand German soldiers were prisoners of war in camps across the United States and were fed, clothed, and housed humanely—in spite of the fact they had fought against the United States. The refugees, however, had done nothing to harm this country, but they were denied everything.[13]

In addition to greater internal commitment, the United States could have demanded more help from both the USSR and Great Britain. The Soviet Union did little or nothing, rejecting all requests for cooperation from the board, and Britain, though somewhat more active in rescue operations than the Soviets, was relatively ineffective. Britain's poor record could well have been better had Roosevelt and his administration pressed harder for cooperation.[14]

The United States offered numerous reasons for not doing more to help the victims of Nazi racial policies:

1. Military efforts (for example, to bomb rail lines leading to Auschwitz or the death mills themselves) would consume vital resources needed to wage the war against German military forces.
2. Axis agents could sneak into Allied countries among the refugees.
3. Help for the Jews in particular would show favoritism to one group of victims.
4. Shipping assets were scarce.
5. Help for the Jews could fuel anti-Semitism at home.

Arguments both for and against these reasons have been advanced, but it seems logical that an earlier and vigorous rescue effort almost certainly would have accomplished more.

In spite of its problems, the War Refugee Board still managed to help save about two hundred thousand Jews and perhaps twenty thousand non-Jews. Where dedicated people and funds came together, the War Refugee Board experienced considerable success. For example, one program called for neutral nations, such as Turkey and Switzerland, to act as escape routes, receiving refugees and then funneling them to sanctuaries in Palestine, North Africa, or the Americas. As refugees departed the neutral countries, they would make room for yet more refugees fleeing Nazi-held territories.

In Turkey, the War Refugee Board's field representative, Ira A. Hirschmann, managed to reduce the fifteen-to-seventeen-week administrative bottleneck in the issuance of documents to at most three weeks. Hirschmann also paid to smuggle Jews through Nazi satellite states and over Black Sea routes to Istanbul. These refugees were then sent via rail to Syria and ultimately to Palestine. Hirschmann's operation was funded by the Joint Distribution Committee and aided by the Jewish Agency for Palestine. The Joint Distribution Committee was an American Jewish organization that sought to evacuate Jews from Germany. Hirschmann is credited with helping to save more than fifty thousand lives.[15]

Roswell McClelland, the War Refugee Board's representative in Switzerland, used money from the Joint Distribution Committee to print many false documents, ship medicine and sanitary supplies into France in large quantities, pay for the release of two hundred wounded guerrillas in France, organize escapes over the Pyrenees, support underground fighters in Slovakia, finance prison breaks in Italy, and smuggle refugees into Switzerland. McClelland scored these successes because he worked with underground groups who knew what they were doing and needed only money and supplies to help the victims of Nazi tyranny to escape.[16] The Joint Distribution Committee raised the money while the War Refugee Board saw to its constructive use.

The War Refugee Board prompted President Roosevelt to warn Germany and its satellites that the time would come when those responsible for the murder of the Jews would be held accountable. On March 24, 1944, the president released the following message to the nations of the world:

> In one of the blackest crimes of all history—begun by the Nazis in the day of peace and multiplied by them a hundred times in time of war—the whole-

sale systematic murder of the Jews of Europe goes on unabated every hour. . . . That these innocent people, who have already survived a decade of Hitler's fury, should perish on the very eve of triumph over the barbarism which their persecution symbolizes, would be a major tragedy.

It is therefore fitting that we should again proclaim our determination that none who participate in these acts of savagery shall go unpunished. . . . That warning applies not only to the leaders but also to their functionaries and subordinates in Germany and in the satellite countries. All who knowingly take part in the deportation of Jews to their death in Poland, or Norwegians and French to their death in Germany are equally guilty with the executioner. All who share the guilt shall share the punishment.

Hitler is committing these crimes against humanity in the name of the German people. I ask every German and every man everywhere under Nazi domination to show the world by his action that in his heart he does not share these insane criminal desires. Let him hide these pursued victims, help them to get over their borders, and do what he can to save them from the Nazi hangman. I ask him also to keep watch, and to record the evidence that will one day be used to convict the guilty.[17]

The War Refugee Board challenged the Red Cross, too, to aid in the rescue mission. The board appealed repeatedly to the International Committee of the Red Cross to "take direct and aggressive action to obtain humanitarian treatment for the helpless minorities being persecuted by the Germans." The Red Cross routinely replied that the Germans would not allow them to intervene, and the Red Cross could not interfere unilaterally in Germany's internal affairs. Such excuses for inaction were not accepted by the board, and the Red Cross continued to hear from the board. In spite of these repeated requests, the Red Cross did not aggressively pursue relief efforts until an Allied victory appeared certain. In the waning days of 1944, Red Cross personnel did gain access to some of the concentration camps and distributed food parcels provided by the Joint Distribution Committee and transmitted by the War Refugee Board. Arthur D. Morse, author of *While Six Million Died*, claims even this last-minute action "undoubtedly saved several thousand prisoners from starvation." The fact that the Red Cross provided such assistance has been attributed to the critical observations of the War Refugee Board. Additionally, the board transmitted $15 million to the Red Cross in Switzerland to pay for supplies and rescue operations. This money came from donations to the United Jewish Appeal.[18]

The Morgenthau Plan

Secretary Morgenthau was committed to winning the war and destroying Hitler's National Socialism, but then, in his own words, he was equally committed "to help win the peace."[19] Inherent in winning the peace was the idea of serving justice. Morgenthau thought the case so clear against the leading Nazis that the Allies could simply round them up and "shoot them." Starting in 1943, with his detailed investigation of the fate of the European Jews, he became more and more convinced that Germany had to be dealt with in an aggressive manner. He thought its war machine had "plans for survival" and that the Germans would continue to "cultivate dreams of world domination even in defeat." Such inclinations, Morgenthau believed, could best be thwarted by removing Germany's capacity for war making and educating its people in the ways of democracy.[20] He perceived the elimination of its war-making abilities as the apex of humanitarianism, by preventing World War III. It was his conviction on this issue that made him infamous—at least in Germany.

Usually, the purview of the secretary of the Treasury does not allow for primacy in foreign policy. Morgenthau, however, did not feel constrained by convention. He perceived disarray and misunderstanding among those responsible for foreign policy and chose to insert his views to the extent the president allowed him to do so. He expressed the reason for the extraordinary nature of his involvement in foreign policy in a conversation with Secretary of State Cordell Hull in 1944: "You know, Cordell, . . . I appreciate the fact that this isn't my responsibility, but I am doing this as an American citizen, and I am going to continue to do so, and I am going to stick my nose into it until I know it is right."[21]

His planning was spurred by what he perceived to be inadequacies on the part of others in Washington and London who leaned toward lenient treatment of Germany. In London, the European Advisory Commission (EAC), led by U.S. Ambassador John G. Winant, Soviet member Feodor T. Gusev, and United Kingdom member Sir William Strang, merely managed to proclaim the Allies would be the supreme authorities in Germany who would exercise control over political, administrative, economic, financial, and military areas—as well as other essential matters. The American team in London went further and expressed the hope that Germany would be left united with a strong economy and a democratic government. The EAC was clearly unable to agree on much.[22]

Military planners on Gen. Dwight Eisenhower's staff at Supreme Headquarters, Allied Expeditionary Force, worked out yet another proposal based on guidance from the Combined Chiefs of Staff in Washington. In broad terms, Eisenhower's planners envisioned:

1.   The arrest of high Nazi leaders and the dissolution of the Nazi Party
2.   A purge of the German courts of all Nazis
3.   A prohibition of all political activity, except that which Eisenhower might approve
4.   The revival of German agriculture and the importation of food and other necessities in order to "prevent disease and unrest"
5.   The restoration of public utilities, coal mine operations, and transportation facilities[23]

To implement these broad goals, Eisenhower's military government officers produced a draft titled "A Handbook for Military Government in Germany." According to this handbook,

1.   The occupying forces were to make certain "that the machine works and works efficiently."
2.   The centralized German administrative system was to be preserved.
3.   Enough light and heavy industry was to be retained to make Germany self-supporting and to keep the European economy as a whole on "a reasonably even keel."
4.   The average food supply for Germans was to be maintained at 2,000 calories per person per day (this was more than the people in neighboring countries would expect to receive).
5.   Military considerations were to have primacy at all times.
6.   The occupying forces were to have authority over economic affairs.[24]

In Washington, the State Department produced a memorandum on German reparations that supported "limited control of the German economy and the elimination of Germany's economic domination of Europe, but the eventual reabsorption of Germany into the world economy." Furthermore, the State Department advocated that reparations be paid in kind from current production with overall production sufficient to maintain a "tolerable standard of living."[25] Of course, this proposal meant the German industrial base would have to be left largely intact, a situation Morgenthau found both dangerous and unjust. Once he became aware of such leniency, Morgenthau decided America's foreign policy needed his personal touch.

On August 19, 1944, Morgenthau met with President Roosevelt and told him, "Nobody has been studying how to treat Germany roughly along the lines you wanted." Following this meeting, Morgenthau appointed three men to define the Treasury's view of the German problem. One of these three, Harry White, shared Morgenthau's ideas: "Germany should never again be in a position to wage war. . . . It might be necessary to reduce Germany to the state of a fifth-rate power."

Morgenthau's objective was to eliminate all German industry that could be used for military purposes, and he believed it unnecessary for the Allies to accept responsibility for the country's economy. As part of this plan, he considered it desirable to shut down Germany's great industrial center, the Ruhr, although he was uncertain as to how to do this. Additionally, Morgenthau wanted a prosperous Great Britain and a cooperative and friendly Russia.[26] While Morgenthau's committee was defining his department's position on postwar Germany, Morgenthau evolved and articulated very definite opinions on the matter. Some of these opinions were unquestionably his own, but he reached others during meetings with President Roosevelt.

In a conversation with Secretary of War Henry L. Stimson, Morgenthau suggested the possibility of simply turning Germany into an agricultural nation of small landowners. He believed that an agricultural lifestyle engendered a contentment that an industrial environment could rarely achieve and that in time the Germans would adjust and enjoy a richer life. On the matter of the Ruhr, an area he eventually concluded should simply be shut down, Morgenthau suggested the Germans who would become unemployed as a result might be put to work on an "international T.V.A. [Tennessee Valley Authority] . . . at work on reclamation and hydroelectric projects all over the world." The factories of the Ruhr, he said, should be dismantled and given as reparations to those countries Germany had devastated.[27] This course of action would have addressed three of Morgenthau's major concerns: (1) the weakening of the German economy; (2) the rehabilitation of the victim states (especially the USSR); and (3) the strengthening of the British economy, as British industry would get the business Germany lost. Morgenthau commented, "I can tell you this, if the Ruhr was put out of business, the coal mines and steel mines of England would flourish for many years." Indeed, he argued to Roosevelt that a healthy European economy did not require a strong German economy.[28]

Morgenthau seems to have derived from President Roosevelt the notion of reorienting German education. Roosevelt thought perhaps those people between twenty and forty years of age should be transplanted to some area such as Central Africa where they would be removed from the rest of German society. The children, he said, could be put in schools managed by former American, British, or Soviet officers where they would learn about democracy. Roosevelt also seems to have planted the idea that postwar Germans be allowed no aircraft, no uniforms, and no marching.

The committee finished its work, and the plan incorporating Morgenthau's ideas was set by September 4, 1944, in time for Roosevelt to take it to Quebec, where he met with Winston Churchill at the Octagon Conference. Morgenthau accompanied Roosevelt, and Roosevelt asked him to explain the plan to Churchill. The plan, entitled "Program to Prevent Germany from Starting World War III," contained several harsh provisions, which, according to Churchill, would have been like "chaining himself to a dead German."[29]

In its most essential form, the Morgenthau Plan called for:

1. The demilitarization of Germany, including the total destruction of all war materials and key industries basic to military strength
2. The cession of East Prussia and southern Silesia to Poland and the USSR
3. The cession of the Saar and adjacent territories bounded by the Rhine and Moselle Rivers to France
4. The designation of an International Zone made up of the Ruhr and its surrounding territory
5. The division of the remainder of Germany into a South German state comprising Bavaria, Württemberg, Baden, and some lesser southern areas and a North German state made up of the old states of Prussia, Saxony, Thuringia, and some smaller ones
6. The restoration of Austria to its pre-1918 borders
7. The establishment of a customs union between the South German state and Austria
8. The stripping, weakening, and controlling of the Rhineland and the territory north of the Kiel Canal so that "it cannot in the foreseeable future become an industrial area." All surviving industrial plants and equipment to be totally dismantled and shipped to Allied nations as restitution. All equipment to be removed from the mines and the mines closed.
9. A prohibition against future reparations, payments, and deliveries, except for forced German labor outside of Germany and the confiscation of German assets outside of Germany
10. The closing of all German schools and universities until an Allied Commission formulated an effective reorganization program. German students could, however, pursue an education in other countries.
11. The discontinuation of all radio stations, newspapers, magazines, and weeklies, and so on until adequate controls could be imposed
12. The control of Germany via Allied military government solely to facilitate military operations and occupation. All responsibility for the German economy and society to remain with the German people using such resources as remained.

13. The control of foreign trade and capital to remain under UN control for twenty years after surrender
14. The punishment of war criminals to be pursued
15. The prohibition of all aircraft, marching, and military uniforms
16. The policing of Germany and its civil administration all to be done via Germany's continental neighbors[30]

Not only was the Morgenthau Plan criticized by Churchill, but American politicians and newspapers rejected it out of hand. Officially secret, its contents were soon leaked to the press. The *Washington Post* reported that there was a rift within the cabinet over the handbook compiled by Eisenhower's staff. The *New York Times*, the *Wall Street Journal*, and the *Evening Star* all reported on and criticized the plan. Governor Thomas E. Dewey of New York charged that the Germans had been steeled by news of the plan and that it had helped the Germans as much as ten fresh divisions.[31] As a consequence of the negative public reaction, President Roosevelt ceased consideration of the plan per se. However, subsequent developments indicate the plan had some residual influence. Certainly a wide assortment of ideas proposing strict treatment for the Germans existed in late 1944, and Morgenthau's committee drew on a number of these ideas as it crafted the Treasury's plan. Specifically, the committee used a British parliamentary report and comments from Bernard Baruch as well as remarks and writings from Warren A. Seavy and James B. Conant of Harvard.[32] The British report called for restraints on the German economy, and Seavy, a law professor, argued the Germans would "menace . . . the future peace of the world" if allowed to retain their industrial wherewithal. Baruch and Conant also believed in strong controls for a postwar Germany. Eisenhower reportedly told Morgenthau he "did not favor a soft peace for Germans." And Morgenthau believed Churchill "wanted the Germans treated in a stern manner."[33] A U.S. Senate subcommittee stated that in order "to crush German imperialism permanently," it was necessary to alter the nature of German industry.[34] Such prevailing ideas would have made a soft peace difficult to achieve at the national level.

As it turned out, the governing U.S. document from war's end until July 1947 was Joint Chiefs of Staff (JCS) 1067, which President Harry Truman first issued on April 26, 1945, two weeks after Roosevelt's death. That document stated unequivocally, "The principal Allied objective is to prevent Germany from ever again becoming a threat to the peace of the world." It was stern, even going so far as to prohibit Americans from associating with Germans on anything other than an official basis. The Germans were given to understand that they were black sheep and that they were to be punished.

With the death of Roosevelt, Morgenthau lost his place of preeminence. Notwithstanding the initial triumph of a hard-line policy toward the defeated Germany, President Truman tended to rely more on the secretaries of State and War for advice with respect to foreign policy and military matters. Morgenthau was not completely swept aside, however. For example, he still was able to get an addendum to JCS 1067, which stated that even in the event of inflation, additional goods would not be brought into Germany, nor would the dismantling and removal of production facilities in fulfillment of the program for reparations, demilitarization, and disarmament be halted.[35] Furthermore, Morgenthau was adamant—and successful—in insisting that the Allies should in no way be held responsible for a German economy gone awry. And the provision that the Allies "should assist in the elimination of industrial capacity deemed dangerous to the security of the U.N." was not inconsistent with the philosophy of the original Morgenthau Plan. All in all, JCS 1067, as revised and reissued by Truman on May 10, 1945, was strict enough to elicit a comment from Secretary Morgenthau to the effect he hoped "somebody doesn't recognize it as the Morgenthau Plan." Of course, it was not the Morgenthau Plan, but the wartime spirit of righteous vengeance that Morgenthau had captured in his plan and that was widespread in the United States—especially after the death camps were opened by advancing Allied armies—was still to be found in the language of JCS 1067. That directive, however, was never fully implemented, and exceptions were regularly made later as the Allies managed Germany on an ad hoc basis.

The Bretton Woods Agreement

Within his usual sphere of activity, Treasury Secretary Morgenthau's most significant peacetime achievement was the Bretton Woods Agreement of 1944. The purpose of the agreement was to stabilize international monetary exchanges and thereby expand trade. Two major postwar financial institutions grew out of Bretton Woods: the International Bank for Reconstruction and Development, also known as the World Bank; and the International Monetary Fund, commonly referred to as the IMF. Bretton Woods bore fruit after Morgenthau's time in office, as this agreement laid the foundation for U.S. economic leadership of the free world. The agreement was not easily accepted in the United States. Isolationists, led by Robert A. Taft, saw the World Bank as nothing more than a new way of deficit spending for the United States. The IMF, the same isolationists argued, would be "like pouring money down a sewer." And both institutions, the isolationists argued, were unconstitutional. Morgenthau countered that although many of the member states needed economic assistance, "The conservative thing to do . . . is to help these people so they won't go either Fascist or Bolshevik. . . . The radical thing is to do nothing and sit by and let them go to hell." Morgenthau also orchestrated a media campaign in which he engaged the assistance of leading papers and journalists to explain the agreement to the American people. He was successful, and the IMF and World Bank came into existence in 1945.[36]

Morgenthau resigned as secretary of the Treasury in July 1945. He was, no doubt, disappointed with the turn of events in his personal career after Roosevelt's death. But he left with a feeling of satisfaction from his many contributions. He could look back and take credit for helping to defeat Hitler and then rescuing at least some of the führer's intended victims. As for the postwar world, he influenced both the occupation of Germany and the international monetary system. He summarized what was probably his most important contribution: "If Hitler had won . . . there wouldn't be any democracy anywhere, here or in England or in Europe. . . . I had an opportunity, thanks to Franklin, to help beat back that threat, and it was the greatest thing in my life."[37]

Henry Morgenthau Jr. lived for twenty-two years after leaving office. He retired to his farm in the Hudson Valley, where he continued to believe that the good life is to be found in the country and that those who enjoy the good life are obligated to help others who are not so fortunate.

Notes

1. John Morton Blum, *From the Morgenthau Diaries: Years of Crisis, 1928–1938* (Boston: Houghton Mifflin, 1959), chap. 1, passim.

2. John Morton Blum, *Roosevelt and Morgenthau: A Revision and Condensation of From the Morgenthau Diaries* (Boston: Houghton Mifflin, 1970), xv.

3. Ibid., 275.

4. Ibid., 280.

5. John Morton Blum, *From the Morgenthau Diaries: Years of War, 1941–1945* (Boston: Houghton Mifflin, 1967), 426.

6. Ibid., v.

7. Blum, *Roosevelt and Morgenthau*, xiii.

8. Ibid., 532–33.

9. Ibid., 564.

10. Ibid., 531–33.

11. David S. Wyman, "The Abandonment of the Jews," in *The Holocaust*, 2d ed., ed. Donald L. Niewyk, Problems in European Civilization series (Boston: Houghton Mifflin, 1997), 257.

12. Arthur D. Morse, *While Six Million Died: A Chronicle of American Apathy* (New York: Random House, 1967), 324.

13. Ibid., 340–41.

14. Wyman, "The Abandonment of the Jews," in Niewyk, *The Holocaust*, 262.

15. Morse, *While Six Million Died,* 316–18.

16. Ibid., 331–32.

17. Ibid., 337–38.

18. Ibid., 324–30.

19. Blum, *Years of War, 1941–1945*, 419.

20. Blum, *Roosevelt and Morgenthau*, 565.

21. Blum, *Years of War, 1941–1945*, 341.

22. Ibid., 329.

23. Ibid., 330–31.

24. Ibid., 331.

25. Ibid., 331–32.

26. Ibid., 327–42, passim.

27. Ibid., 351–52.

28. Blum, *Roosevelt and Morgenthau*, 579.

29. Blum, *Years of War, 1941–1945*, 369.

30. Henry Morgenthau Jr., *Germany Is Our Problem* (New York: Harper & Brothers, 1945), items 1–4 of "The Morgenthau Plan."

31. Blum, *Years of War, 1941–1945*, 377–79.

32. Ibid., 343.

33. Ibid., 335–37.

34. Ibid., 391.

35. Ibid., 455.

36. Ibid., 429–33.

37. Ibid., 474–75.

Suggested Readings

Blum, John Morton. *From the Morgenthau Diaries: Years of Crisis, 1928–1938.* Boston, 1959.

———. *From the Morgenthau Diaries: Years of Urgency, 1938–1941.* Boston, 1965.

———. *From the Morgenthau Diaries: Years of War, 1941–1945.* Boston, 1967.

Morgenthau, Henry, Jr. *Germany Is Our Problem.* New York, 1945.

Morse, Arthur D. *While Six Million Died: A Chronicle of American Apathy.* New York, 1967.
Wyman, David S. "The Abandonment of the Jews," in *The Holocaust.* 2d ed. Edited by Donald L. Niewyk. Problems in European Civilization series. Boston, 1997.

8

Margaret Chase Smith
Wartime Congresswoman

Janann Sherman

On the day following Pearl Harbor, Congress voted to declare war on Japan by a margin of 470 to 1. The lone dissenter was Jeanette Rankin, a representative from Montana. In fact, Rankin stood outside the mainstream in other ways: the first woman in Congress, she had been elected in 1916, four years prior to the ratification of the Nineteenth Amendment guaranteeing the vote to women. Nothing if not consistent in her pacifism, Rankin had voted "No" on the declaration of war against Germany in April 1917; late in her life, she spoke against the Vietnam War. In 1941 her solitary stand on the declaration of war against Japan seemed incongruous even to her constituents. They turned her out at the first opportunity.

Much more in tune with the sentiments of American women—and the American people generally—was Margaret Chase Smith, one of only eight women serving in the House of Representatives in 1941. Smith had "inherited" her husband's seat from Maine in 1940 as a "congressional widow." Winning election to the House in her own right four more times, she went on to serve twenty-four years in the Senate (1949–73).

Smith was a trailblazer, a gritty woman from the blue-collar world who empathized with those who suffered from the dual handicaps of being female and poor. Specializing in national defense issues, Smith quickly won respect for her work on the House Committee on Naval Affairs. From this position, she pushed hard for measures to aid war workers, both male and female, and to advance women's roles in the armed services.

Congresswoman Smith's story is told by Janann Sherman of the University of Memphis in Tennessee. Sherman earned her doctorate at Rutgers University in New Jersey with a specialization in women's history. Her full-length biography of Margaret Chase Smith, *No Place for a Woman: A Life of Senator Margaret Chase Smith*, was published in 2000.

Excerpted from Chapter 5, "Naval Affairs," in Janann Sherman, *No Place for a Woman: A Life of Senator Margaret Chase Smith* (New Brunswick, NJ: Rutgers University Press, 2000), 58–72. Reprinted by permission of Rutgers University Press.

Margaret Chase Smith won her first election to the U.S. House of Representatives in 1940, following the death of her husband, Clyde H. Smith, a two-term congressman from Maine. She went on to serve eight years in the House, followed by twenty-four years in the U.S. Senate. When Smith first assumed office, war was intensifying in Europe, and before the end of her first term, the United States had become a full participant. Scholars continue to debate the liberating potential of wartime for women: did the nation's need for woman-power to fuel home-front production foster permanent advancement or only temporary change? For Congresswoman Smith, wartime exigencies brought a new validity for women in the public sphere and increasing importance to their representation in government.

One of only seven women in the U.S. House of Representatives during the war, Smith worked on a variety of military and home-front issues, representing her gender in the media, the committee room, and on the House floor. Of particular importance was her position on one of the most important committees in wartime: the House Committee on Naval Affairs (NAC). From there, Smith lobbied for the amelioration of discriminatory practices in industry and society, proposed legislation to formalize women's wartime gains, and forcefully pursued a series of measures to expand women's roles in military service.

Within days of her appointment, Smith was named to a seven-"man" NAC subcommittee to investigate vice (a euphemism for prostitution) and a rising venereal disease rate in areas surrounding naval ports.[1] Although vice and its impact on the progress of the war was the impetus, a whole constellation of desperate conditions in congested port cities soon prompted the subcommittee to broaden its focus. Hundreds of witnesses came to complain, to explain, to justify, and to plead for help, poignantly revealing the scope and complexity of the problems. The Congested Areas Subcommittee had a front-row seat on wartime America in its most extreme circumstances.[2]

In port cities, the streets were teeming with people, night and day, in a ceaseless pageant of arrivals and departures. Thousands of men in uniform jostled in the streets with coveralled war workers, male and female, rushing to catch overcrowded buses to get to jobs and home again. Streets leading from the harbor to downtown were lined with honky-tonks, juke joints, bawdy houses, and tattoo parlors, all competing for attention with bright neon signs and loud music. Long lines snaked down the sidewalks and into the streets: lines to get into restaurants, into movies, into taverns, into grocery stores. Men in uniform and men in grimy work clothes slept in the streets, in their cars, in hotel lobbies, on park benches. Life in boomtown was, in short, "life on a more primitive level."[3]

As the hearings opened in Norfolk, Virginia, an array of military and local health officials debated venereal disease rates and described their efforts to control prostitution. Two years earlier, Andrew Jackson May, chairman of the House Military Affairs Committee, pushed through legislation making vice activities near military installations a federal offense. From testimony, it appeared that the net effect of closing these red-light districts had not been the elimination of prostitution, but its dispersal. Moreover, disturbing testimony made it plain that the prostitute's place as a major source of contagion was rapidly being taken by transient young girls, sometimes only twelve to fourteen years old, who were assumed to be unable to resist a uniform. A third group of women straddled the line between professional and amateur. These were chiefly waitresses in restaurants and beer parlors.

Legal definitions of prostitutes were intentionally vague to allow police to assume extensive discretionary authority. "Promiscuous," or simply unescorted, women were picked up, compelled to undergo degrading medical examinations for venereal disease, and, if found infected, forcibly detained for as long as six months. Ignoring obvious violations of constitutional rights, authorities believed repression and detention had proven to be "a practical and thoroughly effective police procedure for the control of venereal disease."[4]

Dismayed by reports of hundreds of women being rounded up and thrown into overcrowded facilities, Smith managed to slip off alone, between sessions, to visit the Norfolk jail. There she found ninety-one women and girls were being held in a space intended for twenty-five. Scattered mattresses, topped with filthy blankets, lay about the floor. There was one lavatory and one table. Forced to wait weeks, even months, before being sentenced or diverted to their home authorities (social workers, health agents, and so on), the women, Smith told the press (who dubbed her the "vice admiral"), "had absolutely nothing to do, not even a place to sit down." Most of the younger girls had been arrested, she found, for being alone on the street, trying to find a brother or a boyfriend in the hustle-bustle of boomtown. Port towns were replete with large numbers of men in uniform; sometimes 70,000–80,000 men were "at liberty" (on leave) in Norfolk. Married women told Smith of finding themselves stranded when their husbands were moved to another area, and of being bored and lonely. They went out unescorted and were promptly arrested.[5]

Vice raids fell most heavily upon lower- and working-class women. Smith was particularly sensitive to their problems because she was one herself. The daughter of a small-town (Skowhegan, Maine) barber and a homemaker who waited tables and stitched shoes to help support their six children, Margaret Chase had been working since she was twelve years old. Beginning as a dime-store clerk and night telephone operator, she briefly taught elementary school after high school graduation before taking a job as a stenographer and girl Friday for her hometown newspaper. She later moved up to the position of office manager of a woolen mill. When she was thirty-two, Margaret married Clyde Smith, a fifty-four-year-old businessman and first selectman (the equivalent of mayor), becoming his aide, secretary, campaign manager, and, as Clyde put it, "partner in public life." Elected to Congress in 1936 and again in 1938, Clyde died in the spring of 1940. His widow fought four difficult campaigns in the next five months to win his unexpired term and a term in her own right.

Because she had spent her entire adult life in pink-collar work and understood the struggles of single women, Smith rushed to defend working women. A girl in Norfolk, she told the subcommittee and city officials, did not have a chance to survive waiting tables or working in beer parlors at starvation wages of only ten or twelve dollars per week (women working in war industry typically made three to four times that amount). Young women without skills, Smith asserted, often found prostitution an economic necessity.[6]

Throughout the hearings, Smith vigorously objected to the unsanitary and neglected condition of the female inmates, the wrongful detention of innocent girls, and the absence of programs for training and rehabilitation. Although she favored detaining the women until they were well, she found it unforgivable that no one was making an effort to see that they were trained to make "a better kind of living." When Smith asked the *Newport News* city manager if anything was being done to "help girls coming in, without jobs or with jobs that don't pay enough, to contact them before they get into the hands of the police," he replied lamely that some social agencies tried to help, but usually the girls were picked up, and those who were not infected were turned back to their home authorities. "I can't think of anything less effective," Smith said sharply, "than sending them home at random."[7]

Discussions of vice were soon overwhelmed by a vast array of social disruptions brought about by the rapid expansion of war industry and military activities in the port cities. Towns had been transformed from largely residential communities into overcrowded industrial centers almost overnight. Few municipalities registered population increases of less than 100 percent since the war began and several on the West Coast had exploded into boomtowns five and six times their normal size within two years. In these areas, as many as fourteen people occupied a single room, sharing one toilet with twenty other families. Federal temporary housing projects, in those places lucky enough to have them, had no streets and no sewers, just flammable wooden shacks in a sea of mud. Food shortages of monumental proportions resulted from rationing programs based upon prewar population figures. Grocery shelves cleared within an hour of opening in Virginia, and two hundred restaurants in San Francisco closed in 1943 after their food allowances were cut in half. Manpower shortages left municipalities without adequate fire and police protection, transportation services, or garbage collection. Raw sewage flowed directly into beach areas, foreclosing recreation and polluting seafood sources. Communities threatened with epidemics of typhus, bubonic plague, and malaria reported critical shortages of doctors and hospital beds.

Moreover, the perceived need for another full complement of city and military services for the "negro" population placed additional burdens on these communities. Race relations, always volatile, grew increasingly tense in the separate but unequal atmosphere of the cities. "Colored" housing was notably inferior to the worst whites had to bear and was often built beyond the reach of public transportation. Black soldiers had no access to USOs or the other meager entertainments; black war workers, male and female, were assigned to the most menial chores and assumed to be infiltrated by "bad elements" who made trouble and were on the verge of being wildly out of control, having too much money to spend on liquor and drugs.

This constellation of problems in congested areas was manifested in individual lives. The average male recruited to work in war industry would arrive to find no housing. He lived out of his car or shared a "hot bed"—rotating an eight-hour sleep shift—in a stifling dormitory. Since it often took two or three hours to reach his ten-hour war job, he left too early to get breakfast at one of the very few restaurants that had enough food to open. At lunchtime, he could hope for a meager meal at work—the cafeteria at the Bethlehem Shipyards, for example, was issued exactly one-tenth of an ounce of meat per meal per man. It was nearly impossible to get food after work because restaurants were constantly running out, and most food stores closed before workers could reach them. The war worker was tired and he was hungry.

Women working in war industry had the same problems as the men plus another full set: working mothers were further burdened by stores that closed early; meal preparation was complicated by rationing and shortages; they struggled with inadequate child care arrangements, insufficient medical services for themselves and their children, and long lines and shoddy merchandise. The subcommittee found the average woman worked thirteen days on, one day off, then worked six days on, one day off, followed by another thirteen days on, and so forth. Most women had full responsibility for the shopping and for the care of their homes, their husbands, and their children. They got their work done at the expense of their sleep and health.

The impact of these problems was, while predictable, profound: absenteeism, often nearly 20 percent of the workforce, and labor turnover rates approaching 100 percent in most West Coast ports. Women's absentee rates were 50 percent greater and their turnover rate was more than double that of men. Uncovering the reasons behind those figures was one major goal for Smith. A steady stream of war industry representatives complained that women were unreliable, often took a day off without warning, and frequently and capriciously quit their jobs. What, Smith asked, was being done to help women handle their dual responsibilities? Was part-time work available, and what about programs for child care? Part-time work was simply too complicated to offer, replied the employment manager of Consolidated Vultee Aircraft Corporation (San Diego) in a typical response; and as for child care, "We have felt that should be handled outside the company," he said, referring obliquely to "undue obligations to employees."[8] Smith insisted the record reflect that women's absenteeism was due to circumstances beyond their control; they were simply being asked to assume too much of the burden. She asked, "Shouldn't we be doing something to help?"[9]

Like most junior members of Congress, Smith had limited ability to influence her colleagues. Her significance rested in her attempts to raise issues that would not otherwise have been addressed. Very few women testified at the Congested Areas Hearings—only 13 of 421 witnesses—and most of them appeared as representatives of federal, state, or local authorities. No one spoke for working-class women—whether prostitute or aircraft welder—and no one spoke for women and children, except Smith. Her suggestions for child care, housing for families with two employed parents, more inexpensive housing for single women, flexible hours, and a recognition that working women juggled at least two jobs reflected a sensitivity to women's situations not apparent in the men serving on or appearing before the subcommittee. Her presence and persistence seemed, too, to raise the consciousness of her colleagues. After a few hearings, Chairman Ed Izac and Rep. John Fogarty started sounding like Smith, seizing the opportunity to point out to industry representatives that women war workers needed assistance, not blame.[10]

Child care became the pivotal issue around which discussions of women's place in wartime revolved. Early in the war, mothers had been specifically exempted from industry's recruiting appeals. Mobilization depended heavily upon the ability of housewives to deal with rationing, shortages, price controls, scarcity, and the extra work involved in shopping, canning, gardening, and raising children in the absence of fathers. When the need for women's labor outweighed those considerations, large numbers of mothers moved into the workplace. But because of conventional attitudes about women and the presumed transient nature of their place in war industry, few provisions were made to help them handle their domestic responsibilities. Not surprisingly, government-sponsored studies concluded that lack of safe, convenient, affordable child care was a major cause of women's absenteeism. As many as 33 percent of nonworking mothers indicated they would take war jobs if they had someone to care for their children.[11] Smith made it a point to get industrial representatives to admit that women who did have access to child care were dependable workers.

The 1941 Lanham Community Facilities Act provided federal funds for the day care of children of working mothers. Like all such programs, a plethora of regulations dictated disbursement, and the flow of funding was hampered by ambivalence at every level. On the local level, resistance was revealed by remarks like that of a school official in South Portland who bluntly stated that he "would not advocate a nursery school. It constitutes juvenile delinquency."[12] The assumption that the alarming increase in truancy and petty crime, not to mention juvenile prostitution, was the fault of mothers who worked, and that those women took jobs out of a selfish desire for high wages, was evident throughout the hearings. When Smith suggested that surely there were some women who had to work and asked, "What happens to their children?" most responded that was a problem for the mother to solve.

These same attitudes were reflected at the congressional level where child-care funding remained precarious, even at the height of the war emergency. Working with five other congresswomen across partisan lines, Smith fought the efforts of Rep. John Taber (R-NY), ranking Republican on the House Appropriations Committee, to cut funding nearly in half—from $127.5 million to $68.6 million—in 1944. In her very first speech on the floor of the House, Smith pleaded for recognition of the difficulties working mothers faced: "We found many women standing in line waiting for medical care, for themselves and their children. We found them waiting hours after work to get their groceries and other necessities. We found children roaming the streets and some even locked in automobiles, not only because their war-working parents were absent from home but also because of the lack of child-care facilities and schools. This is an emergency. We have waited altogether too long to meet it. . . . We can economize, but not when it comes to the care of our children."[13]

Opposing testimony was provided by Clare Hoffman (R-MI), who contended that public child care would be unnecessary "if some of these women, instead of going into beer parlors, would go home and take care of their children." Taber's amendment lost by five votes, 59 to 64, but Smith's was a meager victory. She held the line, but stiff opposition foreclosed any chance to increase funding.[14] At peak capacity, the child-care program administered by the Federal Works Agency enrolled fewer than 3 percent of the children under fourteen of working mothers.[15]

Smith's sensitivity to gender discrimination, heightened through many years in the workplace, also led her to pursue a series of measures during and after the war to equalize opportunities for women. The first bill she submitted to Congress aimed to abolish the differentials in minimum ages for war work, lowering the minimum age for girls from eighteen to sixteen to match that of boys.[16] Later, she joined other congresswomen in attempting to codify equal pay for equal work. Wartime had not erased the boundaries between men's and women's work, but in many instances, the boundaries were redrawn. Many male jobs were modified (most often simplified) into female ones, making unequal wage rates more easily explainable. However, when women began literally taking men's jobs, employers and unions were faced with a dilemma. To pay a woman at a man's wage undermined the barriers that divided women's work from men's, but to pay women in a man's job less undermined the value of the job and threatened men's wage scales when they returned to reclaim those jobs. Primarily because of their desire to sustain male wages, government and labor unions combined in attempts to persuade management to equalize wages. In 1942 the War Labor Board issued General Order 16 permitting employers to balance wage and salary rates between males and females "for comparable quality and quantity of work." This was, however, only a suggestion. In heavy industry, the war increased instead of decreased sex segregation in the workplace. Even at its peak, women held only 4.4 percent of skilled jobs and supervisory positions.[17] In 1945, Chairman of the House Labor Committee Mary Norton introduced legislation mandating equal pay for women. Vigorously opposed by management and chambers of commerce, the bill failed.[18] Two years later, Representatives Smith and Helen Gahagan Douglas introduced equal pay bills. These measures also failed.[19] Clearly, the modest gains women made in the workplace during the war were hard won and short lived.

Controversies surrounding the issues of equal rights, equal pay, and government-sponsored child care reflect the ways in which women's social progress during World War II depended upon the exigencies of war need. They also illuminate the boundaries of acceptable women's roles and the limits to the power of a handful of female representatives. Smith had more success in her efforts on behalf of military women, partly because she had gained increased power within the committee, partly because others more powerful than she desired the same ends, and partly because she had learned to make skillful use of the process.[20]

Just prior to American entry into World War II, Rep. Edith Rogers (R-MA), who had experienced the problems of civilian women working with the army in the previous war during which she served as a Red Cross nurse, proposed legislation to establish the Women's Army Auxiliary Corps (WAAC).[21] Smith testified in support of the bill and, like Rogers, she preferred a women's corps that would be "a regular part of the Army in every way, excepting of course, actual combat."[22]

Four basic themes were stressed by proponents of the WAAC bill, in these as well as in subsequent discussions about women's military service: the efficiency of employing women in times of manpower shortages in order to free men for combat; women's "natural" abilities, which made them better suited for some occupations, notably those that required finger dexterity and involved a significant amount of tedium; the justice of providing women the opportunity to exercise their rights and responsibilities as citizens of the republic; and pledges that women's duties, authority, and length of service would be strictly limited and, unlike civilian volunteers, could be strictly controlled. Despite assurances that the army expressly did not "advocate the creation of an Amazon contingent to supplement combat forces," opposition in Congress rested primarily upon concerns for increased costs and rhetorical defenses of sacred American womanhood.[23] Congressional resistance delayed passage of the WAAC bill for several months, even after the Japanese attack on Pearl Harbor provided the final, decisive push into the war. Prodded by Secretary of War Henry L. Stimson and Chief of Staff George C. Marshall, Congress finally approved a women's auxiliary as adjunct to the army, but not in the army.[24]

In this ambiguous position, the WAAC limped along for a year until Rogers pushed legislation changing the WAAC to the more integral WAC (Women's Army Corps) in 1943. Similar women's units were created in the naval services: navy WAVES (an acronym for Women Accepted for Voluntary Emergency Service), women Marines, and Coast Guard SPARs (from the first letters of the Coast Guard motto and its translation: Semper Paratus—Always Ready).[25] Women's units, mirroring American society, were racially segregated. Limited to 10 percent of the WAC, ultimately 6,520 black women served in the army in segregated units. Barred from the WAVES and SPARs until October 1944, only 72 black women became WAVES and 4 became SPARs by the end of the war, though they were integrated into the corps. Women Marines did not accept black women.[26] Although women's military status still remained somewhat ill defined, the purpose of the women's corps was unambiguous: their service was to be in an auxiliary capacity (in a fixed number of occupational categories) to release men for combat duty. Their numbers and their authority were strictly limited, their military rank topped out at one colonel or captain for the woman who held the position of the women's director, and their length of service was for the duration of the emergency plus six months.[27]

During the Congested Areas investigations, as Smith inquired about military women, she uncovered great reluctance to make use of them. Besides citing the difficulties involved in providing housing for the women, military commanders complained most about the mandate to release a trained man within thirty days of acceptance of a presumably untrained woman. As long as women were considered temporary help, Smith believed, this situation would continue. She filed a report with the NAC urging future consideration of a permanent corps of women in the peacetime military.[28]

Just before Christmas 1944, Smith made an extensive inspection tour of the Pacific war theater with members of the NAC, covering

24,527 miles in seventeen days. She watched carrier battle exercises from the bridge of the USS *Saratoga* with Pacific Fleet Commander Adm. Chester Nimitz and discussed with him the need for WAVES in the Pacific. At every stop, she toured hospitals and interviewed nurses. She was appalled by the conditions under which they worked, with shortages of the most rudimentary supplies, and living conditions best described as crude. Nurses told her, though, that their biggest problem was their job's precariousness. If they got sick or hurt as a result of such duty, they were simply sent home.

Military nurses held temporary status and relative rank (that is, the pay but not the command authority), a compromise made to prevent them from exercising command over male officers. Convinced that women needed regular permanent status in order to have the stability of a military career and respect as equals, Smith came home to propose such legislation for nurses. But it was not until she obtained her own subcommittee with jurisdiction over medical services three years later

President Harry S. Truman signs a bill to establish a permanent Army Nurse Corps and a Navy Nurse Corps, April 16, 1947. *From left*: Margaret Chase Smith, coauthor of the bill; Col. Florence A. Blanchfield, superintendent of the Army Nurse Corps; Lt. Cmdr. Ruth B. Dunbar, assistant superintendent of the Navy Nurse Corps; Maj. Helen Burns, director of dieticians, U.S. Army; and Maj. Emma E. Vogel, director of physical therapy, U.S. Army. Photograph from the Margaret Chase Smith Library Archives, Northwood University, Skowhegan, Maine.

that she was able to make significant progress on this matter. Teaming with Rep. Frances Bolton, who introduced a companion bill for army nurses to match Smith's legislation for the navy, and aided by reports of severe nursing shortages, Smith guided through legislation resulting in the Army-Navy Nurse Act, granting nurses in both services permanent status and regular rank as commissioned officers with commensurate pay and benefits.[29]

Obtaining regular status for nurses was comparatively easy; nursing was regarded as fundamental to the physical and emotional well-being of the masculine military. Considerably more resistance met efforts to broaden roles and benefits for other military women. It took, for example, three tries to pass legislation to simply permit women in the WAVES and Marines to serve overseas. Despite the fact that WACs were stationed in North Africa and the European theater and nurses had already seen action in Bataan and Corregidor, House debate on the WAVES measure was characterized by male demands that American women be defended, hallowed, and kept home. Smith withdrew the bill in the face of certain defeat.[30] Her second try fared better, at least in the House, probably due to increasing pressure from Admiral Nimitz, who indicated he needed 5,000 WAVES immediately at Pearl Harbor to release men for combat duty.[31] The Senate, however, refused to condone overseas service. Senate Naval Affairs Committee Chairman David J. Walsh (D-MA) twice struck the overseas clause (Smith got it through the House in 1943 and again in 1944). "The navy, to my mind," Walsh told WAVE Director Mildred McAfee, by way of explanation, "is a male organization."[32] A compromise measure, finally approved in September 1944, allowed women to serve only in the "American area" (North and South America, Hawaii, Alaska, the Canal Zone, and the Caribbean).[33]

Ironically, the imperative to give permanence to women's military status gathered little support until the end of the war. The process of demobilization, with its massive clerical requirements, heightened the need for women as did the continuing necessity of support for occupation troops. Under increasing pressure to resolve the question of women's peacetime participation in the navy, the House NAC met in May 1946 to consider a proposal to establish a permanent women's naval component. At issue was whether to create permanent regulars and reserves for women, as the men were organized, or restrict women to reserve status only. Men on active duty were designated within the regular navy; those men on reserves were kept in readiness to be called in the event of an emergency. Vice Adm. Louis E. Denfeld, chief of the Bureau of Naval

Personnel, testified that the navy planned to assign "an appreciable number of officers and enlisted women to active duty in peacetime . . . [but] whether we have them in the regular navy or the reserves does not matter." Capt. Jean Palmer, director of the Women's Naval Reserve, stated the obvious: "The women would rather be in the regular navy." Chairman Carl Vinson made it clear, however, that he intended to establish a permanent women's reserve, subject to unlimited active duty and sent home at the discretion of the naval secretary; there would be no women regulars. Using women only when the services needed them, he decreed, was the "happy solution."[34]

Smith did not see it as a happy solution at all. Utilizing large numbers of women on active duty, while designating them as reserves, was unfair and dishonest. A permanent reservist, Smith contended, was a contradiction in terms: "There is no such thing as a service career for a reservist." To her the issue was simple: "The Navy either needs these women or they do not." If it did, then women should be made regulars as well as reservists; and if it did not, then the matter was settled. She offered an amendment to provide "the authority to appoint enlisted women in the Regular Navy and Regular Marine Corps in the same manner under the same circumstances and conditions as such laws or parts of laws apply to the appointment of enlisted men." Surprisingly, Smith's amendment passed, 10 ayes to 2 noes, but it would not hold.[35] Vinson refused to call a vote on the bill, and the Seventy-ninth Congress adjourned without taking further action. A similar WAC bill was reported out of the House Military Affairs Committee during the same session and met the same fate.

Legislation concerning women's integration into military service was resurrected in the Eightieth Congress, where the measures, following unification of the Naval Affairs and Military Affairs Committees, were considered by Armed Services Committees (ASC) in both houses of Congress. Again, hearings were held first in the Senate, and all the big guns the military could muster testified, including Chief of Staff and General of the Army Eisenhower; Fleet Admiral Nimitz; and the directors of the women's branches: WAC Col. Mary A. Hallaren, WAVE Capt. Joy Bright Hancock, and Marine Col. J. W. Knighton. With little variation, they explained that the initial reluctance to accept women in the military had rapidly given way to open admiration and greater reliance upon them. Testimony provided abundant documentation of need and deployment and praised women's striking capacity for patience, attention to detail, and enthusiasm for monotonous work. Military leaders were simply recognizing that clerical work was women's work in civilian life and therefore logical that it should be so in the military. Their motive, as Eisenhower put it, was "plain efficiency"—women cost less and did the job better. From their point of view, anything short of permanent status was not an option "because it would be impossible during peacetime to attract the right kind of women for a period of two or three years on reserve status. . . . They would not be willing to leave [their civilian jobs] for some short period, when there was no security and no retirement benefits attached to them."[36]

After the hearings concluded, the Women's Armed Services Integration Act granting women regular military status was reported out of the Senate ASC on July 16, 1947, and passed the full Senate on a voice vote a week later.[37] But when the bill was sent to the House, ASC Chairman W. G. Andrews (R-NY) and Vinson, now minority leader, refused to consider it. After six months of their inaction, Smith angrily confronted Andrews. She had learned that as a result of "behind-the-scenes, off-the-record" executive sessions with some unnamed members of the Navy Department, an agreement had been reached to jettison the Senate bill. She reiterated the need for women to have permanent regular status or none, urging him to be forthright and to publicly vote yes or no "and not a dodging 'maybe.' "[38] When the measure—for reserve status only—finally came before the House ASC for a vote, the tally was 26 ayes, 1 present, and Smith: no.[39] Andrews, determined to get the matter out of the way quickly, listed it on the consent calendar, a method usually reserved for noncontroversial bills that are reported out of committee and unanimously approved. Smith objected. She would not allow this legislation, she said, to be "railroaded through" the House.[40] Her objection prevented its quick passage by the full House without debate. The chairman had no choice but to bring the issue to the floor.

The floor debate was intense, with dire warnings of biological imperatives and runaway costs soon overwhelming appeals to fairness.[41] Chairman Andrews promoted his bill as the only acceptable alternative, a "compromise" between the two extreme views: that of rejecting the women totally or "injecting" them into the regulars. It passed; opponents then moved to amend it. Smith, in a standing vote, supported Adam Clayton Powell's (D-NY) amendment barring racial discrimination in the women's armed forces; it fell 63 noes to 12 ayes. Then she proposed three amendments of her own. The first was to change the name of the bill to reflect its true intent, from the misleading Women's Armed Services Integration Act to Women's Armed Services Reserve Act.

It carried.[42] Her next amendment gave members a chance to change their minds. Essentially the Senate bill, altered to reflect changes necessitated by the unification of the armed services, it stimulated further debate that ultimately foundered over women's presumed excessive health care costs, and was rejected 66 noes to 40 ayes. Her last challenge to the bill was to amend it to strictly limit the number and manner in which women could be utilized on active duty—to a maximum of ten officers and twenty-five enlisted women and for two years. The issue had not changed, she said; the services either needed the women or they did not. If they did, then they should be taken into the regular military organization. If they did not, then there could be no objection to such limitations. The amendment was rejected 41 noes to 21 ayes. From there the bill, as amended, was sent to a joint conference with the Senate to thrash out a compromise.

Smith's tactical victory came in forcing the issue to the House floor where it could be fully debated, then turned over to joint conferees, at least half of whom supported women's integration. Not content to let the matter rest uneasily with this group, Smith contacted Secretary of Defense James V. Forrestal, demanding he investigate and expose the collusion behind efforts to scuttle the bill. "This, to say the least," Smith wrote, "is duplicity that gravely questions the integrity of the administration of the National Military Establishment." Forrestal, in response, sent emphatic messages in support of the Senate bill to members of the joint conference, who hammered the two bills into one favoring regular status.[43] Public Law 625, the Women's Armed Services Integration Act, was signed into law by President Truman on July 12, 1948. Because policy is collectively made, it is often impossible to assess the impact of one member of Congress on the progress of a particular piece of legislation. This instance is the exception.

Smith came to Congress at a propitious historical moment. The disruptions of wartime profoundly, if temporarily, altered social arrangements. Smith articulated the contradictions between women's new roles and aspirations and traditional attitudes about women's place, and within the limits of her power, attempted to ameliorate some of the resulting burdens. These same circumstances also enhanced her ability to surmount contradictions of her own: the need to remain ladylike while demonstrating she was tough enough to handle the hard issues. Development of expertise in military affairs and consistent advocacy of a strong national defense affirmed that reputation and ultimately defined Smith's thirty-three-year congressional career. In 1948, shortly after the

Integration Act's passage, she became the first woman to be elected to the U.S. Senate on her own, and for most of her twenty-four years in the upper house she was the only woman among ninety-six, later ninety-nine, men. Because of the expertise and experience she acquired in the House, Smith soon secured appointment to two of the Senate's most powerful committees, Armed Services and Appropriations. From those positions, she strongly influenced defense policy and spending through much of the Cold War and two hot ones: Korea and Vietnam. When she involuntarily "retired" from the U.S. Senate in 1973, after losing her 1972 bid for reelection, Margaret Chase Smith was ranking minority member on Armed Services and second on Appropriations, unquestionably the most powerful woman in American politics.

Notes

1. The subcommittee, chaired by Edouard V. Izac (D-CA), included Winder R. Harris (D-VA), John E. Fogarty (D-RI), James W. Mott (R-OR), George J. Bates (R-MA), John Z. Anderson (R-CA), Melvin Maas (R-MN), and Margaret Chase Smith (R-ME).

2. Subsequent discussion herein is based upon U.S. Congress, House of Representatives, Subcommittee of the Committee on Naval Affairs, *Investigation of Congested Areas Hearings*, 78th Cong., 1st sess., March 1943, pts. 1–8 (hereafter cited as *I.C.A. Hearings*).

3. *I.C.A. Hearings*, pt. 3, 1001.

4. *I.C.A. Hearings*, pt. 2, 599.

5. "Girls Behind Jail Bars Visited by a Congresswoman," *Washington Post*, March 27, 1943; press release, March 31, 1943, *Statements and Speeches*, 41 vols., vol. 2, *1943–1944*; Margaret Chase Smith Library Center, Skowhegan, Maine (hereafter cited as MCSLC).

6. *I.C.A. Hearings*, pt. 1, 225–26, 259.

7. *I.C.A. Hearings*, pt. 1, 259; pt. 5, 1193.

8. *I.C.A. Hearings*, pt. 2, 462–66.

9. *I.C.A. Hearings*, pt. 6, 1460–62.

10. *I.C.A. Hearings*, pt. 4, 1060; pt. 6, 1453–55.

11. *I.C.A. Hearings*, pt. 2, 556; pt. 3, 775.

12. *I.C.A. Hearings*, pt. 5, 1242.

13. U.S. Congress, Statement to House Committee on Appropriations, *Hearings on H.R. 4346*, 78th Cong., 2d sess., The First Deficiency Appropriations Bill of 1944, February 24, 1944, 2454.

14. *Congressional Record*, 78th Cong., 2d sess., March 9, 1944, 2440–57.

15. Susan M. Hartmann, *The Home Front and Beyond: American Women in the 1940s* (Boston: Twayne, 1982), 84.

16. U.S. Congress, House of Representatives, H.R. 3332, *Congressional Record*, 77th Cong., 1st sess., February 13, 1941, 996.

17. Ruth Milkman, *Gender at Work: The Dynamics of Job Segregation by Sex during World War II* (Urbana: University of Illinois Press, 1987), 9.

18. U.S. Congress, House of Representatives, H.R. 526, *Congressional Record*, 79th Cong., 1st sess., June 21, 1945, 27.

19. U.S. Congress, Statement before the House Committee on Education and Labor in support of H.R. 4408, February 13, 1948, in *Statements and Speeches*, vol. 5, 127, MCSLC.

20. For a fuller examination of this episode, see Janann Sherman, " 'They Either Need These Women or They Do Not': Margaret Chase Smith and the Fight for Regular Status for Women in the Military," *Journal of Military History* 54 (January 1990): 47–78.

21. *Congressional Record*, 77th Cong., 1st sess., May 28, 1941, 4531–33.

22. U.S. Congress, House of Representatives, Committee on Military Affairs, *Hearings on H.R. 6293*, 77th Cong., 22d sess., January 20, 1942, 51.

23. *Congressional Record*, 77th Cong., 2d sess., March 17, 1942, 2582–2608.

24. Public Law 554, 77th Cong., 1st sess., signed into law May 15, 1942.

25. *Congressional Record*, 77th Cong., 2d sess., July 2, 1942, 5923.

26. Data from Women in Military Service for America Memorial Foundation Inc., Washington, DC.

27. U.S. Congress, Senate, Committee on Armed Services, *The Women's Armed Services Integration Act of 1947: Hearings on S. 1103, S. 1157 and S. 1641*, 80th Cong., 1st sess., July 2, 1947, 11–15.

28. U.S. Congress, House of Representatives, Naval Affairs Committee, *Covering Various Assignments Pertaining to Women in the Naval Services*, H. Rept. 271, 78th Cong., 2d sess., November 24, 1944.

29. U.S. Congress, House of Representatives, Committee on Armed Services, Subcommittee No. 9, Hospitalization and Medical Subcommittee, *Hearings on H.R. 1943*, 80th Cong., 1st sess., February 6, 1947; *Congressional Record*, 80th Cong., 1st sess., March 12, 1947, 1998–2014. The Army-Navy Nurse Act, Public Law 36-80C, was signed into law on April 16, 1947.

30. *Congressional Record*, 78th Cong., 1st sess., April 22, 1943, 3709–28.

31. U.S. House, Committee on Naval Affairs, *Hearings on H.R. 2859*: To Amend the Naval Reserve Act of 1938 as Amended, H. Rept. 119, June 4, 1943, 973–87.

32. Walsh quoted in "Walsh Opposes WAVES Overseas," *New York Times*, June 16, 1943.

33. *Congressional Record*, 78th Cong., 2d sess., September 18, 1944, 7862–63.

34. U.S. Congress, House of Representatives, Naval Affairs Committee, *Hearings on H.R. 5915:* To Establish the Women's Reserves on a Permanent Basis, 79th Cong., 2d sess., May 9, 1946, 3319–39.

35. Ibid.

36. U.S. Congress, Senate, Committee on Armed Services, *Hearings on S. 1103, S. 1157 and S. 1641:* The Women's Armed Services Integration Act of 1947, 80th Cong., 1st sess., July 9, 1947, 10, 91.

37. *Congressional Record*, 80th Cong., 1st sess., July 23, 1947, 9793.

38. *Congressional Record,* 80th Cong., 2d sess., April 6, 1948, A2152–53.

39. U.S. Congress, House of Representatives, *Hearings on S.1641*, 80th Cong., 2d sess., March 23, 1948, 5833.

40. *Congressional Record*, 80th Cong., 2d sess., April 6, 1948, A2152–53.

41. *Congressional Record*, 80th Cong., 2d sess., April 21, 1948, 4711–19.

42. This name accompanied the bill into the joint conference, where the original name was restored.

43. Smith-Forrestal letters in *Armed Services Committee* file, MCSLC.

Suggested Readings

Anderson, Karen. *Wartime Women: Sex Roles, Family Relations, and the Status of Women during World War II*. Westport, CT, 1981.

Campbell, D'Ann. *Women at War with America: Private Lives in a Patriotic Era*. New York, 1984.

Hartmann, Susan M. *The Home Front and Beyond: American Women in the 1940s*. Boston, 1982.

Holm, Jeanne. *Women in the Military: An Unfinished Revolution*. San Francisco, 1983.

Sherman, Janann. *No Place for a Woman: A Life of Senator Margaret Chase Smith*. New Brunswick, NJ, 2000.

Stiehm, Judith Jicks. *Arms and the Enlisted Woman*. Philadelphia, 1989.

9

Harold E. Stassen
Governor, Naval Officer, and Diplomat

William E. Lass

The outlook on the East Coast was usually internationalist; the same could not be said for people in the Midwest. In 1917 the largest number of votes against war with Germany had come from this area. So did many of the negative votes on the League of Nations two years later. Isolationist feelings continued to run high in the Midwest throughout the 1930s.

By the beginning of World War II, Republican leaders from the Midwest were reassessing the positions of their region and party. In fact, many felt that a second great war had erupted in part because America had refused a strong leadership role in the world. Most particularly, many believed that a great chance had been lost when President Woodrow Wilson's brainchild, the League of Nations, had stumbled along without U.S. participation. During the 1930s the League had mustered only ineffective protests when faced with the test of Japanese aggression in China, the Italian invasion of Ethiopia, and German rearmament.

Consequently, by the middle of World War II many Midwestern leaders hoped that their country could prevent a third cataclysm by taking a much more energetic role internationally and by replacing the League with an effective world policeman. In April 1944 the charter of the United Nations was unveiled. One of its strongest supporters was a young Republican from Minnesota, Harold E. Stassen, the "Boy Governor," who had enjoyed a meteoric career and seemed headed for the White House.

William E. Lass, professor at Minnesota State University in Mankato, writes about Stassen. Lass earned his Ph.D. from the University of Wisconsin in Madison; he is noted for his work on the history of Minnesota and the Upper Missouri River region. Among his many publications are five books, including *Minnesota: A History* (1977).

On Monday, December 8, 1941, the day after the shocking Japanese attack on Pearl Harbor, Minnesota's Governor Harold E. Stassen proclaimed that an unlimited emergency existed in his state. From then until his resignation on April 27, 1943, Stassen energetically mobilized Minnesota's home front and promoted the contemplated United Nations organization. For the remainder of World War II he served as an officer in the Pacific Fleet and as a member of the U.S. delegation to the San Francisco Conference at which the United Nations charter was drafted.

Throughout his youth and early political career, Stassen was the stereotypical workaholic. Born April 13, 1907, on a Dakota County farm near the capital of St. Paul, he attended a country school and graduated from high school at age fifteen. His frenetic pace at the University of Minnesota, where he was an honor student, included participating in intercollegiate debate and oratory, captaining a national championship rifle team on which he was the best marksman, and serving as all-university class president. As the leader of the campus Gopher Party named after the school mascot, he paved the way for the formation of the Young Republican League.

In 1929, only two years after receiving his undergraduate degree, Stassen completed a law degree at the University of Minnesota and started practicing law in South St. Paul. In 1930 he was elected Dakota County attorney, a position he held until elected governor on November 8, 1938. As county attorney Stassen built the Young Republican League into a potent political force with the aim of capturing control of the Republican Party and restoring its traditional leadership. The party had been seriously challenged in the 1920s by the upstart liberal Farmer-Labor Party and then shocked in 1930 by the election of the charismatic Floyd B. Olson, the state's first Farmer-Labor governor, who subsequently served for nearly six years. Through the Young Republican League, Stassen challenged his party's old guard, which had been dominated by doctrinaire isolationist conservatives.

Styling himself as a "progressive Republican" who found some New Deal programs acceptable, Stassen easily won his party's gubernatorial candidacy. In the ensuing campaign against incumbent Farmer-Labor Governor Elmer A. Benson, Stassen pledged to make government more efficient and less costly. He also harshly attacked Benson's spoils system and tolerance of Communists, the most radical element in the Farmer-Labor Party. Campaigning vigorously, Stassen sometimes made as many as four or five talks in an evening. After finishing each presentation he characteristically rushed to the exit to shake hands with each departing member of the audience. His centrist ideas appealed to the electorate, which was reacting critically to Farmer-Labor rule and some New Deal policies. Many voters were also impressed by Stassen's appearance. Standing 6'3" and weighing 220 pounds, he exuded a commanding presence. Stassen overwhelmed Benson, who gained the dubious distinction of losing the governorship by the largest margin in the history of the state only two years after having won it by the record margin at the time. Stassen became the youngest elected governor in the nation's history.

In the legislative session of 1939, Stassen accomplished his major goals of instituting a state civil service system; drastically cutting the number of state employees and expenditures; establishing an administration department, whose commissioner was to serve as the state's business manager; and curtailing the power of organized labor. The labor law, which included a provision that unions had to undergo a cooling-off period by submitting to arbitration before they could strike, was the most controversial element in Stassen's program. Stassen contended that such a stipulation would lead to harmonious solutions, which would spare the state's economy from costly strikes. However, the act, which partially repudiated the national Wagner Act, a New Deal cornerstone, was lambasted by some liberals. Stassen managed to gain passage of the law by skillfully exploiting the growing schism between farmers and organized laborers. Once joined by their enmity of railroads and big business, farmers and organized labor started parting ways when unions threatened to organize farm laborers and agricultural processing-plant workers. The labor measure, which was similar to acts passed in Oregon and Wisconsin, and Stassen's insistence on a streamlined government that had a social conscience attracted nationwide attention.

Stassen rapidly emerged as a champion of progressive Republicanism as the United States was increasingly disturbed by Nazi Germany's aggressive diplomacy. In January 1939, President Franklin D. Roosevelt urged Congress to appropriate millions more for defense. Even though Roosevelt proclaimed U.S. neutrality in September 1939, only days after Great Britain and France declared war on Germany in response to the Nazi invasion of Poland, American sympathies were clearly with its old World War I allies. The Roosevelt administration abandoned its ostensible neutrality in early June 1940 when it began aiding Great Britain.

German military successes were the main news of the day as the Republicans prepared for their national convention in Philadelphia. Seeing Stassen as an important symbol of progressive Republicanism, the GOP national committee in mid-April 1940 chose him as the convention's temporary chairman and keynote speaker. His selection was widely interpreted to indicate the ascendancy of the party's young, liberal element, a decided shift away from isolationism toward internationalism and the importance of the Midwest in electoral college strategy.

Noting that the thirty-three-year-old governor was legally too young to be considered for the presidency, *Time* magazine concluded that he "will be old enough some day soon, and may well aspire then to be something solider than a keynoter. Already he is marked as a young man who has come far but should go farther."[1]

In his keynote address of June 24, 1940, delivered as Nazi armies were sweeping through France, Stassen emphasized national defense.

Harold Stassen as governor of Minnesota, c. 1940. *Courtesy of the Minnesota Historical Society, St. Paul, Minnesota*

"Even as we meet," he said, "lights are going out in Europe. Blackouts of dictators take the place of lighthouses of free men. It is our grave responsibility to keep burning brightly the light of liberty."[2] Sharply criticizing the Roosevelt administration's lack of preparedness, Stassen called for strong national defense measures including the creation of highly mobile forces. With the nomination of Wendell L. Willkie, an internationalist, Stassen and his party emerged as vigorous advocates of national defense to ready the country for a war that the United States seemed increasingly likely to enter.

Stassen's keynote address underscored the public concern for national defense, which had become evident by actions of various states. The state of New Jersey had been the first to act. In September 1939, Governor Arthur H. Moore appointed an emergency defense committee. His move helped stimulate the creation of other defense programs. Tennessee and Virginia formed defense councils in May 1940, and within a month Arizona, California, Connecticut, Georgia, Louisiana, and Maine followed suit. Soon after returning from the Republican convention, Stassen formed a civilian defense office headed by Ernest L. Olrich.

As states were organizing defense programs, President Roosevelt, on May 18, 1940, activated the National Defense Advisory Commission (NDAC). The NDAC was soon supplanted by the Office of Civilian Defense (OCD), which Roosevelt created by executive order on May 20, 1941. To facilitate coordination of federal and state defense programs, the OCD had a Division of State and Local Cooperation. This division worked through nine regional civilian defense areas, whose boundaries were coterminous with the War Department's service commands. In the early fall of 1941, after participating in civilian defense planning conferences in Indianapolis, Indiana, and Omaha, Nebraska, Olrich reported to Stassen that Minnesota's program was one of the best in the nation.

Stassen actively promoted Minnesota's civilian defense and that of the nation as well. On Saturday evening, September 13, 1941, he was one of four governors who each delivered seven-minute segments on the Columbia Broadcasting System's radio program, "With States and National Defense." In addition to Stassen, the painstakingly coordinated broadcast, whose presenters spoke from their home states, featured three Democrats—Herbert H. Lehman of New York, Frank M. Dixon of Alabama, and Culbert L. Olson of California. Ten days after the program, Fiorello H. La Guardia, mayor of New York City and director of the OCD, invited Stassen to serve on a board to survey defense production. Consisting of three college presidents, three governors, and three major businessmen, the board was to inventory production of airplanes, tanks, naval and merchant ships, and artillery.

La Guardia was probably well aware that Stassen, through Olrich, had been systematically monitoring defense contracting in Minnesota. Stassen, who saw the manufacture of war materials as a vital boost to the state's economy, had Olrich issue periodic reports. From July 1940, when the first defense contract was issued to a Minnesota company, until July 25, 1941, Minnesota firms contracted to produce $60.5 million worth of gun mounts, artillery, periscopes, clothing, and other goods for national defense. Stassen sometimes participated in well-publicized ceremonies at which major contracts were announced.

In the meantime, the need for sharply improving national defense was highlighted by the passage of the Selective Service Act on September 16, 1940, the first peacetime draft in the country's history. The draft combined with the accompanying mobilization of National Guard units greatly increased the need for production of military supplies; the need was further accentuated by the passage of the Lend-Lease Act on March 11, 1941, under which the president was authorized to advance war materials to any nation whose defense was deemed vital to the United States. Initially intended to aid Great Britain, Lend-Lease was extended by Roosevelt to the Soviet Union on June 24, only two days after the Nazi invasion of that country.

Interest in all aspects of civilian defense was also spurred by the threat of hostilities with Japan. Relations between the United States and Japan deteriorated rapidly after Secretary of State Cordell Hull, in January 1940, refused to negotiate an extension of the expiring commercial treaty because Japanese aggression beyond China into Southeast Asia appeared imminent. Within a five-day period in September 1940, Japan obtained military bases in French Indo-China by a treaty with France's Vichy government and signed an alliance with the Axis powers—Germany and Italy. In response, Roosevelt, with Japan as the most obvious target, proclaimed an embargo on U.S. exports of scrap iron and steel to all countries outside of the Western Hemisphere except Great Britain. After Japan occupied French Indo-China on July 24, 1941, Roosevelt froze all Japanese credits in the United States, thus effectively halting American trade with Japan.

As relations with Japan worsened, Stassen stepped up Minnesota's civilian defense program. Olrich toured the state to encourage the formation of local defense councils and arranged to have civilian defense advocates speak at the seven regional conferences of the League of Minnesota Municipalities. To support the Defense Savings Program, which was started by the federal government in April 1941, Stassen served as the honorary chairman of the Defense Savings Committee for Minnesota. The committee, which included some of the state's most prominent bankers, industrialists, politicians, and civic leaders, helped organize local defense savings clubs. These numerous clubs, in turn, heavily promoted such programs as Bond-a-Month Clubs—bond purchases through payroll deductions and the sale of defense stamps.

Although war had appeared quite likely for some months, Americans were nonetheless surprised by its sudden start. Consequently, the expansion of state civilian defense programs had to be accomplished rapidly. After proclaiming a state of emergency on December 8, the day Congress declared war on Japan, Stassen mobilized Minnesota's civilian defense by a series of executive orders.

He first stipulated that the state's defense organization would be separated into military and civilian divisions, headed respectively by Ellard A. Walsh, state adjutant general, and Olrich. The military division, named the Minnesota Defense Force, was directed to establish an aviation wing including a civil air patrol. Walsh was also charged with organizing an aircraft warning and spotter service, to order and conduct blackouts in any part of the state, to form a defense radio network, and to create a military medical service.

By separate executive orders Stassen created sections of the civilian division, which, when fully constituted, worked with civilian defense councils in the state's eighty-seven counties and nineteen principal cities. He called for the formation of volunteer firefighter, police, and air raid warden units as well as vocational education, nursing, and social welfare units. County and city rationing boards staffed by volunteers were formed to administer the federal rationing program of scarce commodities, and advisory committees were named to promote agricultural and industrial resources and production and to deal with labor relations. Because Stassen chose not to convene a special session of the legislature to deal with the wartime emergency, funding for recruitment, training, and equipping civilian defense forces was provided by the state's Executive Council.

Because of his deep personal interest in involving women in the war effort, Stassen started a Victory Aides Program as a component of civilian defense. His order of January 7, 1942, specified that every Minnesota municipality was to promptly "recruit at least one volunteer Victory

Aide for each square block of built-up area in said municipality, at least one for each half township of rural territory, and at least one for each suburban area containing 100 residents."[3] Recruitment of the approximately forty thousand women who staffed the program was coordinated by the state's civilian defense office and association of women's clubs. Victory Aides, who had to represent residents of their area, performed a number of defense-related tasks. Through personal visits to each household, they kept residents informed of the local, state, and national defense programs as a way of encouraging widespread cooperation with the rationing program, the Victory Garden project, the collection of scrap metals, and Victory Bond drives. The Aides attempted to boost morale by compiling lists of all families who had members in the armed forces and reporting them to local authorities, who thanked the families on behalf of the community. The Aides also reported any welfare needs to governmental agencies and in urban areas conducted surveys of labor and housing resources, both of which became more scarce as the war endured.

On March 27, 1942, Stassen, in a statewide radio network broadcast, informed Minnesotans that the civilian defense program was progressing splendidly. There were more than six thousand uniformed, equipped men being trained for the military division. Volunteers for the civilian division included nearly twenty thousand Victory Aides, more than sixteen hundred emergency firemen, one thousand emergency policemen, and more than fifteen thousand air raid wardens. Thousands of others had volunteered for Red Cross programs. About eighteen hundred were serving on local defense councils and another five hundred were on local rationing boards.

On a day-to-day basis Stassen was especially active in efforts to sharply increase agricultural production. He stressed that "the greatest contribution Minnesota makes or can make to the materials needed to win the war is our contribution to the food supply of our Armies and Navies, our nation, and our allies."[4] The federal government looked to Minnesota, one of the ranking agricultural states, to help solve the problem of looming food shortages. The surplus of farm products plaguing the United States at the outbreak of the European war was rapidly depleted by the needs of the nation's armed forces, Lend-Lease shipments, and increased domestic food purchases spurred by the burgeoning buying power of industrial workers. These factors were compounded by the Japanese takeover of regions in the Pacific that produced coconut oil. Loss of that oil, which was used for a variety of industrial applications, forced the federal government to seek substitute oils from soybeans, flaxseed, and peanuts. As the state with the nation's first soybean oil production plant, Minnesota was naturally regarded as a prime source.

Soybeans were only one of Minnesota's crops deemed vital to the war effort. Others were corn, oats, barley, rye, potatoes, hay, peas, and flax. Vital farm products included milk and its derivatives, hogs, beef cattle, poultry, and sheep. Despite advances in mechanization, farming demanded much labor—especially in such an intensive activity as dairying. The drive to increase dairy production created severe farm labor shortages in some parts of the state. In many cases, dairy farmers who could not find laborers sold their herds, which, in turn, threatened to lower milk production.

Stassen's proposed solution to the dairy farm labor crisis was to request that the federal government defer skilled dairy farmers from the draft. In early October 1942 he conferred in Washington, DC, with Gen. Lewis B. Hershey, the federal draft chief, and Col. Joseph Nelson, director of the Minnesota Selective Service Office. He persuaded them to promptly cancel induction notices and to withhold further induction notices of farm operators and experienced farmhands running dairy and livestock farms that produced substantially above subsistence levels. Stassen's Washington meetings with Paul McNutt, director of the War Manpower Commission, were less fruitful. Stassen asked for a long-range federal farm labor plan, but McNutt responded that it could be considered only after more legislation.

Upset by this rejection, Stassen promptly announced his own farm labor policy for Minnesota. As part of an eleven-point program he established the Minnesota Emergency Manpower Agency (MEMA) within the Office of Civilian Defense. Stassen's detailed program was hailed in a *New York Times* front-page article as the first of its kind in the nation. It included opening rural placement offices, establishing day-care facilities for children of farm workers, and reducing the number of male employees in government and nonwar activities businesses by 20 percent to help create a pool of potential farm laborers.

Soon after forming MEMA, Stassen ordered the start of an agricultural award program to encourage farmers to increase production. Awards in the form of special achievement flags and buttons were to be given to individual farmers, farm communities, and farm processing plants whose production exceeded that of the previous year. Stassen's decisive, imaginative solutions to the wartime farm problem only served to bolster a growing public opinion that he was presidential timber.

While Stassen's civilian defense program was being praised, he attracted far more national and international attention as a strong proponent of a postwar United Nations Organization (UN). The idea of replacing the failed League of Nations was stimulated by Roosevelt and Winston Churchill, Great Britain's prime minister, through their Atlantic Charter announcement of August 1941. In agreeing on common goals they called for the formation of a general security system after aggressor nations had been disarmed. On January 1, 1942, in the spirit of the Atlantic Charter, twenty-six nations, led by the United States and Great Britain, created the wartime United Nations Organization. Ultimately comprising forty-six anti-Axis countries, the UN set winning the war as its priority, but its existence spurred worldwide interest in creating a permanent peacetime UN.

Moving to preempt the peace issue, Vice President Henry A. Wallace, in May 1942, suggested a peacetime UN in principle. His position was reinforced by a Memorial Day speech at Arlington National Cemetery by Undersecretary of State Sumner Welles. As Welles was speaking, Stassen was delivering a Memorial Day address in Cleveland, Ohio, which clearly indicated that Republicans, with an obvious eye toward the next presidential election, would not leave the peace question to the Roosevelt administration.

Unlike Wallace and Welles, Stassen presented a detailed seven-point statement of goals for the postwar UN. First, he specified that temporary governments should be established over each Axis nation until the people in those nations could form a proper government. Four of his points called for international commissions to control international airports, to control the world's major ports, to increase literacy worldwide, and to foster free trade. Nations were to be bound by a code of justice, which would be administered by an international organization. Last, he proposed an international police force. Invoking the memory of Abraham Lincoln, his favorite role model, Stassen proclaimed that "we must now say that government of the people, by the people, and for the people shall gradually spread throughout the earth."[5]

Emboldened by extensive media praise that he actually had a plan rather than merely a general idea for an international organization, Stassen moved to the next stage by proposing its administrative framework. In an address titled "A Proposal of a Definite United Nations Government," delivered on January 7, 1943, to a joint meeting of the Minneapolis and St. Paul branches of the Foreign Policy Association,

Stassen presented a plan for a United Nations whose key body would be a single-house legislative parliament. Its executive function would be in a seven-member council headed by a world chairman chosen by the parliament. This structure, Stassen stated, would then administer the seven-point peace program he had first elaborated in Cleveland.

Although Stassen presented the UN ideas as his own, some journalists thought they bore the imprint of Clarence K. Streit, the longtime League of Nations correspondent for the *New York Times*. Streit's seminal 1939 book, *Union Now: A Proposal for a Federal Union of the Democracies of the North Atlantic*, was a ringing call for creating a world government.

Following the Twin Cities address, Stassen intensified his UN campaign. His major speeches included those to the United Nations Forum at Constitution Hall, Washington, DC, and to the Minnesota United Nations Committee. The Minnesota speech was transmitted nationally over the Mutual Broadcasting System. Using ghost writers, Stassen also composed an article, "We Need a World Government," for the *Saturday Evening Post* of May 22, 1943, and another piece of his "Blueprint for a World Government" was published the next day in the *New York Times Magazine*. Even before his articles appeared, Stassen was nationally recognized as a leading UN advocate. Raymond Moley, in his "Perspective" editorial for *Newsweek*, believed that "if the war leaves people in the mood for greater internationalism, Stassen may well be remembered as one of its major prophets."[6]

Several weeks before his UN articles appeared, Stassen had left the governorship to enter the navy as a lieutenant commander. He had first announced his abrupt career change thirteen months before resigning on April 27, 1943. In his statewide radio address of March 27, 1942, Stassen informed Minnesotans that he would run for a third term that fall and, if re-elected, would serve only through the end of the legislative session. He explained that by then his important work of governing during the first phase of the war, in which civilian defense was organized, would be completed. Then, he advised, the war would move to its second and final phase of the great Allied victory offensive. During that period he believed he could best serve Minnesota and the nation as a member of the armed forces.

Time billed the announcement as "Stassen's Shocker" and, like much of the public, was puzzled by the decision. However, the writer wondered about an underlying motive in commenting that "though even

cynics admitted that Governor Stassen's patriotism was perfectly virtu-
ous, they also pointed out that virtue might well bring more than its
own reward: a bemedaled young hero who had helped win World
War II might look good to many a 1944 President-maker."[7] Others questioned the wisdom of Stassen's decision. Jack Alexander, in a *Life* article, thought that a good home-front governor was more valuable to
the nation than another lieutenant commander and deplored "the fact
that Stassen's talent for bold political thinking is to be stowed away in a
Navy locker for the duration."[8] Stassen's only explanation for his action
was that the "offensive drive for victory against the totalitarian forces
that threaten the future of free men will be conducted in the main by
the young men of my generation. I want to be with them."[9]

Stassen evidently arranged to be commissioned in the naval reserve
with the assistance of Frank Knox, the 1936 Republican vice presidential candidate, who was then serving as Roosevelt's secretary of the navy.
During the spring of 1942, Stassen completed a five-week training course
at the Great Lakes, Illinois, naval station. That fall he and Edward J.
Thye, his hand-picked successor, easily won the governorship and lieutenant governorship. Stassen's resignation was marked by a farewell
dinner in Coffman Memorial Union on the University of Minnesota
campus. With one thousand people in attendance and another two thousand unable to get tickets, the event was featured in a St. Paul front-
page story as "Throng Hails Stassen as Great Leader."[10]

After being inducted on April 29, Stassen spent his first month at
the Great Lakes station and then received further training at the naval
school at Fort Schuyler, New York. In late summer Knox assigned him
as flag secretary for Adm. William F. "Bull" Halsey, the commander of
the South Pacific Fleet. The move was consistent with Knox's philosophy that the navy needed both a strong civilian control and more efficient administration.

By the time Stassen reported for duty at Halsey's headquarters at
Nouméa, New Caledonia, nearly one thousand miles east of Australia,
the United States was on the offensive. Halsey's initial reception of
Stassen was less than enthusiastic. Apparently he resented having what
he regarded as a political appointee assigned to his staff. But he and the
affable Stassen worked well together, and Halsey, famed for his infor-
mality, was soon calling him Harold or "Stass." In time the two became
good friends. As flag secretary, Stassen was a type of general office manager who handled a variety of routine tasks including supervising in-

coming and outgoing mail. Sometimes when Halsey went to sea, Stassen remained at Nouméa. But during the offensive in the northern Solomons, highlighted by the invasion of Bougainville on November 1, 1943, Stassen was sent on a "familiarization cruise" aboard the light cruiser *Montpelier*, which was attacked by Japanese dive bombers. Stassen, who remained on the bridge of the flagship as it was being damaged by bombs, won the admiration of his fellow officers for his coolness under fire. Halsey's naval victories in the northern Solomons and the seizure of Bougainville enabled American forces to isolate the Japanese stronghold of Rabaul, New Britain, and opened the way for an island-hopping advance northward.

While serving in the South Pacific, Stassen was oftentimes the subject of conjecture about his supposed presidential aspirations. Halsey and some of his staff kidded Stassen about being promoted from lieutenant commander to commander in chief. Navy regulations forbade Stassen from taking any overt action to run for the GOP presidential nomination in 1944, but the navy could not control his Minnesota supporters. In December 1943 the Minnesota Republican Party endorsed Stassen as its presidential candidate. Then in the spring of 1944, Stassen's close associates, including Governor Thye and Minnesota's U.S. Senator Joseph H. Ball, entered his name in the Nebraska and Wisconsin primaries. Stassen won Nebraska and finished a respectable second to Governor Thomas E. Dewey of New York in Wisconsin. Any hopes the Stassen backers had of forcing a draft-Stassen movement at the national convention were dashed by Dewey's nomination. Evidently, the Stassen forces did not expect to win, but rather to preview their man for the 1948 campaign.

During a short furlough in late July and early August 1944, Stassen visited his family in South St. Paul and conferred with Navy Department officials in Washington. Soon after his return to Pearl Harbor, Halsey's Third Fleet sailed out to participate in a coordinated attack on the Philippines. Responding to an American troop landing on Leyte Island, the Japanese high command dispatched massive naval forces to the region. Halsey recalled that while discussing strategy with his staff, Stassen urged knocking out the Japanese carriers first. The ensuing Battle of Leyte Gulf, which was really three separate engagements fought over three days in late October, was a smashing American victory. It proved to be not only the last and greatest naval battle of World War II but also the greatest in the history of the world. By the time the Philippines campaign ended with the occupation of Manila on February 23, 1945, Stassen was about to enter the diplomatic phase of his wartime career.

On the recommendation of the State Department, Roosevelt named Stassen to the eight-person U.S. delegation to the San Francisco Conference. The conclave, which was to finalize the United Nations charter that had been preliminarily drafted at the Dumbarton Oaks Conference in Washington, DC, in the late summer and early fall of 1944, was scheduled to open on April 25 with nearly fifty nations represented. Roosevelt carefully crafted the delegation with the aim of later achieving bipartisan support for the charter. It was headed by Secretary of State Edward R. Stettinius, with his predecessor, the seriously ill Cordell Hull, as senior adviser. From the Senate, Roosevelt chose Texas Democrat Tom Connally, chairman of its Foreign Relations Committee, and Republican Arthur H. Vandenberg of Michigan, a member of the committee. He also named two members of the House of Representatives— Sol Bloom, a New York Democrat and chairman of its Foreign Relations Committee, and Charles A. Eaton of New Jersey, the ranking Republican on the committee. Other than Stassen the only appointee who was not associated with the State Department or Congress was Virginia C. Gildersleeve, dean of Barnard College.

Stassen had some obvious qualifications for the assignment. He was recognized as one of the nation's UN experts, and he represented the important constituency of liberal Midwestern Republicans. Furthermore, Roosevelt was impressed by Stassen's ability. After the death of Secretary of the Navy Frank Knox on April 28, 1944, the president had considered appointing Stassen to the post.

Determined to make the most of his new position, Stassen, weeks before the conference opened, embarked on what amounted to a political campaign. In a major address on March 7, "San Francisco—The Golden Gate to Peace," delivered at a meeting sponsored by the Minnesota United Nations Committee in Minneapolis, Stassen described "seven cardinal points of future world policy."[11] They included formation of the United Nations, a willingness by the United States to delegate a limited portion of its sovereignty to that organization, and American cooperation with its major wartime allies in maintaining an international police force. Traveling widely to disseminate his views, solicit opinions, and win Republican support, he met with Governor Dewey in Albany, members of Congress, and many groups, including fifty Harvard University faculty members. The thrust of his message was that "the extreme principle of absolute nationalistic sovereignty is of the

Middle Ages and it is dead. It died with the [advent of the] airplane, the radio, the rocket and the robomb [robot bomb]."[12]

While the pending San Francisco Conference was being heavily publicized, the nation and world were shocked by the death of President Roosevelt on April 12. At the conference, which spanned nine weeks, Stassen chaired the committee that drafted the trusteeship policy and worked closely with the American delegation on other charter provisions. Vandenberg recalled that Stassen impressed the other American delegates by his facile mind, analytical powers, organizational ability, industriousness, and cordial personality. After the conference adjourned on June 26, Stassen remained on leave from the navy for nearly another month in which he met with President Harry S. Truman and gave speeches, including a nationally broadcast radio address on NBC, about the UN.

By the time Stassen resumed his duties on Halsey's flagship, the *Missouri*, the Japanese were virtually powerless. Lacking both a tactical fleet and warplanes, they were suffering through Halsey's bombardment of coastal installations and factories before the United States dropped atomic bombs on Hiroshima and Nagasaki. Stassen was on watch when the radio announcement of Japan's willingness to surrender was received. After the surrender terms were signed aboard the *Missouri* in Tokyo Bay on September 2, 1945, Stassen was put in charge of supervising the release of American prisoners of war from military prisons in the Tokyo-Yokohama area.

Stassen, who had been promoted to captain, was discharged at the Great Lakes Naval Center on November 15, 1945. Two days earlier, he had helped host a Halsey Day in Minnesota. As one of the most popular war heroes, the four-star admiral was honored by a parade from the Twin Cities airport to Northrop Auditorium on the University of Minnesota campus. There he met Stassen and lauded his former flag secretary to an audience of six thousand students.

In 1946, Stassen began his long and ultimately fruitless quest for the presidency. Most thought he had impressive credentials, but many doubted the wisdom of his tactics. Had he challenged Henrik Shipstead, a diehard isolationist who was up for reelection, Stassen would almost certainly have become a U.S. senator in 1947. Instead, he backed Thye, who easily beat Shipstead, and announced that he was running for president in 1948. Although his decision was heavily publicized, it was generally regarded as premature. However, Stassen believed he could better establish a political base outside of the Senate. During the long interim he traveled extensively in Europe where he conferred with all heads of state including Joseph Stalin of the Soviet Union.

In the spring of 1948, when he finished first in the Nebraska and Wisconsin primaries, Stassen enjoyed commanding poll leads over Truman. But after he was edged out by Dewey in the Oregon primary his fortunes declined. While serving as the president of the University of Pennsylvania, he vied for the Republican nomination in 1952. He won the Minnesota primary, but his cause collapsed after the heavy Minnesota write-in vote for Dwight D. Eisenhower. Philosophically close to Eisenhower, Stassen served in the administration as the director of the Foreign Operations Administration, special assistant to the president for disarmament, and chief American representative to the 1957 London Arms Control Negotiations.

By the time Stassen ran for the Republican presidential nomination in 1960, 1964, and 1968 he was being ridiculed as "Childe Harold" by some former supporters. Clearly, the image of the man by then stood in sharp contrast to his World War II years when he was at the zenith of his public acceptance while serving his state and his nation as a governor, naval officer, and diplomat.

Notes

1. "Republican Keynoter," *Time*, April 29, 1940, 16.

2. *Official Report of the Proceedings of the Twenty-second Republican National Convention* (Washington, DC: Judd & Detweiler, 1940), 45.

3. State of Minnesota, Office of Civilian Defense, General Orders No. 4, January 7, 1942, in Governor Stassen, Harold E. Records, Box 7, Minnesota State Archives, Minnesota Historical Society, St. Paul.

4. Transcript of radio address by Governor Harold E. Stassen and Victor Christgau, Emergency Manpower director, delivered over Radio Station WCCO and other stations on October 15, 1942, in Stassen Papers, Box 5, Minnesota Historical Society.

5. "Stassen's Seven Points," *Time*, June 15, 1942, 10.

6. "Perspective," *Newsweek*, April 5, 1943, 92.

7. "Stassen's Shocker," *Time*, April 6, 1942, 14.

8. Jack Alexander, "Governor Stassen: The Republican Party's Minnesota Hopeful Plans to Get Re-elected and then Join the Navy," *Life*, October 19, 1942, 133.

9. Transcript of March 27, 1942, radio address, in Stassen Papers, Box 5.

10. "Throng Hails Stassen as Great Leader," *St. Paul Pioneer Press*, April 27, 1943.

11. Harold E. Stassen, "San Francisco—The Golden Gate to Peace: Seven Cardinal Points of Future World Policy," *Vital Speeches of the Day*, March 15, 1945, 338.

12. "Stassen's Creed," *Time*, March 12, 1945, 19.

Suggested Readings

Blegen, Theodore C. *Minnesota: A History of the State.* Rev. ed. Minneapolis, 1975.

Clark, Clifford E., Jr., ed. *Minnesota in a Century of Change: The State and Its People since 1900.* St. Paul, 1989.

Lass, William E. *Minnesota: A History.* 2d ed. New York, 1998.

Stuhler, Barbara. *Ten Men of Minnesota and American Foreign Policy, 1898–1968.* St. Paul, 1973.

III
The Sharp End

10

Arthur W. Radford
Aviation Trainer and Combat Commander

Jeffrey G. Barlow

In common with the other branches of the armed forces, the U.S. Navy grew exponentially in size and capability during the war. It also realigned its force structure. When the big-gun, heavily armored battleships sank into the mud of Pearl Harbor, the navy turned to its aircraft carriers, which fortunately were at sea on December 7, 1941, and thus escaped damage. In two critical fleet engagements in the following spring, American carriers halted major Japanese offensives at the battles of the Coral Sea and Midway. These actions assured the primacy of the aircraft carrier; it would reign for the rest of the century as the U.S. Navy's principal sea-control and power-projection weapon.

Making possible the triumph of naval aviation were farsighted pioneers who developed the operating techniques and basic equipment of the carrier some years before the start of the war. Among these officers was Arthur Radford, whose wartime career oscillated from fleet assignments to staff duty ashore. While the fighting forces garnered the publicity, essential naval work was also done by the commands engaged in training and development.

Delineating Radford's wartime career is Jeffrey G. Barlow, a historian at the Naval Historical Center at the Washington Navy Yard in Washington, DC. Having written extensively on the modern U.S. Navy, Dr. Barlow has published *Revolt of the Admirals: The Fight for Naval Aviation, 1945–1950* (1994). His advanced degrees come from the University of South Carolina in Columbia.

Arthur Radford was one of a group of naval officers who for reasons of seniority, initiative, and, above all, personal competence rose to positions of considerable responsibility in the U.S. Navy during World War II. A naval aviator thoroughly grounded in the variety of aerial challenges both ashore and at sea, Radford was promoted to rear admiral in July 1943, thus serving for the remainder of the war as one of the navy's flag officers.

Arthur William Radford was born in Chicago, Illinois, on February 27, 1896, to John Arthur Radford, a Canadian-born electrical engineer, and Agnes Eliza (Knight) Radford.[1] The eldest of four, young

Arthur proved to be a bright and energetic boy. When he was six, his family moved to Riverside, Illinois, a suburb west of Chicago. John Radford, who worked for the Commonwealth Edison Company, was named the managing engineer of Chicago's new Fisk Street Power Station, which possessed the first steam turbine-driven generators in the United States. Radford remembered that his father would occasionally take him down to see the facility.[2]

The boy's initial years of schooling were spent at Riverside Public School. An excellent but a somewhat reserved student, Radford demonstrated an interest in a naval career at a young age. A schoolmate from those days recalled: "As early as fourth grade . . . he was continually drawing sketches of warships. As I remember, they all looked like the battleship *Maine*. Most of them were cross-sectioned showing compartments, engines, ammunition hoists, bunkers, crew's quarters, etc. These intrigued me no end."[3]

In the summer of 1910 the family moved to Grinnell, Iowa, but Arthur only attended Grinnell High School for a year and one-half before deciding to apply for an appointment to Annapolis. He received the district congressman's appointment to the U.S. Naval Academy and, having passed the examination for admission after several months of tutoring at an Annapolis prep school, he entered the Academy in July 1912. He was only sixteen years old.[4]

Although a mediocre student in his first year at Annapolis, Radford (or "Raddy" as he had quickly become known) thereafter began to apply himself to his studies. When he was commissioned in 1916, he stood 59th in a graduating class of 177.[5] Following duty in the battleship *South Carolina* during World War I, Radford served tours as aide and flag lieutenant to two battleship division commanders before reporting to Pensacola, Florida, for flight training in 1920. During the 1920s and 1930s, he alternated between duty at sea with various aircraft squadrons and fleet staffs and stateside tours in the Bureau of Aeronautics (BuAer).

He joined the aircraft carrier *Yorktown* as executive officer in May 1940. After serving almost a year in that ship, Radford served a brief period of duty in the office of the Chief of Naval Operations (CNO) before being designated commander of the Naval Air Station in Trinidad, British West Indies, in July 1941.[6] The assignment was not much to his liking because it looked as if it would keep him sidelined too long. As he recalled, "When originally informed I was to be ordered to duty in Trinidad I had protested because I thought it would mean I would spend the next three years there."[7] Fortunately for Radford, three months after taking over, he received orders for duty in BuAer.

The reason for this sudden change of station was an organizational realignment within the bureau. By mid-1941, given the strains imposed by the expanded fleet training program, it had become apparent that fleet squadrons no longer could continue the standard practice of training pilots after they reported to the fleet. Because of the vastly increased performance of service aircraft over those used at Pensacola, aviators who had completed flight training required extensive flying time in fleet aircraft before attaining combat proficiency.[8] As a result of such problems, senior officials in the Navy Department agreed in November 1941 to create a separate Training Division within BuAer to be headed by "an officer of wide experience in the training of naval aviation personnel."[9] Several weeks earlier, Artemus L. Gates, the assistant secretary of the Navy for Air, had visited Radford in Trinidad and had been impressed by the officer's determination and zeal. He quickly persuaded Rear Adm. John H. Towers, the chief of the Bureau of Aeronautics, to transfer Radford back to Washington to take charge of this new division.[10]

Radford assumed his new duties on December 1, 1941, just a week before the Japanese surprise attack on the fleet at Pearl Harbor brought the United States into the war. An officer just starting what was to become a meteoric wartime rise to prominence, the 6'1"-tall, 170-pound Radford possessed a keen intelligence, a decision-making style that was direct but not abrupt, and a ready smile that softened his no-nonsense approach to his work. He got down to business at once. In order to facilitate coordination with the Office of the Chief of Naval Operations and the Bureau of Navigation (BuNav—reorganized and renamed the Bureau of Naval Personnel in May 1942), Raddy was given additional duty assignments as director of Aviation Training in both organizations. He later quipped about this situation, "I could practically write a letter to myself in the Bureau of Naval Personnel or the Office of the Chief of Naval Operations—then prepare and sign the answer."[11]

From the outset Radford was determined to build up the physical facilities of the training establishment as quickly as possible. He soon learned that accomplishing the myriad of tasks that had to be done seemed a never-ending job. Like the other divisions in BuAer during those hectic months, the Training Division worked from dawn to dark seven days per week. Radford later recalled that in those busy months in Washington, walking from his apartment to work and back was his only exercise.[12]

During 1942 the administrative organization for aviation training was put into place and refined. By the end of that year the basic components had been established. Within BuAer, Radford's division consisted of a number of specialized sections: Administration, Physical Training, Service Schools, Training Devices, Flight Training, Gunnery, Operational Training, Technical Training, Radar, and Training Literature. Out in the field, four semiautonomous commands were operating to instruct the aviation personnel required: Air Primary Training Command, Air Intermediate Training Command, Air Operational Training Command, and Air Technical Training Command.[13]

Primary Training Command exercised supervision over the Pre-Flight Schools and the network of Naval Reserve Aviation Bases around the country where aviation cadets received their initial instruction. Intermediate Training Command administered the large facilities at Pensacola and Corpus Christi, Texas, where trainees completed their formal flight instruction and received their wings. Operational Training Command, headquartered at Jacksonville, Florida, controlled the education of new pilots between the time they left the training centers and the time they joined fleet squadrons. Finally, Technical Training Command supervised teaching at the wide variety of aviation technical schools—enlisted men's schools for such courses as aviation maintenance, parachute matériel, bombsight maintenance, aerography, and Link trainers; and officers' schools for air combat intelligence, air operations, fighter direction, gunnery, and engineering.[14]

One officer who recalled Captain Radford's highly efficient style of managing the Training Division was then Lt. Comdr. Robert J. C. Maulsby. A naval aviator, Maulsby had spent much of 1941 in England as a naval observer attached to the American embassy. While there he had attended a series of specialized British courses in what was known as fighter direction—the use of radar plotting and two-way communications to vector defending fighter aircraft against incoming enemy bombers.

Maulsby returned to the States in November 1941 as the U.S. Navy's expert in this highly technical skill. Because of the secrecy accorded to radar at that time, he wryly recalled, "If you wanted to mention the word radar you found yourself a secure closet, [and] established a Marine guard outside."[15] When Radford took over the Training Division, he quickly assigned the younger officer to its Technical Training Section to handle fighter direction matters.

Because of the small number of people in the division who understood radar in those first months, Bob Maulsby made it a practice to go straight to Radford on issues that needed to be settled. He found the captain's working style very practical and efficient. He recalled: "When I'd go in with something that . . . had to be authorized outside Training, he'd tell me to go and see so-and-so who had that as his responsibility. I'd go in and start to make my . . . request, and whomever [*sic*] it was would get on the phone and say, 'Raddy, who the hell is this you've sent around here?' 'Well, . . .' [Radford] would tell him . . . 'give him what he wants.' " Maulsby commented further, "His colleagues . . . had enough respect for him . . . [so] that if he wanted something done . . . they'd do it."[16]

Radford's utilization of personnel was equally productive. In fact, his seemingly innate understanding of how best to employ and motivate people was one of his greatest strengths. John Jenkins, a reserve officer who was involved during the war in evaluating men selected for aviation training, later wrote to Raddy, "It was a pleasure to work on the cadet selection program under your cognizance, for I was always sure that you would approve and support what was technically sound and reject what was merely expedient."[17]

Raddy picked the Naval Academy's All-American football star Tom Hamilton to develop sports training programs to condition naval aviation trainees. In creating this part of the new V-5 program for cadets, Hamilton was able to call upon the expertise of some of the country's top men in the coaching and physical education fields, including the heads of the athletic programs at Harvard, Ohio State, and Penn State. The result of Hamilton's efforts was the creation of a first-class conditioning regimen for the U.S. Navy.[18] In another example of innovative thinking, Radford became convinced early on that the navy's aviation training program could benefit by employing women for intricate but repetitive tasks such as running flight simulators. When BuNav responded that there were no plans to bring women into the service during the war, Radford took the idea to Congressman Carl Vinson, the chairman of the House Naval Affairs Committee. Within days, the bureau was asking Radford how many women reserves could be used in the aviation training program. Once initiated, the new effort burgeoned, and by the end of the war, there were some twenty-three thousand WAVES in the navy's aeronautical organization.[19]

A further demonstration of his talent for making the best use of personnel assets were the two schools he established at Quonset Point, Rhode Island—the Aviation Indoctrination School and the Air Combat Intelligence (ACI) School. These courses of instruction made splendid use of well-educated business and professional men who had volunteered for this training. Radford later commented, "In the Squadrons the pilots and the mechanics were simply superb but the Aviation Ground Officers and the ACI Officers added a maturity of judgment and experience which made the total effort in most cases, magnificent."[20]

By the beginning of 1943, with the navy's aviation training program in full operation, Radford was having trouble keeping together the outstanding group of assistants he had assembled. One by one they were being sent on to other assignments. Raddy, too, was getting restless for combat duty. His turn finally came in mid-April 1943, when he was ordered to report to Commander Air Force, Pacific Fleet (COMAIRPAC) for duty as a carrier division commander.[21] The new assignment was an official confirmation of just how highly he was thought of in Washington, since with it came a promotion to rear admiral. Raddy had not yet held a major ship command, which was traditionally required before an officer was selected for flag rank.

After visiting U.S. bases in the South Pacific and Southwest Pacific during May and early June 1943 as a member of an official inspection party headed by Assistant Secretary Gates, Radford reported for temporary duty to Rear Adm. Frederick C. "Ted" Sherman, Commander Carrier Division (COMCARDIV) TWO, at Pearl Harbor, Hawaii. His first weeks in the islands were spent in so-called makee learn status, riding one or another of the aircraft carriers operating out of Pearl Harbor and observing flight operations and carrier tactics. Radford was fascinated with the tremendous improvements in carrier operations that had taken place in the months since he had left the *Yorktown*. He commented, "I was particularly impressed with the operation of carriers [*sic*] task groups in circular formations and maneuvering with simultaneous turns to land or take off planes. This new tactic permitted groups to present concentrated anti-aircraft fire in case of air attack."[22]

At the end of June 1943, Radford was ordered to Mare Island, California, where he joined the *Independence*, one of the new small, 10,000-ton aircraft carriers built on light cruiser hulls. Admiral Towers, who had since become COMAIRPAC, had decided that since Radford was slated to command a carrier division, which included several of these small carriers, it would be a good idea for him to get acquainted with how they operated before he took over. Cruising back to Hawaii on the *Independence*, Raddy quickly noticed that the light carriers were much more sensitive to heavy seas than were the older, larger carriers such as the USS *Enterprise* or the *Essex*-class carriers that were just then entering the fleet.[23]

On July 21, 1943, he was detached from duty with Carrier Division TWO and ordered to command Carrier Division ELEVEN. The following day Radford was promoted to temporary rear admiral.[24] His command initially consisted of the small carriers *Independence* and *Princeton* and the new *Essex*-class carrier *Lexington*. During the rest of July and the entire month of August, Raddy kept his carriers busy in the waters off Pearl Harbor refining their training evolutions and flight operations. While this was going on, plans were being drawn up at Pearl Harbor for conducting a brief foray into the Central Pacific.

Baker and Howland Islands are small, uninhabited islands located some five hundred miles east of Tarawa and the Gilbert Islands, which were scheduled to be seized later that fall. The idea was to build a landing field on Baker from which American land-based P-40 fighters could operate. With American air facilities already in existence in the Phoenix Islands southeast of the Gilberts and in the Ellice Islands to the southwest, the construction of an airstrip on Baker would complete the network of air bases needed for launching significant aerial attacks to soften up the Japanese-held Gilberts.[25]

The outfit for the Baker Island operation, Task Force 11, was led by Rear Adm. Willis A. Lee, Commander Battleships, Pacific. Radford led the covering force, which consisted of the small carriers *Princeton* and *Belleau Wood* and four destroyers. The initial landings on Baker Island began on September 1, 1943. While Raddy's carriers operated some fifty miles to the east of the island, providing air cover, one of his destroyers, with a fighter director on board, was positioned some fifty miles to the west of Baker, in the direction of expected enemy air activity. During the first eight days of the operation, fighters from the carriers managed to shoot down three Japanese "Emily" four-engine flying boats without letting them get close enough to spot Lee's surface forces. The airstrip on Baker was successfully completed on September 10, and the following day Army Air Forces P-40s were flown in from Canton Island to begin operations against the Gilberts.[26]

Since the Baker operation had gone so smoothly, Radford believed that the carriers should "work over" Tarawa and Makin atolls before returning to Pearl Harbor. He sent a message to Admiral Towers, asking him to send an *Essex*-class carrier to join them. Towers immediately agreed with the suggestion and convinced Adm. Chester W. Nimitz, the

Commander in Chief, Pacific Fleet (CINCPACFLT), that it would provide good training for the carriers. Nimitz ordered Task Force 15, built around the *Lexington*, sent out. It was under the command of Rear Adm. Charles A. Pownall, whom Nimitz had recently appointed Commander Carriers Central, Pacific Force.[27]

Radford's force joined up with Pownall's ships on September 15. Raddy transferred to the *Lexington* for a conference with Pownall on the morning of the 16th. After conferring, the two commanders decided that Tarawa would be attacked at daylight on September 18 and that Makin and Apamama would also be separately targeted by the task force. Although Radford hoped that the carriers would be able to launch a second series of air strikes against Tarawa atoll on the following day, Pownall refused to commit himself to this idea ahead of time.[28]

Task Force 15 remained undetected by the Japanese on its run in to the target area on the night of September 17–18. The first attack was launched before dawn, and five other carrier strikes were sent out during the morning and early afternoon. Despite the heavy antiaircraft fire they encountered at Tarawa, the American fighters, dive bombers, and torpedo planes quickly worked over their targets. Only four U.S. planes were lost in the strikes. Nonetheless, a nervous Pownall decided to forego a second day of attacks, and when the last planes from strike six were recovered, he ordered the task force to set course for Pearl Harbor. Raddy, who believed that a second day of attacks would prove even more successful, was puzzled by his senior's faintheartedness.[29]

Back in Pearl, the carrier division commanders and their staffs reviewed the details of the operation, looking for measures that would improve the effectiveness of future carrier strikes. One of the issues that quickly caught Radford's attention was the carriers' lack of night fighters to fend off snooping Japanese aircraft that could vector land-based bombers into nighttime attacks on the American ships. He was aware that a night fighter school had been established before he had left Washington and that fighters equipped with radar for night flying were then in training, but these specialized planes were still weeks away from being deployed in the fleet. Raddy began pondering how he might create an interim night-fighting capability in his command.[30]

The next operation he took part in was the air attack and cruiser bombardment of Wake Island on October 5–6, 1943. For it, Radford shifted his flag to the *Lexington*. The two days of strikes went off smoothly, and it was evident that these small offensive operations, combined with intensive training in Hawaiian waters, were readying the

American carrier forces for their part in impending large-scale operations in the Central Pacific.[31] The first such assault was not long in
coming. The Pacific Fleet's move into the Gilberts—the capture of
Tarawa, Makin, and Apamama, codenamed Galvanic—was scheduled
for mid-November. It would be the first time that American carriers
would be required to operate against Japanese land-based air power in
strength and would have to fight it out with the Japanese for command
of the air while U.S. Marine and Army ground forces captured the heavily
fortified, enemy-held islands.

For this show, Radford was given command of Task Group 50.2,
the Northern Carrier Group, consisting of the *Enterprise* and the small
carriers *Belleau Wood* and *Monterey*. He transferred his flag to the *Enterprise*. When Radford and Rear Adm. Alfred E. Montgomery, who was
to command the Southern Carrier Group, were first briefed on the Galvanic plan, they were not happy about the way the carriers were to be
tied closely to the surface forces during the operation. Radford, in particular, believed that the fast carriers could provide far more protection
for the surface forces if they took the offensive against Japanese air power
in the nearby Marshall Islands prior to D day, eliminating enemy aircraft and damaging the existing airfields so that they were no longer a
factor in the operation. With Towers's permission, they presented their
alternate idea to Vice Adm. Raymond A. Spruance, the force commander,
but he remained unswayed. Looking back on the operation years later,
Radford commented, "I am quite certain that Task Force 50 could have
done a much better overall job of protecting our surface forces if we had
struck first—hard and often enough to eliminate enemy air power in
the Marshalls before D-Day."[32]

Radford's carrier group left Pearl on November 10, headed toward
Makin. During the voyage, Raddy huddled with the *Enterprise*'s Air
Group commander, Lt. Comdr. Edward M. "Butch" O'Hare, on the
problem of developing an interim night fighter unit. O'Hare, an outstanding pilot, had won the Medal of Honor in February 1942 for single-
handedly shooting down four Japanese "Betty" bombers and heavily
damaging two others during an enemy bombing attack on the original
Lexington.[33]

During the course of the following week, O'Hare worked with a
number of other officers to develop a plan for the employment of
what he called Black Panther groups. Two such groups were actually set
up—each consisting of an airborne radar-equipped TBF-1C torpedo
plane and two F6F-3 fighters. They were to be launched after dark, as

necessary, to seek out and attack enemy snooper aircraft and break up nighttime raids by torpedo planes.[34]

The invasions of Tarawa and Makin began on November 20, 1943, and Radford's Northern Carrier Group was kept busy during the next few days with strikes on Makin in support of ground operations. On the evening of the first day, the threat that Radford had been preparing against emerged, when Japanese torpedo planes carried out a dusk attack on Montgomery's task group off Tarawa. The small carrier *Independence* was torpedoed and had to retire from the war zone.[35] Radford's turn came on the night of the 26th (D+6—six days prior to the start of the operation), when his task group was targeted by fifteen torpedo bombers. The *Enterprise* quickly launched the first of its Black Panther teams, with Butch O'Hare piloting one of the F6Fs. Although the night fighters shot down two of the Betty bombers and helped to break up the Japanese attack, O'Hare's plane was lost in the melee. Raddy's makeshift night fighter unit had saved the task group from being torpedoed, but its success had exacted an unwelcome price.[36]

When Radford returned to Pearl Harbor on December 4, 1943, he was detached from duty as COMCARDIV ELEVEN and ordered to report as chief of staff and aide to Admiral Towers, COMAIRPAC.[37] For the next several months he worked diligently, helping, among other tasks, with the final planning for the next big Central Pacific operation—Flintlock—the capture of the Marshall Islands. Raddy recalled, "As Chief of Staff, I attended most of the high-level planning conferences in December [on Flintlock], which even at that late day were ironing out important details that should have been settled some time before."[38] Having hopes for another sea command when he completed his duty with AIRPAC, Radford was unpleasantly surprised to learn in early March 1944 that he was being ordered back to Washington as assistant Deputy Chief of Naval Operations (DCNO) (Air).[39]

He thus reported to his new boss, Vice Adm. John S. McCain, on April 1, 1944. Although apologetic about pulling Radford back from the Pacific, McCain quickly put him to work on specific problems that required his administrative skills. The sheer pace of his new assignment kept Raddy from brooding about his luck. As he wrote to Rear Adm. Ralph Wood just days after he arrived in Washington, "I . . . can't say that I appreciate the job very much; however, time does not hang heavy on my hands."[40] One thing that did concern him, though, was an awareness that the cooperative, "can-do" spirit so evident in Washington during the first disastrous months of the fighting had been replaced by a certain bureaucratic inertia now that the war was being won.[41]

The first major problem that Radford tackled was the need to establish a navy policy for the retirement of worn-out aircraft and for the development of an integrated aviation maintenance, matériel, and supply program based on this policy. On April 12 he was appointed senior member of a four-man informal board to study these matters.[42] During the course of the next three weeks, the Radford Board held fifteen meetings.[43] When issued, its report on the integrated aeronautic program was adopted within the Navy Department almost without change.[44] Later that year, Radford headed a second board, which reviewed the functioning of the new integrated aeronautic program and examined other steps necessary to ensure its effective operation.[45] The competence with which he handled these duties did not go unnoticed by the new secretary of the Navy, James V. Forrestal.

McCain had told Raddy when he had taken the assistant DCNO (Air) assignment that the problems he would be working on should only occupy him for about six months, and he had promised to help Radford get back to the Pacific once they were completed. Although McCain had left Washington for duty in the Pacific before Raddy's six months were up, he had left word with his successor, Vice Adm. Aubrey W. Fitch, that Radford had been promised orders to sea on or about October 1. Happily for Raddy, the orders came through as expected.[46]

Arriving in Pearl Harbor on October 7, Radford soon received orders to report to the Commander FIRST Carrier Task Force as COMCARDIV SIX. He headed first to Kwajalein and then on to Saipan. Here he was held over from the 22d to the 26th—the period during which the Battle of Leyte Gulf, destined to become the largest naval action in history, was occurring in the waters surrounding the Philippine Islands. From Saipan, Raddy flew to Ulithi, where he reported to Admiral McCain, who had just become Adm. William F. Halsey's fast carrier commander.[47]

He spent his first two months in "makee learn" status, riding as a passenger in the *Ticonderoga*, which was part of Rear Adm. Ted Sherman's Task Group 38.3. He found it a useful experience but was somewhat troubled by his assessment that the task force's air groups did not seem as well trained as they had been in 1943. He wrote to his successor in Washington, Rear Adm. John H. Cassady: "Frankly, the Fast Carrier Task Force is . . . certainly not as good as it was a year ago. . . . The recent changes in carrier air group composition have lowered their overall efficiency. . . . We will probably . . . be able to protect ourselves eventually [from the Japanese kamikaze suicide planes], but I don't think we will be able to hurt the other fellow as much."[48] While with Sherman's task group, Raddy witnessed supporting air strikes against southern

Arthur Radford as commander of Carrier Division SIX, ashore at Ulithi, March 29, 1945. *Courtesy of the National Archives and Records Administration, Washington, DC*

Luzon and the Visayas and antiair and shipping attacks on northern Luzon and Manila, and rode out the December typhoon that seriously battered Admiral Halsey's Third Fleet.

On December 29, 1944, Radford unexpectedly was ordered to assume command of Task Group 38.1 from injured Rear Admiral Montgomery. The fleet sortied from Ulithi the next day and headed for scheduled air strikes on Formosa and Luzon. During the middle portion of that month, it operated for the first time in the South China Sea, attacking Japanese targets in French Indo-China and Hong Kong.

During February, under Admiral Spruance's command, the redesignated Fifth Fleet directed strikes against the Tokyo area and launched air attacks in support of the invasion of Iwo Jima. Radford, commander of Task Group 58.4, was in his element as a combat commander. Following strikes against Japanese navy ships in the Inland Sea in mid-March 1945, the fleet began its sustained slugging match with Japan's kamikazes during the three-month-long Okinawa campaign.[49] During the fighting, Radford's innovative leadership kept paying dividends. He continued to push the use of night fighters in his group. On the evening of the Okinawa invasion, following several days of successful night attacks against shadowing Betty bombers, Raddy sent a message to the ships of his task group, "WELL DONE ON THE NIGHT OPERATIONS. . . . MAYBE THESE NIPS WILL FINALLY UNDERSTAND IT ISN'T SAFE TO BOTHER THIS GROUP AT NIGHT."[50]

Following completion of its efforts off Okinawa in mid-June, Radford's Task Group 38.4 returned to combat during July and August 1945 as part of Halsey's Third Fleet in attacks on the Japanese home islands of Honshu and Hokkaido, striking airfields, merchant shipping, and ground targets. At sea with his force when he received the message on August 15 to "cease all offensive operations against Japan," Radford signaled his ships, "TO EVERY OFFICER AND MAN IN THIS SPLENDID GROUP WELL DONE[.] IN THE LAST 45 DAYS YOU HAVE CONTRIBUTED MUCH TOWARD THE VICTORY ANNOUNCED TODAY AND I AM PROUD OF YOU."[51] He then sat down to write his wife that the war was over and that through God's grace his life had been spared; he also told her how fortunate he felt in having been able to play an important part in the war.[52]

In the postwar period, Radford continued his climb to positions of ever-increasing responsibility in the U.S. Navy. From January 1948 to April 1949 he served as vice chief of Naval Operations. He was commander in chief of the Pacific and Pacific Fleet throughout most of the

Korean War. His final duty was as chairman of the Joint Chiefs of Staff during the first Eisenhower administration.

Arthur Radford's rise to prominence during World War II had much to do with his rare combination of innovative combat leadership and extraordinary administrative finesse. He was representative of a group of outstanding career naval officers who reached their maturity in time to lead their service during that great conflict.

Notes

1. Information on Radford's family background comes from Officer Data Cards and personnel forms found in a folder entitled "Information on R." in Box 27 of Radford's papers in the Naval Historical Center's Operational Archives (hereafter cited as OA); biographical material contained in the folder entitled "Radford, Arthur W. Admiral USN" in Box 516 of the Officer Bios Collection (hereafter cited as Officer Bios), OA; and a September 11, 1950, *Time* cover story on Radford entitled "Men at War: Waiting for the Second Alarm," 22.

2. Arthur W. Radford, *A Brief Résumé of the Life and Experiences of Arthur W. Radford, Admiral, United States Navy (Ret.)—February 4, 1966*, 3; Xerographic copy of a typescript manuscript with penciled corrections, "Radford, A. W. Adm. (1 of 4)" Folder, Individual Personnel Section, Post 1 Jan 46 Command File, OA. The original manuscript is located in the archives of the Hoover Institution on War, Revolution, and Peace at Stanford University. For a partial edited version, see Stephen Jurika Jr., ed., *From Pearl Harbor to Vietnam: The Memoirs of Admiral Arthur W. Radford* (Stanford, CA, 1980).

3. Letter from Edward D. McDougal Jr. to Commander M. U. Beebe, CINCPACFLT staff, November 4, 1949, 2; "Information on R." Folder, Box 27, Radford Papers, OA.

4. Radford, *Life of Arthur Radford*, 5–11.

5. Numerical ranking of graduates of the class of 1916, in the U.S. Naval Academy Alumni Association, Inc., *Register of Alumni: Graduates and Former Naval Cadets and Midshipmen, 1845–1995* (Annapolis, MD, 1994), 138. For additional information on Radford's standing during his First Class year, see *Annual Register of the United States Naval Academy, Annapolis, MD.—October 1, 1916— Seventy-second Academic Year, 1916–1917* (Washington, DC, 1916), 52–53.

6. "Three Off-Shore Naval Air Stations Established," Navy Department Press Release, June 30, 1941; "Radford, Arthur W. Admiral USN" Folder, Box 516, Officer Bios, OA.

7. Radford, *Life of Arthur Radford*, 201.

8. Historical Unit, Deputy Chief of Naval Operations (Air), *United States Naval Administrative Histories of World War II*, vol. 14, *Aviation Training, 1940–1945*, unpublished typescript manuscript, n.d. [1946], 10; Rare Book Collection, Navy Department Library, Naval Historical Center (hereafter cited as NDL).

9. Letter from CNO to secretary of the navy, Op-22-B serial 0114122, November 6, 1941; quoted in ibid., 15.

10. Letter from Gates to Beebe, November 1, 1949; "Information on R." Folder, Box 27, Radford Papers, OA.

11. Radford, *Life of Arthur Radford*, 207.

12. Ibid., 212–14.

13. DCNO (Air), *Aviation Training, 1940–1945*, 27–28.

14. Ibid., 24–27.

15. Interview with Capt. Robert J. C. Maulsby, USN (Ret.), Fort Belvoir, VA, June 16, 1995.

16. Ibid. Although his career had moved in another direction, Maulsby continued his interest in the navy's development of radar control techniques after the war. See letter from Maulsby to Radford, May 22, 1947, and the letter in response from Radford to Maulsby, June 10, 1947; attached in "Norfolk Files 'M' 'Z' " Binder, Box 28, Radford Papers, OA.

17. Letter from Professor John G. Jenkins, chairman of the Department of Psychology, University of Maryland, to Radford, February 21, 1946; "Admiral Radford's Correspondence" Binder [second of two], Box 28, Radford Papers, OA.

18. Radford, *Life of Arthur Radford*, 214–18. See also letter from Radford to Captain O. O. Kessing, April 22, 1946; "Admiral Radford's Correspondence" Binder [second of two], Box 28, Radford Papers, OA.

19. Radford, *Life of Arthur Radford*, 220.

20. Ibid., 224.

21. Ibid., 227. The exact date of his relief (April 19, 1943) comes from a copy of the citation for the Legion of Merit awarded to him for his service as director of Aviation Training in BuAer (BuPers document Pers 328, signed for President Roosevelt by Secretary of the Navy Frank Knox on February 5, 1944); in "Radford, Arthur W. Admiral USN" Folder, Box 516, Officer Bios, OA.

22. Radford, *Life of Arthur Radford*, 232.

23. Ibid., 233.

24. Ibid., 234; "Rear Admiral Arthur W. Radford," unnumbered BuPers document, n.d.; "Radford, Arthur W. Admiral USN" Folder, Box 516, Officer Bios, OA.

25. Clark G. Reynolds, *The Fast Carriers: The Forging of an Air Navy*, rev. ed. (Annapolis, MD: Naval Institute Press, 1992), 83.

26. Radford, *Life of Arthur Radford*, 234–36; and Reynolds, *The Fast Carriers*, 83.

27. Radford, *Life of Arthur Radford*, 236; Clark G. Reynolds, *Admiral John H. Towers: The Struggle for Naval Air Supremacy* (Annapolis, MD: Naval Institute Press, 1991), 433.

28. Radford, *Life of Arthur Radford*, 237.

29. Ibid., 237–39.

30. Ibid., 239.

31. Ibid., 242–43; Reynolds, *The Fast Carriers*, 87–88.

32. Radford, *Life of Arthur Radford*, 247.

33. For information on Butch O'Hare's feat, see Steve Ewing and John B. Lundstrom, *Fateful Rendezvous: The Life of Butch O'Hare* (Annapolis, MD: Naval Institute Press, 1997), 128–42.

34. For details on the O'Hare concept, see memorandum from COMCARDIV ELEVEN to COMAIRPAC, Subj: "Carrier Night Fighter Operations," no serial, n.d. [ca. December 1, 1943], with enclosure; unlabeled folder, Box 27, Radford Papers, OA; and Ewing and Lundstrom, *Fateful Rendezvous*, 246–51.

35. Reynolds, *The Fast Carriers*, 103.

36. The most thorough and accurate account of the engagement is in Ewing and Lundstrom, *Fateful Rendezvous*, 263–98. Radford's own comments on the reasons for Butch O'Hare's loss are contained in a letter he wrote to naval historian Samuel Eliot Morison. See letter from Radford to Morison, February 23, 1951; "Acknowledgements and Criticisms, 1950–1953" Folder, Box 33, Samuel E. Morison Office Files, OA. Ewing and Lundstrom's account, however, corrects Radford's version of events on several vital points.

37. The reason for Radford's new assignment is discussed in Reynolds, *The Fast Carriers*, 90.

38. Radford, *Life of Arthur Radford*, 258.

39. Ibid., 271. There is a thorough discussion of Towers's activities as COMAIRPAC during the time that Radford was chief of staff, in Reynolds, *Admiral John H. Towers*, 448–66.

40. Letter from Radford to Wood, April 5, 1944; "Admiral Radford #1 Personal Corres., 1944 April–July" Folder, Box 27, Radford Papers, OA.

41. See Radford, *Life of Arthur Radford*, 272–73.

42. For information on the Radford Board, see Historical Section, Deputy Chief of Naval Operations (Air), *United States Naval Administrative Histories of World War II*, vol. 10, *Aviation Planning*, unpublished typescript manuscript, n.d. [1946], 171–216; Rare Book Collection, NDL.

43. A copy of the Radford Board's report is included as Exhibit "L" in ibid., 420–40.

44. See DCNO (Air), *Aviation Planning*, 171ff.

45. Ibid., 204–7. The report of the second Radford Board is included as Exhibit "V" on pages 596–607 of the history.

46. Radford, *Life of Arthur Radford*, 273, 278–79; Radford's itinerary, as listed on First Endorsement on BuPers 060281 orders Pers-3160-ME-5 dated September 13, 1944, from CINCPACFLT to Radford, P16-3/00, October 7, 1944; "R. Adm. A. W. Radford Personal File" Folder, Box 27, Radford Papers, OA.

47. Ibid., 279–82. See also First Endorsement to CINCPAC Orders P16-3/00 serial 8670 dated October 10, 1944 from COMAIRPAC to Radford, P16-4/00 FF12-5/60-bt, October 18, 1944; in "R. Adm. A. W. Radford Personal File" Folder, Box 27, Radford Papers, OA.

48. Letter from Radford to Cassady, December 7, 1944, 1; "R. Adm. A. W. Radford Personal File" Folder, Box 27, Radford Papers, OA.

49. Detailed statistical data on Carrier Division SIX's operations during Radford's tenure as commander can be found in a typed ten-page action summary in "R. Adm. A. W. Radford Personal File" Folder, Box 27, Radford Papers, OA.

50. Message from CTG 58.4 to Task Group 58.4, 012330Z April 1945; unlabeled folder, Box 27, Radford Papers, OA.

51. Message from CTG 38.4 to TG 38.4, 150320Z August 1945; ibid.

52. Radford, *Life of Arthur Radford*, 409–10.

Suggested Readings

Baer, George W. *One Hundred Years of Sea Power: The U.S. Navy, 1890–1990.* Stanford, CA, 1994.

Jurika, Stephen, Jr., ed. *From Pearl Harbor to Vietnam: The Memoirs of Admiral Arthur W. Radford.* Stanford, CA, 1980.

Morison, Samuel Eliot. *The Two-Ocean War.* Boston, 1963.

Reynolds, Clark G. *Admiral John H. Towers: The Struggle for Naval Air Supremacy.* Annapolis, 1991.

———. *The Fast Carriers: The Forging of an Air Navy.* Rev. ed. Annapolis, 1992.

Taylor, Theodore. *The Magnificent Mitscher.* Reprinted with an introduction by Jeffrey G. Barlow. Annapolis, 1991.

11

James M. Gavin
Pioneer in Airborne Warfare, Battlefield Commander, and Military Maverick

Spencer C. Tucker

Of the ninety divisions on the U.S. Army's order of battle in World War II, five were airborne formations designed to seize key areas from the enemy by surprise aerial assault. Made up of parachute and glider components, the airborne divisions drew their men as volunteers from other units. Controversial from the beginning for skimming off the cream of the army's soldiery, the elite divisions were also criticized for their large aircraft requirements. Skeptics complained too that airborne operations scattered the elite troopers ineffectively across the countryside, which left them vulnerable on the ground to conventional enemy formations. Notwithstanding these objections, U.S. airborne soldiers fought in the European theater in such pivotal conflicts as the invasions of Sicily, southern Italy, and Normandy, the Battle of the Bulge, and the crossing of the Rhine River.

The prototypical paratrooper was James Gavin, a soldier who believed in leadership by personal example. Physically tough, energetic, and innovative, Gavin rose with startling speed from the rank of captain in 1941 to major general by 1944—an advancement that would have taken two decades or more in the peacetime army. One of the very few soldiers in the army to make and survive four combat jumps, Gavin by 1944 commanded the 82d Airborne Division, dubbed by a top British officer as "the greatest division in the world."

Writing about this iconoclastic American soldier is Spencer C. Tucker, holder of the John Biggs Chair of Military History at the Virginia Military Institute in Lexington. Tucker, who earned his doctorate from the University of North Carolina at Chapel Hill, served in U.S. Army Intelligence and has published twelve books on military and naval history. His latest work is the three-volume *Encyclopedia of the Korean War* (2000).

James Maurice Gavin was a pioneer in airborne warfare and one of the most brilliant battlefield commanders of World War II. A soldier's soldier and authentic war hero, he became the youngest major general in the army during the conflict and made more combat jumps than any other general officer in U.S. military history.

He was born in Brooklyn, New York, on March 22, 1907, the illegitimate son of Katherine Ryan, a recent immigrant from Ireland. A ward of the city of New York, at eighteen months he was adopted by an Irish Catholic coal-mining couple, Martin and Mary Gavin of Mount Carmel, Pennsylvania. Acutely conscious of his illegitimacy, James Gavin believed from youth that he was different. He liked his weak-willed stepfather, but he also wanted to be different from him; certainly he disliked his stepmother, a heavy drinker who never showed him any affection.

A good student, Gavin was interested in history and especially the Civil War. Then and later he was fascinated by Thomas "Stonewall" Jackson and his brilliant 1862 Shenandoah Valley Campaign. Gavin wanted to attend college but his stepparents told him that eighth grade was sufficient education and that he would then have to go to work full time. He had already worked part-time as a newspaper boy, coal picker, and barber's assistant. For the next three years Gavin was first a clerk in a shoe shop and then manager of a filling station. In March 1924, at age seventeen, he left home for New York City; the next month he enlisted in the army.

Gavin then cast off his foster family entirely and took a new family—the U.S. Army. Sent to the Panama Canal Zone, he became a clerk and quickly made corporal. The base library was a refuge and he seized the chance to remake himself. Sensing his ability, his first sergeant urged Gavin to apply for an army school that prepared enlisted applicants for the U.S. Military Academy at West Point. Gavin did so, and although he struggled academically, his hard work paid off and he passed the entrance exam. He reported to West Point in July 1925.

Less prepared academically than most of his classmates, Gavin found the classroom work "extremely difficult."[1] Nonetheless, in June 1929 he graduated 185th out of 299 in his class. Gavin selected the infantry as his service branch. Years later he described his choice in these words: "I went forth to seek the challenge, to move toward the sound of the guns, to go where danger was the greatest, for there is where the issues would be resolved and the decisions made."[2] But his choice of the infantry rather than the cavalry or engineers was probably also prompted by his financial straits and rather unimpressive academic record.

At West Point he first discovered his magnetism for attractive women, who were drawn to Gavin throughout his life. He met Jean Emert in the summer of 1928; they were married in September 1929. Later he claimed that he had not wanted to marry her. In any case he was not faithful to her and had a succession of mistresses. The two finally divorced in 1947, when Gavin married Jean Duncan, sixteen years his junior. He had one daughter by his first wife and four by his second.

Gavin's preoccupation was the army, and he always believed that innovation and new techniques would win wars. A new era of warfare had dawned, marked by swift movement and machines, and he wanted to be a part of it. His quest led him to Brooks Field, Texas, and to army aviation. But for obscure reasons Gavin failed flight school. Failure never sat well with him, and he seldom talked about the experience. Gavin then applied for and received an assignment to the remote post of Camp Harry J. Jones, Arizona, which was close to the Mexican border and home of the all-black 25th Infantry Regiment, officered by whites.

In the summer of 1933 Gavin was assigned to the Infantry School at Fort Benning, Georgia. The timing was fortuitous as its academic department, led by George C. Marshall with Joseph "Vinegar Joe" Stilwell as head of tactics, had initiated the "Benning revolution," a search for new directions and techniques for the U.S. military. Many of the individuals there at this time—Marshall, Omar Bradley, J. Lawton Collins, Courtney Hodges, Matthew B. Ridgway, and Walter Bedell Smith—would figure prominently in Gavin's future. The instructors stressed simplicity, effectiveness, and innovation.

Gavin was particularly impressed by Stilwell, who demanded much of the students and told them that they should always be able to do themselves what they asked of their men. Gavin never forgot this lesson and came to believe that a leader had to be as tough or tougher than the men he was to inspire. Until late in life when arthritis from a jump injury and the effects of Parkinson's disease slowed him, Gavin's hallmark was physical fitness. He seemed younger than his age and maintained a spartan regimen based on heavy manual labor, long-distance marches, and simple diet. He despised generals who lived better than their men. Gavin, who came to be known for his immaculate dress, was often called "Gentleman Jim" or "Slim Jim." Later he was known for the identifying hallmarks of glider patch, M-1 Garand rifle, and perfectly polished paratrooper boots.

Following Benning, Gavin found assignment at Fort Sill, Oklahoma, then commanded by Lt. Col. Lesley McNair. Just as Gavin arrived, Lt. Maxwell Taylor (a graduate of West Point's class of '22) was leaving. Gavin had taken a dislike to Taylor when the latter had been an instructor at West Point from 1928 to 1932; the two became intense lifelong rivals, whose careers would cross many times over the next decades.

Gavin took advantage of Fort Sill's library to become proficient in military history and strategy, reading such classic writers as Carl von Clausewitz and such innovators as Basil Liddell Hart and J. F. C. Fuller. He kept the careful notes he took with him throughout his career.

In 1936, Gavin was posted to the Philippine Islands. Assigned to the 57th Infantry (Philippine Scouts), he was shocked by the lack of preparedness and modern weapons ("Our weapons and equipment were no better than those used in the First World War," he recalled), and the fact that the principal military maneuver was practicing a withdrawal into the Bataan Peninsula.[3]

In the fall of 1938, as war clouds gathered over Europe, Gavin was promoted to captain and assigned to the 3d Infantry Division at Vancouver Barracks, Washington. In the summer of 1940 he received a plum assignment to West Point as instructor in tactics. By now, Europe was engulfed in war and the German blitzkrieg was at full tide. Gavin noted the "quantum jump" made by the Germans militarily. Convinced that the United States would soon be fighting them, he became knowledgeable about German tactics and military equipment, in particular the brilliant May 1940 assault on the supposedly impregnable Belgian fortress of Eben Emael.

Gavin became convinced that thoroughly trained, elite units utilizing surprise could turn the course of battle. This belief led to his decision in February 1941 to apply for airborne duty and parachute training. The superintendent opposed his transfer, and, not surprisingly, the army turned it down. Repeated efforts, including several trips to Washington, DC, to a friend in the infantry personnel office, finally brought success. Ordered to Fort Benning in July, Gavin completed parachute training the next month.

The U.S. Army had experimented with paratroops shortly after World War I at Kelly Field, Texas, but only the Russians and the Germans correctly foresaw their potential. The Russians developed most of the early techniques, but the Germans demonstrated the effectiveness of airborne forces, not only in the May 1940 capture of Eben Emael but also in the May 1941 assault on Crete.

These successes encouraged the British and Americans to follow suit, which was ironic because Hitler had become disillusioned with airborne forces as a consequence of the German experience in Crete. Thanks to radio intercepts (the "Ultra" secret), the Allies knew of the German invasion plans, and although the Germans were ultimately successful, they took prohibitive casualties: 6,698 men (3,352 dead; of these the majority—1,653—were paratroopers). Nearly two hundred German aircraft were also lost in the invasion of Crete. A shocked Hitler declared an end to airborne assaults, and for much of the rest of the war Gen. Kurt Student's paratroopers fought as infantry.

Army Chief of Staff George Marshall played the key role in the development of U.S. airborne forces. In June 1940, a month after Eben Emael, he ordered the creation of the first all-volunteer, parachute test platoon at Fort Benning and, in October, the formation of the first U.S. parachute battalion. But in spring 1941, U.S. Army airborne forces were hardly impressive. There was no paratroop unit larger than a battalion and no established doctrine as to how to employ them, much less the airlift capacity to get them into combat. The first American airborne divisions were not activated until after Pearl Harbor. Eventually the United States had five such divisions: the 82d and 101st, followed by the 11th, 13th, and 17th.

At Benning, Gavin first served as a company commander in the 503d Parachute Infantry Battalion; he then became the battalion S-3, in charge of training. Col. William C. Lee of the 503d was his mentor. Lee had been the driving force behind the development of U.S. airborne forces, and Gavin's well-known dedication to the "art and science of war" led Lee to give him the task of developing paratrooper doctrine. With this assignment in October 1941 came Gavin's promotion to major.

Gavin then wrote a training manual, *Tactics and Techniques of Air-Borne Troops*. Basing it on a thorough study of Russian and German practices and his own innovations, he dealt with organization and equipping of paratroop units up to the regimental level. He stated that the war the United States was now about to enter would be one of rapid movement and shifting front lines, which would require paratroopers to be flexible and self-reliant. The manual attracted notice, and he later attributed his rapid rise in the airborne to it.

On December 7, 1941, the Japanese attacked Pearl Harbor and the United States became a belligerent. In February 1942, Gavin attended an abbreviated course at the Command and General Staff School at Fort Leavenworth, Kansas, which qualified him for divisional assignment. He returned to Benning to the Provisional Airborne Group and immediately set about designing the first airborne division. The army selected the 82d Infantry Division at Camp Claiborne, Louisiana, commanded by Maj. Gen. Omar Bradley with Brig. Gen. Matthew B. Ridgway as executive officer. In June, Ridgway became its commander and oversaw its transformation into the 82d Airborne Division.

Ridgway, one of Marshall's protégés, knew nothing of the airborne, but he learned quickly and became the preeminent American airborne general of the war; certainly he had a profound influence on Gavin's subsequent career. By the end of the war Ridgway was a three-star general in command of an airborne corps. Indeed, the airborne spawned three remarkable future leaders of the U.S. Army: Ridgway, Taylor, and Gavin.

Chief of Army Ground Forces Gen. Lesley McNair wanted U.S. airborne divisions modeled on German operations, with two glider regiments and one of paratroopers. The paratroops would land first and secure the airhead to be used by the glider forces. Gavin and Lee disagreed: they wanted the new divisions to have a preponderance of paratroopers. But McNair had his way; the original U.S. airborne divisions were constituted along his lines. In August 1942, Gavin received command of the 505th Regiment; shortly thereafter he became a full colonel. The 505th was the first paratroop regiment to be built from scratch. An exacting commander, Gavin believed in thorough, realistic training, physical toughening, and innovative, even daring, techniques, such as free-fall parachuting when other units were using static-line jumps. According to historian Clay Blair, the 505th "may well have been one of the best-trained and most highly motivated regiments the Army had ever fielded." An 82d Division staffer recalled, "They were awesome. Every man a clone of the CO, Gavin."[4]

In February 1943 the 82d was selected over Lee's 101st to deploy to North Africa to participate in Operation Husky, the Allied invasion of Sicily. Paratroopers who were dropped behind enemy coastal defenses to protect the landing beaches were a key element in the Allied plan. The 82d was probably chosen over the 101st not only because Ridgway was one of Marshall's protégés but also because the 82d did not have enough craft to deploy its two glider regiments in combat. Gavin's 505th Regiment took the place of the 326th. Ridgway was pleased, for he had high regard for Gavin and his men. Gavin's regiment joined the 82d in March. Before it was deployed to North Africa it staged the first mass regimental parachute drop in American history, near Camden, South Carolina.

The invasion of Sicily was the largest airborne assault to that date. Both Ridgway and Lt. Gen. Sir Frederick A. M. "Boy" Browning, father of British airborne forces, wanted their own troops to have pride of place, and the rivalry became bitter. Ultimately, General Dwight D. Eisenhower had to allocate the aircraft himself. His decision meant that on D day Ridgway was able to deliver only one regiment, reinforced by a battalion.

Ridgway selected Gavin's 505th, recognizing that Gavin was senior in rank to Col. Reuben "Rube" Henry Tucker III and that the 505th was better trained than Tucker's 504th. Thus, Gavin commanded the first regimental parachute assault in U.S. history. With the additional battalion, Gavin's command became the 505th Regimental Combat Team. Its mission was to establish an airhead between enemy reserves at Caltagrione and the assault beaches of the 1st Infantry Division, blocking any German counterattacks. The remainder of the 504th Regiment would arrive the day after the attack began (D+1) in drop zones secured by the 505th and the one 504th deployed battalion. Gavin disagreed with Ridgway's plan to save weight by substituting mortars for bundle-dropped 75 mm. pack howitzers, but Ridgway finally gave in.

Gavin worked hard to prepare his men. His attention to detail and insistence on realistic training were to the point of obsession. Still, Gavin had serious misgivings about the attack. He wrote on May 16, "It is clear that the effort will be a very risky and costly one. . . . The risks are great, but the rewards are greater. Many lives will be lost in a few hours, but in the long run, many lives will be saved."[5]

The assault took place on the night of July 9–10. High winds and poor navigation produced a widely dispersed drop. Many British gliders were lost in the sea and most of Gavin's men landed well outside the designated drop zones. Even by the 12th, Ridgway reported to Gen. George Patton that of 5,000 paratroopers who had jumped into Sicily he had only 400 under his operational control. But the dispersed drop proved to be an advantage as it confused the defenders and led them to believe they were confronting a much larger force than was actually the case. As in later assaults of the war, "Jumping Jim" Gavin was the first out the door of his aircraft. As one of his men later put it, "He could jump higher, shout louder, spit farther, and fight harder than any man I ever saw."[6]

The men of the 505th did not know that they would soon be contesting with German panzers of the Hermann Göring Division. This information, available through Ultra radio intercepts, had been deliberately withheld from the 82d. The troopers' only weapon against the tanks was the 2.36 in. bazooka.

Gavin spent the next day in firefights with small enemy units and collecting his men. On the critical day of July 11 his forces linked up with the 45th Division and American lines near Vittoria. By chance,

Gavin came on Biazza Ridge, which dominated the exposed left flank of the 45th Division and right flank of the 1st. Gavin soon demonstrated his coolness in combat by taking and holding the ridge and blunting a counterattack by the Hermann Göring Division with Tiger tanks, 88 mm guns, 120 mm mortars, and infantry, all supported by the Luftwaffe. The Germans were bent on smashing the Americans on the beachhead. The paratroopers had no heavy weaponry, and their bazookas proved ineffective against the frontal armor of the Tigers. Gavin himself got to within ten feet of one Tiger, only to see a bazooka projectile bounce off it. After a desperate stand by the paratroopers, U.S. naval gunfire and additional land support in the form of Sherman tanks saved a precarious situation. The U.S. victory in the Biazza battle was vital in protecting the invasion beaches.

In the fighting, Gavin demonstrated his belief that generals command best with their troops; in his memoirs he was sharply critical of General Eisenhower for his remoteness from the battlefield and for often being out of touch with the situation at the front. Gavin always led from the front, which resulted in a number of close brushes with capture, and he preferred to carry the M-1 rifle that was issued to every common soldier. Very much a hands-on commander, he made a point of talking to soldiers of all ranks and questioning them on their roles. And he developed what became a lifelong habit of arising at 4 A.M. and beginning his workday shortly thereafter.

Unlike the action on Biazza Ridge, most of the subsequent fighting for the 505th on Sicily was a series of small-scale engagements. On July 22 the 505th reached Trapani, covering on foot some one hundred fifty miles of difficult terrain with a speed that surprised even Patton. Many of the men believed they would have gotten there sooner but for Ridgway's interference and his dressing down of some of the officers. Throughout the war, Gavin believed that U.S. commanders were too quick to dismiss subordinates for single errors in judgment. He wrote in his memoirs: "I have a haunting memory that does not diminish with the passage of time of how unfairly and thoughtlessly we treated some of our senior officers."[7]

Ridgway recognized Gavin's performance on Sicily by awarding him the Distinguished Service Cross and putting his name in for promotion to brigadier general. Not only Ridgway, but now Patton and Bradley also knew Gavin and were impressed by his accomplishments.[8] After Sicily the debate was renewed over the airborne concept and whether paratroopers made a critical difference. The 505th had been scattered all over Sicily, there was the obvious problem with the 504th Regimental drop, and the British drops had also gone badly. There was general agreement that the 505th had been by far the most successful of the paratrooper regiments, yet Gavin himself was shaken by the experience. Thirty-five years later, the image of all the dead bodies waiting to be buried still haunted him. After Sicily he was determined not to waste men if there was any way to avoid it.

One lesson of Sicily was that the ineffectiveness of the bazooka against German tanks left the paratroopers vulnerable. Gavin had his men train with the bazookas on German tank hulls to probe for weak spots but the problem essentially remained unsolved throughout the war. Troop Carrier Command also needed better training, particularly at night. One important innovation suggested by Gavin was the addition of Pathfinders to mark the drop zone for the mass drop that would follow.

A plan to drop the 82d Airborne on Rome (Operation Giant II) to take the Eternal City in a coup de main was scrubbed because of doubts about Italian assistance and the arrival of two German divisions near Rome. Ridgway had fought against the plan, and he and Gavin both later concluded it would have been a failure. Instead the 82d was employed on the Italian mainland in support of the Allied landing at Salerno, which had run into serious trouble. A crisis situation had developed with the Germans threatening to push the Allies into the sea. Lt. Gen. Mark Clark decided to use the 82d, dropped right on the beach lit by flaming gasoline drums, to reinforce the beachhead. Tucker's 504th was dropped on the night of September 13–14, 1943. It went well and Gavin always thought it was the decisive turning point at Salerno. Certainly it provided an important psychological lift. Clark then canceled the 505th's planned jump at Capua and ordered it to join the 504th at Salerno. The regiment jumped the next night, again on target. On October 1 the 505th reached Naples and participated in the liberation of the first major Italian city. The regiment was then sent north in a drive to the Volturno River. On the 8th it resumed occupation duties in Naples.

On October 10, Gavin received his star as temporary brigadier general and became assistant divisional commander of the 82d. On November 17, Ridgway sent him to London to advise on airborne operations in planning for the forthcoming Allied invasion of France. That month the 82d, minus the 504th Regiment, sailed for Northern Ireland to begin training and refitting for the invasion of France.

In London, Gavin encountered obstacles in the persons of Browning and Air Chief Marshal Sir Trafford Leigh-Mallory. Supreme Allied

Commander General Eisenhower, also skeptical about the use of airborne forces, wrote General Marshall on September 20, 1943: "I do not believe in the airborne division."[9] Eisenhower thought airborne divisions too large and wanted regimental combat teams instead. The airborne concept found few friends, but among them were Bradley and Marshall, who insisted on the deployment of the airborne as divisions; Eisenhower gave way. Marshall wanted to see the airborne divisions employed en masse well behind enemy lines, but Eisenhower wisely vetoed that idea.

Gavin warned that precise positioning of the drop zones was essential. Dropping the airborne troops too far in the enemy rear would put them at the mercy of more heavily armed German units. Airborne troops would also be of little use in the invasion assault. Their place should be to the immediate rear of the enemy. Gavin also worked to standardize airborne practices between the British and Americans, and in late 1943 he published the first document on the subject, "Training Memorandum on the Employment of Airborne Force."[10]

Airborne troops were to be used in the Normandy invasion on a much larger scale than before. Three divisions were employed: the U.S. 82d and 101st and the British 1st. On February 16, 1944, Gavin returned to the 82d and at the same time the division moved from Ireland to northern England. Gavin then took charge of training the division for the assault.

On the night of June 5–6, 1944, Gavin led his men to France in support of the U.S. VII Corps on Normandy's Utah Beach. Their mission was to secure key bridges, set up blocking positions, and link up with the 101st. The drops of the 101st and 82d were widely dispersed, although not as badly as on Sicily; still, unit cohesion was almost nonexistent and most of the paratroopers were in groups of only up to fifty men. The dispersed drop was largely the result of poor training in Troop Carrier Command. But, as on Sicily, this tactic confused the Germans as to the strength and direction of the Allied attacks.

Many of the subsequent paratrooper battles were not for their military objectives, but simply for survival. Nonetheless the men of the 82d and the 101st managed to complete their most critical mission of securing the exits from Utah Beach. In heavy fighting the 82d took the town of Ste-Mère-Église and a key bridge over the Merderet River near Chef-du-Pont. Casualties came to 10 percent; although less than some feared, they were nonetheless quite heavy for a single day of fighting.

By mid-August, and behind schedule, the Allies broke out of the Normandy beachhead. As the advance east across France unfolded, Gavin was in an even more important position. On August 15, at thirty-seven, he became commander of the 82d, the youngest officer ever to hold divisional command in the war. He had that command for the remainder of the conflict. In the subsequent fighting, Gavin and his division became almost legendary. The 82d was credited with covering the most ground, spending the highest number of days continuously in combat, and accounting for the highest number of enemy casualties. Much of this success can be attributed to Gavin's leadership.

The 82d Division won its greatest renown in Operation Market-Garden. This operation of September 17 to September 26, 1944, was Field Marshal Bernard Law Montgomery's plan to win the war in one bold stroke before the end of the year. Convinced that German defenses had crumbled, Montgomery planned to outflank the German West Wall, cut the land exit of German troops through Holland, and allow the Allies to drive into the German industrial heart of the Ruhr. In part the plan arose from pressure to use the three Allied airborne divisions then recuperating in Britain, but Montgomery can be much criticized for the failure to carry out the detailed staff planning to make it work. The operation involved three paratroop divisions—the U.S. 82d and 101st and the British 1st—a Polish airborne brigade, and the British Second Army. "Market" was the airborne segment and "Garden" was the ground portion. "Market" would drop airborne forces to secure bridges over the Maas (Meuse), Waal (Rhine), and Lek (Lower Rhine) Rivers. In "Garden" the Second Army, led by XXX Corps, would race up a narrow corridor from Belgium along a sixty-mile-long causeway over marshy ground across the succession of rivers to secure Arnhem on the far side of the lower Rhine. The paratroops were to drop ahead of the Second Army, seize the key bridges, and then hold them until the ground troops came up. Montgomery and his airborne commander, Lt. Gen. Browning, selected the British 1st Airborne to secure the farthest bridge, at Arnhem. The U.S. 82d and 101st were given the tasks of taking the bridges at Nijmegen and Eindhoven, respectively.

In Market-Garden the dominant theme was Allied overconfidence. Factors in the operation's failure included arrogance and the refusal to adjust the plan. The Allies failed to coordinate with the Dutch underground and heed its warnings as well as late photographic evidence that the German 9th and 10th SS Panzer Divisions were recuperating around

Arnhem. And the land attack was only along one narrow road. But the greatest tactical mistake was to drop the British 1st Airborne too far away from the highway bridge at Arnhem. German panzers were able to isolate it. On September 17 the British 1st Airborne Division dropped beyond the "bridge too far" at Arnhem and the tanks of Lt. Gen.

Gen. James Gavin checks his equipment before boarding a plane for the airborne invasion of Holland, September 17, 1944. *Courtesy of the U.S. Army*

Brian G. Horrocks's XXX Corps began their slow roll north across Holland while men of the U.S. 82d and 101st Airborne floated out of the skies to clear their path. In this largest airborne attack of World War II, 1,400 aircraft carried 34,000 paratroops and glidermen (20,000 men on the first day), but three lifts over three days were required.

The airborne troops at Arnhem, reinforced by the Polish brigade, which was dropped too late, had been expected to hold only two to three days. But only five hundred men made it to the principal bridge before the Germans sealed the drop zone. Nonetheless, the British held out for nine days before evacuating across the Rhine. The operation ended on September 26. Market-Garden, which Montgomery later termed as "ninety percent successful," was in fact a failure.

Gavin's portion of the operation went well, although fighting was fierce. His men made a costly and daring attack to seize the Nijmegen Bridge, only eleven miles from Arnhem. Braving the fast waters of the River Waal and intense fire from German guns, on the 20th they crossed the river and took the bridge, which was many stories high and 1,800 feet long, capturing it intact against determined German resistance. Gavin always believed that the American airborne divisions never received proper historical credit for their role in Operation Market-Garden.

In October, Gavin was promoted to major general, the youngest man to hold that rank in the U.S. Army since George Armstrong Custer. The 82d also won renown in Hitler's counteroffensive in the Ardennes, known as the Battle of the Bulge (December 16, 1944–January 16, 1945). It joined the fight on December 19 and helped bolster the northern flank.

Gavin was only an observer in Operation Varsity, the March 24, 1945, airborne assault by the British 6th and U.S. 17th Airborne Divisions to secure Montgomery's bridgehead across the Rhine River taken the night before. Gavin was horrified by the slaughter of the daylight attack, noting, "At one point I counted 23 transports or gliders going down in flames, trying desperately to make it back to the west bank." He found himself wondering if the operation had really been necessary and if ground troops could not have done the job at less cost in lives.[11]

The 82d continued to fight on the ground in the Allied drive east until the defeat of Germany in May 1945. At the end of April the 82d had crossed the Elbe, and on May 2, Gavin had the extraordinary experience of accepting the surrender of the entire German Twenty-first Army Group—150,000 German soldiers with all their equipment.

At the end of the war the 82d was poised for an airborne assault on Berlin. The city was by then a political, rather than military, target and had been assigned to the Soviet zone of occupation. Eisenhower, preoccupied with a nonexistent German "Alpine Redoubt," wanted to end the war as quickly as possible with the least cost in American lives. With estimates of up to one hundred thousand lives to take the German capital, he rejected the idea. Gavin was confident that such an operation would have been successful, but, as he noted in his memoirs, this was not a military decision alone. After briefly sharing in the occupation of Berlin as part of the joint Allied command with his division, Gavin returned to the United States in December 1945 and remained in command of the 82d at Fort Bragg until 1948. His book *Airborne Warfare* was published in 1947.

Gavin then served as chief of staff of the 5th Army. In April 1949 he was assigned to the Office of the Secretary of Defense as the army representative on the Weapons Systems Evaluation Group. In 1951 he became chief of staff, Allied Forces, Southern Europe; from 1952 to 1954 he was commander, U.S. Army VII Corps in Germany; he then returned to the Pentagon as assistant chief of staff, Plans and Operations. In 1955 he became deputy chief of staff, Plans and Research, the same year he was promoted to lieutenant general, the military's youngest. Between 1955 and 1957 he was chief of research and development. In these posts Gavin was an articulate, zealous advocate for a strong and mobile military force.

Appalled by the army's poor performance in the Korean War (1950–53), Gavin was an early proponent of tactical nuclear weapons. He pushed the Pentagon to let the army develop long-range missiles, weapons later given to the air force and the navy, although the army did retain tactical missiles. He made an important contribution to the tactical use of helicopters as troop carriers, which came to fruition in the Vietnam War. But Gavin disliked the rear-echelon generalship in which he found himself and was in turn disliked by many army leaders for his criticisms of U.S. strategy and military policies.

For the most part he was not successful in the Pentagon battles for new methods and weapons. He often found himself at odds with the administration of his former commander-in-chief, Dwight Eisenhower. Gavin strongly opposed the New Look military policy of Defense Secretary Charles E. Wilson, which favored nuclear weapons for conventional forces ("More bang for the buck," as it came to be known). Gavin's argument was that while nuclear forces were necessary, limited wars were more likely to occur. He was also critical of the role of the Joint Chiefs of Staff, urging that the body be limited to planning and that actual operations be carried out by integrated "unified command staff" to ease interservice rivalries. In this too he was prescient.

Despite his criticisms, Gavin was slated for promotion to four-star rank. But in 1958, on the eve of his promotion and assignment as commander of the Seventh Army in Europe and after thirty-three years in the military, he abruptly resigned from the army in frustration, saying, "I won't compromise my principles, and I won't go along with the Pentagon system."[12] Also in 1958, Gavin wrote *War and Peace in the Space Age,* a critique of the New Look, which held that the United States needed strong conventional forces to deal with limited wars. Such ideas found credence in the early 1960s during the Kennedy administration.

After retirement from the military, Gavin became a vice president of Arthur D. Little, an industrial research and consulting firm in Cambridge, Massachusetts. In 1961, President John F. Kennedy appointed him as U.S. ambassador to France, probably in large part because of his independence of mind. He held that position only into 1962 and then returned to Arthur D. Little. He was chairman of the board from 1964 to 1977.

Gavin strongly opposed U.S. involvement in Vietnam. In 1967 he traveled to South Vietnam and returned convinced that "we are in a tragedy." He argued strongly for an "enclave strategy" whereby U.S. forces would hold coastal enclaves and leave most of the fighting to the Army of the Republic of Vietnam. He also believed that Vietnam distracted U.S. energies from more important areas of the world vital to U.S. interests, such as the Middle East. In 1968, Gavin's *Crisis Now* was published, and he briefly flirted with the idea of running for president. Some Republicans sought to promote him but the idea soon fizzled, and he quietly dropped from the public scene. He retired from Arthur D. Little in 1977. He died in Baltimore on February 23, 1990, of complications from Parkinson's disease.

Notes

1. T. Michael Booth and Duncan Spencer, *Paratrooper: The Life of General James M. Gavin* (New York: Simon and Schuster, 1994), 43.

2. Ibid., 50.

3. Ibid., 62.

4. Ibid., 81, 90; Clay Blair, *Ridgway's Paratroopers: The American Airborne in World War II* (Garden City, NY: Dial Press, 1985), 51.

5. Booth and Spencer, *Paratrooper*, 92–93.

6. "Lieutenant General James Gavin," *Annual Obituary, 1990* (Chicago: St. James Press, 1991), 113.

7. Booth and Spencer, *Paratrooper*, 113–14; James M. Gavin, *On to Berlin: Battles of an Airborne Commander, 1943–1946* (New York: Viking, 1978), 232.

8. Booth and Spencer, *Paratrooper*, 114.

9. Ibid., 151–53; Gavin, *On to Berlin*, 53, 93–94; Blair, *Ridgway's Paratroopers*, 178.

10. Gavin, *On to Berlin*, 88–90.

11. Ibid., 278.

12. "Lieutenant Gavin," *Annual Obituary, 1990*, 113–14; "Lieutenant General James Gavin," *New York Times*, February 25, 1990.

Suggested Readings

Ambrose, Stephen E. *D-Day. June 6, 1944: The Climactic Battle of World War II*. New York, 1994.

Blair, Clay. *Ridgway's Paratroopers: The American Airborne in World War II*. Garden City, NY, 1985.

Booth, Michael T., and Duncan Spencer. *Paratrooper: The Life of General James M. Gavin*. New York, 1994.

Breuer, William B. *Drop Zone Sicily*. Novato, CA, 1983.

D'Este, Carlo. *Bitter Victory: The Battle for Sicily, 1943*. New York, 1988.

———. *Decision in Normandy*. New York, 1983.

Devlin, Gerard. *Paratrooper*. New York, 1979.

Gavin, James M. *Airborne Warfare*. Washington, DC, 1947.

———. *On to Berlin: Battles of an Airborne Commander, 1943–1946*. New York, 1978.

———. *War and Peace in the Space Age*. New York, 1958.

Gavin, James, with Arthur T. Hadley. *Crisis Now*. New York, 1968.

Goelhoed, E. Bruce. *Charles E. Wilson and Controversy at the Pentagon, 1953–1957*. Detroit, 1979.

Graham, Dominick, and Shelford Bidwell. *Tug of War: The Battle for Italy, 1943–1945*. New York, 1986.

Hastings, Max. *Overlord: D-Day, June 6, 1944*. New York, 1984.

Keegan, John. *Six Armies in Normandy*. New York, 1983.

Liddell Hart, Basil H. *History of the Second World War*. New York, 1970.

MacDonald, Callum. *The Lost Battle: Crete, 1941*. New York, 1993.

MacDonald, Charles B. *A Time for Trumpets: The Untold Story of the Battle of the Bulge*. New York, 1985.

Marshall, S. L. A. *Night Drop*. Boston, 1962.

Morris, Eric. *Salerno: A Military Fiasco*. New York, 1983.

Perret, Geoffrey. *There's a War to Be Won: The United States Army in World War II*. New York, 1992.

Ryan, Cornelius. *A Bridge Too Far*. New York, 1974.

Trevelyan, Raleigh. *Rome '44: The Battle for the Eternal City*. New York, 1981.

12

Kenneth R. Martin, James Howard, and the Pioneer Mustang Group

Thomas A. Hughes

Although James Gavin envisioned an important role for the airborne division in the war, other army planners believed that air power, used to bomb the enemy's homeland, would be the shortest route to victory. As noted in the Introduction, these visionaries based their hopes on precision strikes against enemy industry, not on the terror bombing of cities. To hit Axis factories from an altitude of four miles or more, American bombers would fly in the daytime and with their heavy machine guns fight through enemy fighter defenses.

Unfortunately, major raids undertaken in the summer of 1943 showed how costly such efforts could be. On August 1, 177 B-24 Liberator bombers attacked Ploesti, Romania, the major source of German oil. Fifty-three of the big bombers were shot down; another 50 were badly damaged. On August 17, 361 B-17 Flying Fortresses made their first raid against targets deep in Germany: the ball-bearings plants at Schweinfurt and the Messerschmitt aircraft plant at Regensburg. Losses were once again depressingly high: 60 bombers destroyed outright, and another 11 so damaged that they never flew again. Such heavy casualties threatened the entire American bombing effort and the hopes of its advocates for an independent air force after the war.

A solution for the problem resided in the long-range escort fighter, which could accompany the bombers to the target and there tangle with German fighters. Such challenging missions required fighters of great range, speed, and maneuverability. The Army Air Forces (AAF) found the P-47 Thunderbolt and the P-51 Mustang most suitable for the task. To fly these high-performance aircraft, the AAF needed pilots with the "right stuff"—men such as Kenneth Martin and James Howard of the 354th Fighter Group.

Writing about these two fine airmen is Thomas A. Hughes, a faculty member of the Air War College at Maxwell Air Force Base in Alabama, the senior professional educational institution of the U.S. Air Force. Having received his doctorate from the University of Houston, Hughes published *Over Lord: General Pete Quesada and the Triumph of Tactical Air Power in World War II* (1995). He is currently working on a biography of Adm. William Halsey for Harvard University Press.

O n January 11, 1944, in Boxted, England, men of the 354th Fighter Group woke up early and ate a hurried breakfast. At 4:00 A.M., while ground crews readied the fighter planes, pilots listened to Group Commander Lt. Col. Kenneth R. Martin explain the day's job in a briefing hut filled with charts and wall maps. Ninety minutes after waking, the flyers strapped themselves into cockpits, throttled their engines, and climbed into the sky. As Squadron Leader Maj. Jim Howard set course to escort a flight of heavy bombers making an attack on German aircraft manufacturing plants, each of the forty-nine pilots knew that anything could happen.

After intense antiaircraft fire over the target, bomber crews and fighter pilots alike hoped for an easy return. A maelstrom of German planes ambushed the formation over Belgium, however, and in the melee that followed Howard found himself alone near a group of American B-17 heavy bombers. Within minutes, thirty German fighter planes pounced on the bombers. Pledged to protect the vulnerable big planes, Howard chopped his throttle, dropped his flaps, and slashed in like a man possessed. For him, the decision to fight against such long odds was simple: "I seen my duty and I done it."

Bomber pilots saw it differently. "It looked like one American against the entire Luftwaffe [the German Air Force]," recalled one. "He was over us, under us, across the formation and around it. For sheer determination and guts it was the greatest exhibition I have ever seen." Howard shot down five planes that day, protecting well over two hundred Americans in the bombers. For the day's work the quiet, lanky thirty-year-old with a slow smile and huge nose won the Congressional Medal of Honor, the nation's highest award for valor in combat. Fewer than one in twenty thousand earned that award, and Howard became famous, for a while.[1]

Other than his family, perhaps the man most proud of Howard's accomplishments was Ken Martin, his boss. The war had forced Martin into seasoned adulthood sooner than he had ever expected. At twenty-seven, the lieutenant colonel was responsible for seventy-five of the best planes in the world, about one hundred ninety pilots, more than one thousand ground soldiers assigned to his 354th Fighter Group, and equipment worth more than $500 million in today's dollars. He had done his job well, and by the time of Howard's feat that January he was well liked, indeed beloved, by most members of the group.

His own day of fate came exactly a month after Howard's big day. February 11 began like January 11, with the group preparing to battle

Kenneth Martin upon graduation from pilot training, 1938. *Courtesy of the National Archives and Records Administration, Washington, DC*

James Howard as a colonel in 1946, shortly after the end of the war. *Courtesy of the National Archives and Records Administration, Washington, DC*

in the skies of Europe from their base in England. The mission was a difficult escort of bombers to the heavily defended city of Frankfurt. Martin led the operation himself. German planes rose in droves as the American bombers and fighters neared the city. Martin, in the lead plane, eyed a German flying straight into the American formation in an attempt to break up the attack. Aiming his craft at the German, the attacker engaged in a high-stakes game of chicken with the defender.

Neither man relented. Their planes collided in a fatal impact greater than the speed of sound. Instantly, the heart and soul of the group was gone.

It was a bittersweet moment the next day when a general came to promote Jim Howard and give him command of the group. Howard was admired, especially after his own heroics. But as one officer wrote later, "It was not possible to put into words how greatly the loss of Colonel Martin was felt." For Howard and the others in the 354th, the war had become very real. The exhilaration of great success and the pain of immense loss were now part of their own history. They were the war's new veterans, knowing already the face of battle that awaited the million troops slated to invade Nazi-occupied Europe just three months later.[2]

The story of Ken Martin, Jim Howard, and the 354th Fighter Group reveals more than courage under fire, however. History tends to hide an entire set of World War II leaders. The discipline's enduring fascination with the high command on the one hand—people like Dwight Eisenhower and Douglas MacArthur—and the innate drama of battlefield leadership on the other hand—people like those glorified in the movie *Saving Private Ryan*—has pushed the multitude of midlevel leaders from memory. Yet these men in the middle occupied the critical crossroads of command in World War II. Conflict in that war was complicated and choreographed; each operation spawned huge bureaucracies laced with innumerable headquarters and countless planning committees. Somehow the grand schemes of the Eisenhowers and MacArthurs had to filter through the organizational maze to realization at the front lines. Time and again it was men like Martin and Howard, leaders of midlevel units, who fused the big picture to the efforts of the multitude. How well such welds held together under the strain of battle could determine the results of any given operation. An examination of Martin, Howard, and the 354th Fighter Group, then, can offer a rarer glimpse into the experience of World War II, a view that values the contributions of midlevel commanders, reveals the everyday essentials of prosecuting modern war, and sees human conflict through the lens of men in the middle of large bureaucracies designed to prepare, plan, and execute war.

Kenneth Martin sprang from ordinary stock in the center of the nation. He was born in 1917 and spent his early youth in the small town of Leeds, Missouri. The Great Depression pushed his family to Kansas City, and Martin graduated from its Central High School in the spring of 1935. While going to college in Kansas City, he enlisted in the U.S. Marine Air Reserve to satisfy his restless spirit. By the fall of 1936, however, Martin, tired of his safe and familiar environment, determined to pursue his dream of flight full time. He left college early to enter the Army Air Corps (the forerunner to the U.S. Air Force) in February 1937 and spent the next year as an aviation cadet.

Like many men of his generation, once in uniform Martin found a dedication that had escaped him while he was a civilian. From 1938 to the Japanese attack on Pearl Harbor on December 7, 1941, he rose steadily, if unspectacularly, through the ranks. As a result, he had nearly five years of solid experience as a pilot and junior officer when America entered World War II. Although still a first lieutenant, Martin had at least entered the service before the massive influx of enlistments as war drew nearer, and his seniority over those other men his age meant that he would rise even faster as the nation mobilized for war and expanded the armed forces.[3]

Mobilization exploded the size of the American military. The national force structure grew from a few hundred thousand soldiers, sailors, and pilots to more than ten million men by war's end. For its part, the Army Air Corps grew nearly geometrically. The American air forces in World War II were organized, from the bottom up, into squadrons, groups (containing three squadrons), wings (two or more groups), divisions (two or more groups or wings), and numbered air forces (two or more wings or divisions). The three squadrons in every group had about 25 planes, anywhere from 50 to 75 pilots, and more than 1,000 ground personnel. Each group, then, typically had 75 planes, about 180 pilots, and more than 1,000 ground troops. The organizational structure above the group level often varied, so the group became the basic unit of organization and accounting for the air forces. It was through groups, then, that the nation's air arm grew: from just a handful in 1941 to nearly 200 by war's end.[4]

All that growth required a huge influx of people, and those men already in the service rose in rank swiftly. Before World War II a traditional army career meant upward of fifteen years in the ranks of lieutenant and captain. Most men retired as majors, and only the very successful officers reached lieutenant colonel or colonel, usually in their late forties or early fifties. Only the brightest rose to general, a mere handful among thousands. World War II changed all that, and the nation asked those already in uniform—and who were good—to step up to an incredible level of responsibility in a short period of time.

Ken Martin was one of those men. He was promoted from first lieutenant to captain on March 6, 1942, just three months after Pearl Harbor. Before the war, soldiers could spend as long as twelve years as a captain, gaining maturity and seasoning as leaders. Martin, however, was a captain for a month and a day, becoming a major on April 7. With that promotion he also became a squadron commander in the 353d Fighter Group, responsible at the tender age of twenty-five for 24 fighter planes, 67 pilots, and 328 other soldiers. This assignment would have represented the pinnacle of most careers before the war; after Pearl Harbor it was often a short stop on the way up. So it was for Martin, who soon became one of the boy-wonder group commanders of the war.[5]

One of the many groups created to accommodate the surging air arm, the 354th first saw life on November 15, 1942, at Hamilton Air Field, California. Martin arrived eleven days later to assume command, and by year's end the group had accumulated 34 officers and 545 enlisted men along with its first aircraft, a few P-39 fighter planes. The war soon made the P-39 Airacobra obsolete, but in 1942 it represented one of the army's more advanced fighters, and Martin's job was to prepare his men to bring the plane to bear against the enemy. Accordingly, in January 1943 he moved the group to a gunnery range in Nevada for two months so his pilots could practice firing guns and dropping bombs. By the summer he had moved the 354th once again, this time to Portland, Oregon, in anticipation of heading into the far Pacific to battle the empire of Japan. During all this time the group grew steadily, reaching a strength of 112 officers and 868 enlisted men on June 1, about 90 percent of its final complement.[6]

Capt. Jim Howard was one of the men who joined the group that spring. He shared some things in common with Martin. Like his new boss and nearly everybody else, Howard was young: he turned thirty on April 8, 1943. He was like Martin, too, in the respect that both shared the common American sense of restlessness and adventure that seems to keep the country continually on the move. Last, again like Martin, Howard had found a sense of place and a degree of contentment in the military, joining the navy in the same year that Martin had joined the Air Corps.

The similarities did not extend to all aspects of their lives. Howard was born in Canton, China, where his dad, a medical doctor, worked in the eye department at Canton Christian College. Except for two furloughs home, Howard lived in China until he was fourteen. The family then moved to St. Louis, and Howard went to an exclusive boarding school near Philadelphia. He then attended Pomona College in southern California, oblivious of the Great Depression and the hordes of destitute Okies who migrated to California in search of a better life. By his senior year, Howard was heading, inexorably it seemed, to a secure life in law or medicine. Then he heard a talk by a navy pilot. "I made up my mind then and there that I wanted to do something exciting and challenging," he recalled many years later. "I knew that the path to being a naval aviator had many treacherous and devious turns. If I could make it, I was sure I'd find romance and adventure of the highest order."[7]

He was correct about both romance and adventure. After successful completion of the grueling navy pilot training at Pensacola, Florida, Howard headed to San Diego and service aboard one of the nation's new aircraft carriers. He spent 1938 and 1939 shuttling between San Diego and Hawaii, a small cog in a navy machine trying to figure out how best to use airplanes in naval warfare. Honolulu was a wide-open town catering to the navy in those days, and it had a healthy underworld of prostitution dominated by a madam of iron will who hid her business in a middle-class house. One night, Howard and his buddies sought out the place.

> We rang the bell and the door opened. I half expected to be met by a 250-pound native *kanaka*, but instead a cute Japanese girl in traditional island dress was standing there. Someone said the password (like "George sent me") and we were ushered in and took seats around the living room. Soon the lady of the house made her entrance, a seemingly pleasant and slightly plump woman in her forties. She didn't appear to be quite the dragon lady we had anticipated. Drinks were served to everyone and for the next forty minutes we had an enjoyable visit. I guess she just liked company, since there was no charge for her hospitality. On another evening our visit to the house turned out differently.[8]

In late 1940, Howard learned of a secret plan to send American pilots to help China in its war with Japan. "President Roosevelt," a recruiter for the secret organization told Howard and a group of naval aviators, "is intent on furnishing some sort of military assistance to China so that she can survive. I am here to offer all pilots who are reserve officers the opportunity to resign from your service and join a volunteer organization in the Far East." Howard was interested, but his buddies were not so sure. "Why do you want to sacrifice your years in the Navy for this?" one argued. "China! They'll probably send you home in a coffin." Howard saw it differently: "I sure didn't join [the navy] for the pay or even a career. We both know we'll be old duffers before we get any rank." Besides, Howard thought, the place of his birth and child-hood—China—needed help. He added his name to a list of those inter-ested, and half a year later, on June 12, 1941, he received orders from the Navy Department, detaching him from service and releasing him to Claire Chennault, head of the new secret Flying Tigers group heading for China and war.[9]

Chennault had been one of the most contentious officers in the Army Air Corps in the 1930s, but once in China he and his Flying Tigers soon became famous, even though they were supposed to be a secret. Operating on a shoestring budget in an unfamiliar place far from home, against overwhelming Japanese forces, and officially separate from the U.S. military establishment, the Flying Tigers were romanticized as the war's first American heroes. Chennault, Howard, and the other 309 volunteers did gallant battle with Hirohito's forces. Many of them, in-cluding Howard, become aces in the air with five or more kills against Japanese planes. After Pearl Harbor and America's entry into the war, however, the days of the Flying Tigers were numbered. War planners wanted to bring the Flying Tigers back into the formal American force structure in the Far East, and President Roosevelt disbanded the Tigers on July 4, 1942. Howard went home to St. Louis and prepared to don his third uniform in as many years: the outfit of the U.S. Army Air Forces.[10]

Howard came to the 354th Fighter Group in the spring of 1943. Ken Martin recognized immediately what he had in Howard. "My group was new, and most of us were young with little experience in life and no experience in war," he recalled. "But Jim Howard was a veteran and an ace pilot. Although he was also young, he was a little older than the rest of us and had lived a lot more. I knew if we did not use him well we would have lost a tremendous resource." Richard Turner, another pilot in the group, agreed, believing that Howard "epitomizes all those self-less qualities of courage, skill, and determination" of an outstanding combat leader. Accordingly, Martin soon made Howard one of his three squadron commanders and a key deputy.[11]

Together the two men forged the 354th into an effective fighting organization. Martin was mindful of his command responsibilities and kept his focus on larger issues of leadership. An ex-Marine, he was a quiet, soft-spoken man of average height and build. His nickname was Sleeper because of his low-key leadership style and his unflappable dis-position. Although he was as anxious as anyone to get into combat, his calm demeanor helped the men of the 354th focus on the task at hand, working on all the small, often mundane details that go into good war preparation. He never smoked and rarely drank; his friends liked to tease him about his straitlaced morality. But Martin's troops admired the courage of his convictions, and he had an abundance of one crucial leadership trait: He was a great listener. "What struck me most at our first meeting," Howard later wrote, "was the way he listened so intently while I spoke."[12]

Martin delegated the actual combat training of his group to those who had been to war, which meant Jim Howard. "As I looked over the human material I had to work with," the Flying Tiger veteran recalled. "I realized there was a significant age difference between me and my pilots. While I was only thirty, the pilots of the squadron were still in their low twenties. The one thing I had brought back from combat flying in Burma and China was a hardening of resolve and a remembrance of the tragic loss of my friends, and at first, my new pilots seemed almost like children who hadn't yet been weaned." But practice at the gunnery range in Nevada, and more training in Washington State learning low-level maneuvers and flight interception, slowly changed all that. By midsummer 1943, Howard had whipped his men into fighting shape, so much so that his squadron won numerous awards. They had, in Howard's words, "achieved a certain pride of accomplishment."[13]

The group had expected to ship out for the Pacific in the late summer of 1943. Plans are often the first casualty of war, however, and so it was with Martin's group. At midnight on October 5 the group and its equipment filed into four long trains to begin a four-day, cross-country journey to Camp Kilmer, New Jersey. After last passes into New York City, the 354th embarked onto the HMS *Athlone Castle* with other Americans for passage to England and war with Germany.

With six thousand men crowded aboard, the passage was no picnic. The officers were fairly well off. They were quartered three or four to a cabin, and Martin was selected as the troop commander for the entire ship, which meant he had his own berth right next to the captain's. But the enlisted men were sandwiched in from the hold to the top deck in four-tier bunks and hammocks. Although no German submarine threatened their crossing, for the rank and file the voyage was a miserable fifteen-day ordeal. Mealtimes were a constant chow line from six in the morning to eight at night, and the men had to wait in continuous lines to use the few bathrooms. To make matters worse, they sat in an English port for three whole days before British customs officials allowed them to enter the country. For seventy-two hours the crowded men looked longingly at land and yearned for the freedom to move about, stretch, and breathe air untainted by the harsh Atlantic salt.[14]

On November 4 the men of the 354th left the *Athlone Castle* and learned their journey had really just begun. They moved through five bases in the next weeks as the group slowly reconstituted itself. It seemed each day presented something unexpected to deal with, a new obstacle to overcome, on the way to war. It was also the rainy season in England, and the constant downpour further dampened spirits.[15]

One surprise was welcome, however. Instead of the P-39s, the group learned it was to fly the new P-51 Mustangs. This switch added yet another delay as the pilots learned about their new planes, but that was fine with them. The Mustang was the best plane of its kind in the world. It was one of the fastest in existence, could fly at high altitudes, and with its long range and four machine guns it was capable of escorting and defending the big bombers on raids deep into Germany. "It was a fighter pilot's dream," Howard remembered. Moreover, the 354th was the first combat group to have the planes, and the men thereafter adopted the moniker Pioneer Mustang Group. All this meant that higher commanders had a lot of confidence in the 354th. Accordingly, it was not long before the Mustangs were pressed into escort service over the hostile skies of Europe.[16]

The whole group was happy when Lt. Col. Don Blakeslee from the veteran Fourth Fighter Group showed up on December 1 to lead the 354th in its first missions across the English Channel. That afternoon, Blakeslee gathered the group in preparation for the maiden mission the next morning. There were three options when German planes attacked, Blakeslee explained: shoot down the enemy plane, make the enemy break off the attack, or, if the enemy fails to break off, proceed on a collision course to force the issue. There were no other alternatives in the harsh calculus of war. "We will never turn away from a head-on attack. If we do, the word will get back to the Luftwaffe pilots that Americans break first. . . . If they do not break . . . you will have earned your flight pay the hard way."[17]

As was customary, the group's first few forays were relatively easy flights on the outer edges of the Nazi empire. The 354th flew missions on December 2, 5, 11, 13, and 16 under Blakeslee's leadership. Martin led the group into combat for the first time on December 20, and the 354th made its first kills against German planes at about that time. The group hosted a party for orphans in the vicinity of the Boxted airbase on Christmas Day, an activity that raised the morale of the troops as much as it did that of the children. On New Year's Eve the 354th flew yet another mission, this time tallying three kills in exchange for one loss. The group finished the year with five kills and two losses, hardly spectacular but good enough to foster optimism among the pilots for 1944. As one pilot wrote in a diary, 1943 had been "a year filled with work and fun, hopes and fulfillment. . . . Tomorrow the New Year would begin a new year in which we could prove our worth. The Group is ready and waiting, trained and tried, proud and confident. Bring on the New Year."[18]

This optimism was well placed, as 1944 brought plenty of good things to the Pioneer Mustang Group. As the first group to have the vaunted P-51, the 354th was often assigned to escort bombers on routes known to be heavily defended by the German air force. This led to many dogfights with the enemy. January 11, the day Howard shot down five enemy planes and won the Medal of Honor, was also marked by more than a dozen other kills. Press coverage of the group expanded as its prowess grew. At one point more than 100 correspondents converged on the little field at Boxted to interview Howard and other new aces, and even the German propaganda machine took note of the Pioneers. There was plenty of attention to go around, and the group was fast developing the kind of esprit de corps reserved for those individuals who literally pledge their lives to one another.[19]

Sometimes that pledge was all too real. Contact with the enemy meant defeat as well as victory. Ten pilots lost their own duels with the Luftwaffe in January alone, and Martin's tragic aerial collision the next month was a real blow. "We will all remember the personality, the stature, the friendly manner and the firm purpose of the man who undertook to make us," praised one group officer. In the days following the accident, Howard remembered, "a spirit of gloom fell over the base."[20]

Unknown by his men, Martin had remarkably survived his crash. Blakeslee's words "never break for a German" had echoed in Martin's mind as he hurtled toward the German plane. The impact of collision threw both pilots clear of their wrecked planes. Martin fell eight thousand feet before regaining consciousness. "I frantically reached for the D ring of my parachute," he later related. "My fingers were numb and my left arm was smashed. I finally found the ring and pulled on it with all my might. The chute snapped open, and I glided down where I fell in a bloodied and crumpled heap in an open field." German villagers quickly took him to a hospital where he recuperated next to his adversary, who had also miraculously survived. He wound up at a prisoner of war camp in eastern Germany, and after the Gestapo stopped bothering him he survived tolerably well. He escaped just before the war ended and managed to visit his old group before returning to the United States.[21] Colonel Martin lived to receive the Distinguished Flying Cross and to see the 354th honored and commended.

The group's pilots could not know of this, of course, and they mourned his loss. But as painful as this and other losses were, the 354th struggled through. "We must finish what Colonel Martin began so ably," wrote one pilot. "The group will go on about its work. With us, still, is our old attitude, 'Just watch us.' " Howard, after he was promoted to command the group, determined to honor Martin's memory by "rallying our forces for new onslaughts against Nazi Germany."[22]

Their attitude and their efforts, along with countless thousands more, began to pay off as the Allied invasion of Europe neared in the spring of 1944. Aided by fighter plane escort, the big-bomber campaign against Germany finally began to affect the Nazi war machine. In one five-day span in February, bombers dropped almost ten thousand tons of ordnance on German factories. For a week, American, British, and German fighters swirled about the bomber fleets in some of the war's greatest air battles. Collectively, these dogfights cost the Luftwaffe the balance of power in the air, and it never regained its edge. Planes from the 354th flew more than three hundred times in support of these air raids, and group leaders won praise from bomber generals for "the magnificent support your fighters rendered." Gen. Pete Quesada, Howard's immediate boss, agreed, writing to his own mother that "we seem to have the Hun [wartime slang for German] on the run."[23]

The Allied forces kept their adversary running in the months that followed. In March and April both British and American air forces continued to pound German factories, roads, electric power plants, and railroad yards. As the June invasion neared, pilots in the 354th and other groups began to focus closer to the actual landing zone, attacking railheads and bridges in northwestern France. In these weeks the 354th flew more than thirty missions and totaled nearly two hundred fifty victories against the Luftwaffe with just twenty-four losses. The performance of the group led Quesada to offer Howard another promotion and a special assignment at IX Fighter Command headquarters. Howard declined at first, not wanting to leave the Pioneer Mustang Group. But in late April he relented, pinned on the eagles of a full colonel, and moved to Uxbridge to help direct the air traffic for the impending invasion and serve on Quesada's personal staff. The group was sorry to see him leave, but yet another of its members was promoted to command, and the Mustangs went about the business at hand.[24]

Prewar theory on air war held that bombers attacking an enemy could destroy both an adversary's will and capacity to wage war. World War II proved otherwise, but the bomber campaigns in the spring of 1944 did mortally wound the German air force. This victory paid huge dividends when the Allies invaded Europe on June 6, 1944. The British and American forces flew more than twelve thousand sorties that day to protect and aid the ground forces wading ashore in Normandy, France (a sortie is one flight by one plane). The Luftwaffe responded with fewer than two hundred sorties. Even so, the invasion was a hard-won affair. It is difficult to imagine how it would have succeeded if the Allies had not had overwhelming air superiority.[25]

For this crucial advantage, the 354th Group, and many others, deserved credit. The Pioneer Mustang Group finished World War II with 701 aerial victories, more than any other American unit in the European theater. The group accumulated 39 individual aces, an unprecedented number. Many factors went into that accomplishment. Not the least among them was the leadership of Martin and Howard. Martin nurtured the group from its infancy. Despite his youth, he knew how to foster teamwork and demand perfection. From Howard the group learned the details of combat flight, air tactics, and mutual support. There were no hotshot flyers in the 354th, only excellent pilots.[26]

Perhaps the greatest testament to the influence of these two men was the group's performance after their departure. The Pioneer Mustangs, after all, logged far more victories after Martin and Howard left than while they led the group. Combat in World War II was sophisticated and complex, and how well units trained before they entered the fray was critical. It fell to leaders to make sure their charges were ready when their turn to fight came. Martin and Howard, men alike in some respects but very different in other ways, forged the Pioneer Mustangs into one of the war's elite units. War is, among other things, a shared experience. Ken Martin, from the middle of the nation, shy and reserved, and Jim Howard, born in China, rowdy and sophisticated, found friendship and common purpose in the war.

Like so many others who served in the war, both Martin and Howard returned to civilian life once the fighting stopped. Ken Martin went home and began a family and a small business. As a member of the U.S. Air Force Reserve, he returned to active duty during the Korean War and once again fought enemy planes over a distant land. By the late

1950s he was firmly established as a businessman. Jim Howard also longed for normalcy after World War II. Eschewing chances to remain on active duty, he left the service in 1946 and returned to St. Louis. Although he eventually rose to the rank of brigadier general in the Air Force Reserve, the desire for a regular life was strong. He married in 1948 and eventually found his way to Washington, DC, where he began a small electrical research concern that later merged with Control Data Corporation.

Both Martin and Howard are now dead. Exceptional in some respects, their stories are but two of thousands that could be told about Americans at war. World War II was a defining moment in the nation's history, and in the period's extraordinary circumstances ordinary people found uncommon strength, will, and capacity. While societies will always have their Dwight Eisenhowers and Eleanor Roosevelts, the truly amazing thing about the war was the exceptional performance of everyday people—thousands and thousands of them—both at home and abroad. People such as Ken Martin and Jim Howard are mostly lost to history but deserve to be remembered.

Notes

1. James Howard, *Roar of the Tiger* (New York, 1991), 215–35; 354th Group History, Air Force Historical Research Agency (hereafter cited as HRA).

2. 354th Group History, HRA.

3. 354th Group History, HRA; letter from James Howard to Tom Hughes, April 14, 1993; in possession of author.

4. For a recounting of the Army Air Forces growth in World War II, see W. F. Craven and J. L. Cate, *The Army Air Forces in World War II*, vol. 1, *Plans and Early Operations* (Washington, DC, 1948), 101–50, 234–70.

5. 354th Group History, HRA.

6. 354th Group History, HRA.

7. Howard, *Roar of the Tiger*, 8.

8. Ibid., 52–53.

9. Ibid., 57.

10. Martha Byrd, *Chennault: Giving Wings to the Tiger* (Tuscaloosa, AL, 1987), offers an excellent account of Claire Chennault and the Flying Tigers.

11. Richard Turner, *Big Friend, Little Friend* (New York, 1969), 14.

12. 354th Group History, HRA; Howard, *Roar of the Tiger*, 185.

13. Howard, *Roar of the Tiger*, 187.

14. 354th Group History, HRA.

15. 354th Group History, HRA.

16. Howard, *Roar of the Tiger*, 195.

17. Quoted in ibid., 198.

18. Cited in 354th Group History, HRA.

19. 354th Group History, HRA.

20. Cited in 354th Group History, HRA; Howard, *Roar of the Tiger*, 242.

21. Cited in Howard, *Roar of the Tiger*, 241.

22. Cited in 354th Group History, HRA; Howard, *Roar of the Tiger*, 242.

23. Both cited in Thomas Hughes, *Over Lord: General Pete Quesada and the Triumph of Tactical Air Power in World War II* (New York, 1995), 118.

24. Howard, *Roar of the Tiger*, 276.

25. For an accounting of the air forces in the European invasion, see Hughes, *Over Lord*.

26. Howard, *Roar of the Tiger*, 272; Craven and Cate, *Army Air Forces in World War II*, vol. 7, *Services Around the World*, 614–22.

Suggested Readings

Copp, DeWitt S. *Forged in Fire: Strategy and Decisions in the Air War over Europe, 1940–1945*. New York, 1982.

Crane, Conrad C. *Bombs, Cities, and Civilians: American Airpower Strategy in World War II*. Lawrence, KS, 1993.

McFarland, Stephen, and Wesley Newton. *To Command the Sky: The Battle for Air Superiority over Germany, 1942–1944*. Washington, DC, 1991.

Overy, R. J. *The Air War, 1939–1945*. New York, 1981.

13

Brooks E. Kleber
An Infantryman's War

Brooks E. Kleber

Too frequently forgotten in the successful Normandy campaign is the frightful cost inflicted by a tenacious and skilled enemy. The drive across northwestern France was terribly hazardous for the man "on the sharp end." During much of the summer and fall of 1944, U.S. combat infantry units in Europe suffered casualties averaging 90 percent in six weeks. The life expectancy of a lieutenant commanding a rifle platoon in the 90th Division was slightly more than two weeks. One man from that division, Brooks Kleber, landed on Utah—the "easy beach"—but was soon captured while leading a patrol behind German lines.

Kleber's autobiographical account focuses first on the dynamics of one of the most difficult of battlefield "transactions": surrender. With the long range of machine guns and rifles, a man who was seen courted a quick death. Thus, many soldiers remembered an "empty battlefield" on which they glimpsed an enemy only on the rarest of occasions. In such an environment, to take a prisoner or to be taken was challenging and hazardous.

Also difficult, but in an altogether different way, was the life of a prisoner of war. Although U.S. soldiers in German hands did not face the deadly sort of maltreatment routinely meted out by the Germans to captured Soviets, or by the Japanese to American prisoners, Kleber shows that his existence was quite hard—and that the dangers of "friendly fire" were not peculiar to Vietnam or the Gulf War.

Brooks Kleber survived these testing experiences and returned to college, ultimately earning a doctorate from the University of Pennsylvania in Philadelphia. During his career as an army historian, Kleber coauthored *Chemicals in Combat* (1966). For the fiftieth anniversary of World War II, he chaired the Department of Defense committee that provided the U.S. Postal Service with the subjects for its five-year series of commemorative postage stamps.

I was drafted by the army in August 1941 and went to Camp Croft, South Carolina, for basic training. I had graduated from Dickinson College in Carlisle, Pennsylvania, in 1940 and had spent a year in graduate school at the University of Pennsylvania, pursuing an advanced degree in history. My record at both schools was not outstanding. I was

211

inattentive at Dickinson and still immature when I was at Penn. So the draft, which might have been a near tragedy for some young men, was a welcomed respite to me.

From Camp Croft I went to Fort George G. Meade, Maryland, where I was assigned to the Headquarters Company of the 58th Brigade, 29th Infantry Division. This National Guard organization, still in the grips of its prewar command structure, was in the process of triangularization

Brooks Kleber at Fort Custer, Battle Creek, Michigan, in 1942, having just graduated from Infantry Officer Candidate School. *Courtesy of Brooks E. Kleber*

(that is, going from two brigades and four regiments to no brigades and three regiments). The organization was not all that efficient. Eventually, I ended up as a radio operator in the 29th Division Signal Company where I learned to send and receive messages. During breaks in the tedious learning process, I listened to the best of Glenn Miller.

Eventually, I was accepted by the Infantry Officer Candidate School (OCS) at Fort Benning, Georgia. The three months I spent there proved to be the most beneficial of my military career. Some of my unpleasant habits, such as singing as I made my bunk each morning, were mentioned in several surveys by barrack mates about their fellow soldiers. I learned from this criticism and by the end of the course was named the most improved candidate in my platoon. I had stopped singing.

Upon graduation from OCS in August 1942, half of the class was sent to Fort Custer, Battle Creek, Michigan, to activate the 94th Infantry Division. Our battalion cadre consisted mostly of recent OCS graduates with a good sprinkling of reserve captains. There was only one West Pointer in the battalion. Because most of the OCS graduates had had previous experience as noncommissioned officers, their performance in initial assignments was considered superior to that of their West Point colleagues.

The 94th Division soon moved to Camp Phillips in Salina, Kansas, where it received soldiers directly from the induction centers. After a year of training, we went on Tennessee maneuvers and then to Camp McCain, Grenada, Mississippi, where we reverted to small-unit problems after having worked at the division level. One day my good friend Lt. John Paxton came to the field and told me he had volunteered both of us for overseas duty. I acquiesced almost willingly. But for fifty-four years I have regretted departing without saying good-bye to my platoon, which had won two training honors—Best in the Battalion (out of nine) and later second Best in the Regiment (out of twenty-seven). After sailing from New York on a former British liner, the *Samaria,* we spent time in Somerset before embarking five days after D day for the Utah section of the Normandy coast. I was assigned to the 90th Infantry Division.

All this is a prelude to a short account of my time in the European theater, most of which was spent as a "guest" of the German army—a prisoner of war (POW). Rather than relate a detailed day-by-day story of my captivity, I have selected three episodes that illustrate aspects of my experience: an account of my capture, a light story that relates my acquisition of a wheel of Polish cheese, and a description of my travels through southern Germany at the end of the war. I conclude with some reflections on liberation.

"For You, the War Is Over"

As a replacement officer in Normandy, I was assigned to the 359th Infantry Regiment of the 90th Infantry Division. My battalion was already bloodied. Although the 90th had not landed on D day, my battalion had filled in for units of the 4th Infantry Division, whose transport had been sunk. The 90th Division in Normandy was not a well-functioning organization. As a matter of fact, it was so poorly run that the textbook on leadership written after the war by the Command and General Staff College devoted a chapter to the 90th as the best example of a unit gone bad because of inept leadership.

As a weapons platoon leader of an infantry company, I spent two weeks going up and down the Cotentin peninsula always heading for a fight but never quite getting into one. I made mistakes as I learned the ropes. The worst was finding myself looking up at my sergeant from the ditch into which I had thrown myself after my initial experience with incoming artillery fire and being told that it really hadn't landed as close as I imagined. Still, I felt I had won over the men in my platoon. In fact, the night before I was captured my platoon sergeant quietly told me so.

One day my company commander called me to his foxhole and said that I was to take out a patrol. It was a surprising announcement; weapons platoon leaders normally did not go on patrols. Reading my thoughts, he told me it was time I saw a little action. Just before we set out, the three of us who were to lead patrols that night were summoned to battalion headquarters for a pep talk, not from the battalion commander, which would have been expected, but from the regimental commander. Division officers were not being aggressive, he said. Patrol leaders were stopping just beyond the outposts, sitting on their rear ends for an hour and returning with negative reports. This had to stop. "Remember your mission," he roared. "Remember your mission!"

My mission was simple: to determine if there were enemy positions at a particular crossing of secondary roads some distance beyond our forward outposts. I had memorized the map's maze of hedgerows and trails and extensively briefed the other three men on patrol. Although the captain had settled on the weapons platoon leader to head the patrol, he rounded it out with a sergeant and two privates from one of the infantry platoons. No doubt, they were better qualified for patrol duty than my machine gunners and mortarmen. The problem was I had never seen them before. We left behind all unnecessary gear—helmets, web belts, wallets. Stocking hats and rifles—I had a carbine—were the order of the day. During June, evening twilight comes late in Normandy, so we didn't pass through our outposts until after 11:00 P.M.

The gently rolling Norman countryside is marked by hedgerows, which delineated small rectangular fields. The hedgerows, ancient earthen walls about four feet high, were covered with brush and dotted with small trees. Gaps in these barriers enabled farmers and their cattle to pass from field to field. All of us on the patrol knew of the German fondness for booby traps. These miserable devices were uniquely appropriate for use in these narrow passages. I took special pains to inspect each gap for telltale wires as I led the patrol from one field to another. After a half dozen probings, I suggested to the sergeant that he take us through a few gaps.

The briefing for the patrol had not included the location of the German front line, although it seemed obvious that we would have to breach it to reach our goal. The farther we went, the more cautious we became. Midway through one field, we tensed as, off to the right, a cough peppered the night air. Almost simultaneously, someone to the left lit a match. In the crazy patchwork that was the *bocage* country, this particular field was intersected halfway up each side by two hedgerows. A careless sentry stood at each of these junctures. Through pure luck, we had hit a gap in the German lines. With the sentries behind us, we continued toward our objective, which, when we reached it, turned out to be a crossing of two sunken paths that had never seen anything more belligerent than an angry cow.

We had accomplished our mission. Now we had to get back. Retracing our steps proved difficult, and we were hurried by the prospect of an early dawn. I missed the gap in the lines. Suddenly from the darkness an ominous figure bellowed a guttural "Halt." We froze until a point-blank shot sent us scurrying to the rear. Regrouping, we made our way laterally along the rear of the German positions. One of us, I'm not sure who, tripped a flare and our immediate area turned bright as day. We loped on, hoping to find another gap in the line. Instead, off to the left, I could see a group of German soldiers in animated conversation. Now, day was breaking. I headed for a hedgerow perpendicular to the German line. The men followed. I hoped to hide in the brush and to hole up throughout the daylight hours.

As dawn broke, we could see a group of German soldiers becoming larger and more animated. They paid no attention to us until suddenly a shout came for us to surrender. We hugged the ground. Another coarse warning was followed by a burst from a Schmeizer automatic pistol, a burp gun that surely made one of the war's most unpleasant noises. There was a second burst and I stood up. So did the last man in line. The two in the middle must have risen at the same time as the second burst. The sergeant, with one round through the side of his head, was quiet. The man behind him had wounds in his groin. Both were alive. The stock of my carbine was shattered. There was a jagged hole in the armpit of my shirt and my right ear was numb. I began to shake, not from fear but from anger and chagrin.

German soldiers surrounded us. They produced a stretcher and indicated that I and the unwounded soldier were to carry our comrades to the command post. We took the sergeant first. I quickly understood why the American army assigned four men to a stretcher. The load was heavy and the distance was far. Physically and emotionally spent from the night's activities, we made frequent stops. During one of them, I bent over the sergeant's face to see if he were still alive. A fragment from an incoming American mortar shell flashed between our faces and buried itself harmlessly into the ground. I was too numb to flinch. The sergeant was dead.

Leaving the body at the command post, we went back for the other man. When we returned, the Germans placed the body of the dead sergeant and the badly wounded private on a crude, horse-drawn wagon. German soldiers were removing the shoes from both men. Outraged, I yelled at the German officer. He just shrugged. His men were equally passive. Searching the sergeant's body, they discovered a German Bible. They were surprised, as was I. "Was he married?" one asked. "Did he have children?" It was painful for me to admit that I did not know the answers. Another German said to me, almost plaintively, "For you, the war is over." Later, I discovered how common it was for a German captor to say this to a newly captured American prisoner.

Nine months of captivity ensued. An escape from a train in France failed. At Oflag 64 in Poland, the permanent camp for American ground officers, the senior American decreed that escape was no longer feasible. And later, after a miserable forty-five-day move from Oflag 64 to Hammelburg, a small group of us spent one night of freedom during General Patton's abortive attack on the prison camp. In between, there were dangerous train rides, little food, the cold and hungry winter trek, even boredom. But in the conventional sense, my German captor was correct: For me, the war *was* over.

The Polish Wheel of Cheese

In January 1945, Soviet troops forced the Germans to evacuate the American prisoners from Oflag 64 in Schubin, Poland. We were to go ten kilometers and get a train. But there was no train, so forty-five days and more than three hundred miles later, the remnants of that column arrived at a point north of Berlin where it entrained for another POW camp at Hammelburg.

The winter of 1944–45 was bitterly cold. Each day of the three-hundred-mile march, a German guard and an American officer bicycled ahead to find a place for us to sleep and to prepare a meager supper. They did their job well. We almost always bedded down in barns, out-buildings, or occasionally in a church or schoolhouse. Then we were given a piece of bread and a bowl of soup.

On a particularly memorable night, I was sitting in a rather small schoolroom with a portrait of Göring looming over my desk. Someone came by and said that a group of Polish émigrés, also moving west, were out back trading wheels of cheese for American cigarettes. I hurried out. The man in line in front of me got his wheel for three packs; mine cost me five packs, and I understand the POW after me paid ten for his cheese. The cigarettes came from our American Red Cross packages. My buddy, Red O'Connor, contributed half the cigarettes to my purchase and got half the cheese. The wheel of cheese was frozen so it took some time to hack it into two parts. We stowed our treasures in the makeshift backpacks we had fashioned out of shirts and Red Cross boxes. In the following days, we would make cheese sandwiches with the bread in the middle. We were the envy of our comrades. I can't remember how long our cheese lasted, but I do remember several events prompted by the cheese.

The first incident involved only me. I must explain that I love dogs and always have had one. My care for my pets included an examination of their stool as a barometer of their health. For the seven months of my captivity, I had adopted the same test for my own well-being. It seemed to work; at least it was reassuring. A short time after the acquisition of the cheese, while undergoing this examination, I was horrified to discover a pile of rather small, round pellets. My immediate thought was that something had perforated in my digestive system and that my normal elimination was being filtered as through a sieve. Then it dawned on me that goats, like rabbits, produce that type of stool and that the quantity of green goat's milk cheese I had been eating was not only providing welcome nutrition but also giving me this goatlike signature. It was disquieting, but I learned to live with it.

And goat's milk cheese *is* nutritional, a fact brought home to me by a lieutenant colonel who had been my barracks commander at Oflag 64. A West Pointer, he had commanded a battalion in combat. Quite formal, even in prison camp, he occasionally sought out junior officers for a game of chess. The lessons of the battlefield could be found on the chessboard, he would intone. It was no reflection on him or on my erstwhile profession, but at that time I didn't much give a damn about the lessons of the battlefield. Late one afternoon, as we were settling down for the night, my chess-playing commander approached me. "Kleber," he began, "if I had my choice of any kind of food I could take on a trip like this, do you know what I'd take?" Well, of course I knew, but I put on an expressionless face and answered, "No, Sir." "Cheese," he said, "because of its great nutritional value, its durability, and its relatively small bulk." He went on and on. I don't remember saluting, but I did thank him profusely as I walked away.

The third cheese incident places me in a more generous light. One miserable afternoon we were trudging through large quantities of snow near a small Polish village. Conditions were terrible. I saw a dead horse just off the road whose rump had been carved bare by hungry villagers, and I wondered how the horse had died. A fellow prisoner with whom I had become friends—tall, quiet, good-looking John Carlson from Rhinelander, Wisconsin—was just ahead of me. Suddenly, he darted off the side of the road and swept up a dead white chicken and thrust it under his coat. I also wondered how the chicken had died. That night, Carlson plucked, cleaned, and cooked his chicken. A bit later, he offered to trade part of his meal (I forget which part) for some of my cheese. Although I rejected the trade, I did share a generous piece of my cheese with John.

Two months later, after we had arrived at Hammelburg, having survived General Patton's escape episode and having spent some time in Nürnberg, we were leisurely making our way south through Bavaria. The war was all but over, and the guards were now very friendly, especially the one who went from prisoner to prisoner explaining that he had once worked in the Buffalo post office. On April 15, 1945, I celebrated my twenty-sixth birthday. I cooked some potatoes, without salt but with a stray carrot. I also made a mess of fresh wild mustard. It was a beautiful meal—white, orange, and green. Then John Carlson appeared. In his hand he had a pack of Lucky Strike cigarettes tied with a sprig of pussy willow. It was my birthday present. He could have used the cigarettes for a significant trade with a German villager, but he gave them to me.

For years afterward, I always remembered John's cigarettes as the most meaningful birthday present I had ever received. Later, in presenting me with her own annual gifts, my wife always acknowledged John's. I tried to contact John Carlson after the war but never succeeded. But he, and the cheese and cigarettes, are indelibly etched in my book of significant memories.

Springtime in Bavaria

Springtime in Bavaria is beautiful, even for a prisoner of war—or, better, especially for a prisoner of war. Gone were the snow and biting winds of the previous winter when we had trekked from a prison camp in Poland to a point somewhere north of Berlin. Two boxcar rides had taken us to Nürnberg. Now, in April 1945, it was time for the open road again.

Most of the marchers had mixed feelings. In a way it was good to be back on the move. The harrowing experience at Hammelburg and the failed raid to rescue us were worth forgetting. And the attractions of the transient camp at Nürnberg had not been so great as to cause regret upon leaving. The change in the weather meant a lot, too. It was nice having a warm sun shine on us. And everything was green, a comforting color after a winter full of cold grays.

On the other hand, the opening hour of the march was difficult. Improvised packs cut into muscles softened from inactivity and had to be adjusted. The accordion-like movements of a long column swinging into action compounded this trouble. But these matters were only physical. More important was the fact that once again great effort was about to be expended in order to reach an unknown destination, a seemingly minor inconvenience that must be experienced to be appreciated. Matters were not helped much by the nature of the most persistent rumor: Hitler planned to corral his prisoners in his mountain fastness and use them for bargaining purposes.

In midmorning, as the head of the column entered a small town, a group halfway back sighted an American fighter plane hovering high above. Even at its great altitude we could recognize it as one of ours—there was no camouflage to hide its silvery beauty. Eyes followed the darting plane as if hypnotized into an unawareness that it could bring death, even to American prisoners. The spell was broken as the fighter, sighting its target, began a swift descent. Other planes joined it.

The target was not immediately apparent to those in midcolumn, but they couldn't risk the chance that they, themselves, would be the victims. Prisoners and guards alike broke from the road, stampeded across a narrow field, and ended their dash in the comparative safety of some neighboring woods. The bombs fell ahead. The column slowly regrouped. As the march resumed, it was hard to determine who had suffered the most embarrassment from this panic: the American prisoners or the German guards.

The mystery of the attack soon became clear for those of us in midcolumn. Several hundred yards down the road we came to the railway yard of the town that had been the target of the fighter bombers. Here the highway and tracks were parallel, and, unfortunately, some of the prisoners had been hit. Their bodies lay under blankets and greatcoats by the side of the road.

Doubtless we had erred in streaming from the road, although it was an error attributed to instinct and training, not to premeditation. In the future, admonished the senior American colonel, if sighted by American aircraft, we would remain in our tracks. To those piloting fast-moving planes the identity of a column of soldiers was hard enough to determine. If we took to the ditches like frightened rabbits a doubtful pilot might become convinced that this indeed was the enemy.

Several days later the part of the column that had viewed the attack from halfway back now formed the leading element. The reason for the change was simple. In any marching group, difficulties in keeping pace increase in proportion with the position. In order to distribute the discomforts of the march, the American colonel directed the various elements of the column to take turns in forming the van. It was nice being in front. In addition to having easier marching conditions because the accordion-like motions were absent, there was a degree of excitement in being in the lead. You were the first to see the new village, the first to know what was around the long bend in the road.

It was late in the morning when we saw something we didn't want to see—more silvery objects in the clear sky. This time there was no lingering admiration, just a memory of the colonel's admonition and the bodies by the road. We were within earshot of the colonel, and his word was to continue marching and to remain on the road in case we were sighted. The colonel's orders were passed back. The column silently moved on. Several more planes appeared, collecting, as if in interest.

The business of being first in line was no longer attractive. The fighter planes by now were obviously aware of something below. And this time there was no nearby community with a tempting railroad center. The colonel crisply called for the column to halt and to stand in place. Again, his orders were quickly relayed to the rear. There was no doubt now that our column had attracted the American fighters. They were circling off to the front at medium altitude. Without wanting to, we stood there watching—knowing that standing in the road was our best bet but feeling that only flight to the ditches or to the woods would really satisfy our impulses.

Suddenly, one of the planes peeled off from the group and streaked earthward. At the bottom of the dive it veered to the left and roared down the road directly toward us. It was at treetop level. The pilot, his aircraft armed with .50-caliber machine guns, was more than capable of plowing all of us under. It is hard to recall how I felt with the plane bearing down on the column. If recollection serves me, it was a matter of having heavy feet and a light stomach—and a feeling that the speedy plane was covering the distance with amazing slowness.

Finally, it was upon us. It is anticlimactic to say the pilot didn't open fire; he buzzed the entire column and gave his wings a friendly waggle in recognition. I later determined that the red markings on the plane were the signature of the all-black fighter unit stationed in Italy.

And that's the way it ended. We were recognized and word of the column of prisoners would now get back to American authorities. In reality, this episode was far from an anticlimax. It meant contact with our own, no matter how fleeting, and it meant renewed hope that the whole miserable business would soon be over. But most of all, I guess, it meant that we had not been strafed. Still standing there with our stomachs in our throats, some of us didn't even hear the American colonel give the order to resume marching.

Liberation

My psychological reaction to liberation was peculiar. Throughout my time as a prisoner, I never doubted that I would return. In fact, that day was always right around the corner, which made the news at Christmas 1944 of Allied reverses in the Battle of the Bulge all the more disheartening. Nevertheless, I had moments of concern after I was liberated; I got the feeling that I wasn't going to make it home.

On the day that Patton's 14th Armored Division liberated us at Moosburg, the German guards fought among themselves over the degree of resistance to be offered. One of the prisoners in my barracks was killed in this exchange. Then another was killed by a stray shot at Camp Lucky Strike on the Normandy coast. Some weeks later, on the ship taking us home, which was the first not to travel in convoy, I was sure that there was a U-boat lurking out there that had not gotten the word that the war was over or whose captain wanted to sink one more Allied ship for the führer. Finally, the taxi from Fort Dix, New Jersey, to my uncle's home in Trenton stopped on the opposite side of the street. Crossing the street was my last psychological obstacle; when my uncle opened the door, the feeling was over.

Worse captivities produced different reactions. The moving account of several German nurses, upon being freed in the Vietnam conflict, tells of their huddling together in the airplane taking them home, fearful of what was to come. A British lieutenant in World War II, upon liberation, hesitated before taking a ride to his unit because back in his barracks were six bars of soap, 300 cigarettes, and a greatcoat. The explanation? The experience of liberation is almost as traumatic as that of capture. When one is captured, a psychological spring is wound up; when one is freed, it is released.

The saddest story is told by Viktor Frankl, the deceased Austrian psychiatrist who spent three years in Nazi concentration camps. Upon liberation, he and some friends walked in a meadow trying to comprehend the meaning of freedom. A colorful rooster provided their first spark of joy. But that evening, one prisoner asked another, " 'Tell me, were you pleased today?' And the other replied, feeling ashamed as he did not know we all felt similarly, 'Truthfully, no!' We had literally lost the ability to feel pleased and had to relearn it slowly."*

I suspect few former prisoners would go as far as Alexander Solzhenitsyn who, because his terrible ordeal had nourished his soul, concludes *The Gulag Archipelago* with: "Bless you, prison, for having been my life." But I have not found anyone who will disagree with the idea that prison camp is a marvelous teacher of human nature. Someone said that he could learn more about man in two years in prison camp than in two decades of normal life.

*Viktor E. Frankl, *Man's Search for Meaning* (New York, 1984), 95.

For me, in addition to the bittersweet nostalgia of the experiences and comradeship, my period of captivity formulated and shaped my overall outlook, understanding, and sensitivity. If it did not "nourish my soul," it proved to be the ultimate factor in shaping my philosophy of life.

Suggested Readings

Ambrose, Stephen. *D-Day, June 6, 1944: The Climactic Battle of World War II*. New York, 1994.

Durand, Arthur A. *Stalag Luft III: The Secret Story*. Baton Rouge, 1988.

Hackett, John Winthrop. *I Was a Stranger*. New York, 1978.

Hubbard, Preston J. *Apocalypse Undone: My Survival of Japanese Imprisonment during World War II*. Nashville, 1990.

Lomax, Eric. *The Railway Man: A POW's Searing Account of War, Brutality, and Forgiveness*. New York, 1995.

MacDonald, Charles. *Company Commander*. New York, 1978.

———. *The Mighty Endeavor: The American War in Europe*. New York, 1969.

14

Mack Morriss
Guardsman to Yank Combat Correspondent

Ronnie Day

Ultimately, the Allied triumph in World War II resulted from the combined efforts of the three greatest countries, Great Britain, the Soviet Union, and the United States, assisted by the lesser Allied powers. Despite the extreme claims of some advocates of air, sea, or land power, the American victories came from the joint efforts of the army, Army Air Forces, navy, and Marines backed by the outpouring of the nation's farms, factories, and scientific establishment. Without the lavish support from the home front, the fighting forces would have been starved for modern weaponry. Without the successes of the U.S. Navy against the German submarines and the Japanese fleet, the strategic bombing campaigns and the landing operations against those two enemies would have been impossible. Without control of the air, naval and ground advances would have been fatally handicapped. Without soldiers and Marines seizing key territory, the war could never have been pushed to the enemies' homelands. Ultimately, "boots on the ground" proved as essential as air or naval operations.

The GI, especially the infantryman, did a disproportionate share of the fighting and bleeding. Chronicling his sacrifices was the newspaper *Yank*. The paper, published for and by enlisted men, offered a clear-sighted view of the army's war, notwithstanding the restrictions of censorship. One of *Yank*'s most successful correspondents was Mack Morriss, a professional journalist and Tennessee National Guardsman who had the unusual experience of reporting on the war in both the European and the Pacific theaters.

Recounting Morriss's story is Ronnie Day, a professor at East Tennessee State University in Johnson City. Day earned his advanced degrees at Texas Christian University in Ft. Worth, is the editor of Mack Morriss, *South Pacific Diary, 1942–1946* (1996), and has written on such disparate subjects as the early American frontier, the Tudor navy, and World War II in the Pacific. In furtherance of the last interest, he has traveled to Guadalcanal and other South Pacific sites.

New Year's Eve fell on a Sunday at the end of 1944. Mack Morriss was in Paris, still smarting from the fact that he had been relieved at 1st Army Press Camp at Spa, Belgium, the day before the Germans launched their counteroffensive, and so had missed the Battle of the

225

Bulge. He was becoming bored with Paris, and friends told him later that he had welcomed in the New Year with a cognac toast drunk from an ashtray. On New Year's Day he nursed a hangover and looked for transportation, which he finally found. On January 2 he left in an open Jeep for a bitterly cold drive to Belgium and arrived in Brussels sometime on the 3rd where he spent the night. The next day he went on to Spa where he spent three days at 1st Army Press Camp. While he was there he went down to Stavelot to write a story on the stubborn fight his old outfit, the 117th Infantry, 30th Division, had just put up against the 1st SS Panzer Division. By January 8 he had arrived at 9th Army Press Camp at Maastricht in the Netherlands. It had been an uneventful week, he wrote his wife.[1]

In light of what he had seen and experienced, it was. Morriss went into the army with "A" Company, 117th Infantry, 30th Division, in September 1940 when the National Guard was called up for one year's service. He quit his job as editor of the Elizabethton, Tennessee, *Star*, an afternoon daily, to join his hometown unit. Part of his motivation was that he did not want to await the uncertainties of the draft; part of it was that he wanted to prove his manhood in the company of men he had grown up with. At the station in Johnson City where he boarded the troop train with the rest of his company, he told a reporter, "No punching a typewriter for me. I want to get out in the field carrying a rifle."[2]

He did both. During his first year at Camp Jackson, later Fort Jackson, in Columbia, South Carolina, he trained in the field, helped build the installations (the camp, left over from World War I, was nothing but "sagebrush and sand" when the troops arrived in 1940), and punched a typewriter. From the beginning, he had agreed to do a column on life at Jackson for his newspaper back home, and he did. His newspaper experience came to the attention of Lt. Robert M. White II, a member of an established newspaper family in Mexico, Missouri, who had been charged with setting up the division's Public Relations Office (PRO). Consequently, Morriss began working part time for the PRO, and in the summer of 1941, as German armies drove deep into Russia and tension between the United States and Japan reached the breaking point, he worked full time for the PRO during the Tennessee maneuvers. When the developing crisis prompted President Franklin D. Roosevelt to extend the Guard's service indefinitely, Morriss again worked for the PRO during the Carolina maneuvers held in the fall of 1941.

Like many other men in uniform, he waited for the war that now seemed sure to come; and when the Japanese attack on Pearl Harbor on December 7, 1941, ended the suspense, he experienced a kind of relief. He had planned to marry Helen Davis during his Christmas furlough, explaining to his father, "We don't want to lose whatever happiness we may be able to have before the world goes to hell." He was able to do so during a much reduced leave at home in December. Back at Fort Jackson after the briefest of honeymoons, Morriss waited for what the new year and the war would bring. During the winter, he toyed with the idea of either applying for Officer Candidate School or of asking for a transfer to the Air Corps, but when the wildflowers bloomed again at Fort Jackson, he was still with the infantry, a sergeant in command of a machine-gun squad.

Unknown to him at the time, the decision was shortly to be made for him. Miles from the sage and sand of Jackson, New York advertising executive Egbert White was lobbying the War Department to create an army magazine, a fighting man's paper to be known as *Yank*. The language of White's subcommittee of the Joint Army and Navy Committee on Welfare and Recreation belied the group's staid name and called for a paper that would instill in the men a desire to "fight like hell" and "make every soldier want to get 'one of the bastards' before lunch." But because they were good advertising men, who remembered that the paper had to sell itself, the committee's report also declared, "We must not be too holy to engage in an occasional use of leg art."[3]

Thus was born *Yank, the Army Weekly*. White collected a talented group of writers, artists, and advertising executives and put the first dummy together in the art department of *Mademoiselle* magazine in a nonstop thirty-hour session. Secretary of War Henry Stimson was pleased with the result, but Mrs. Stimson insisted that the pinup had to go. It did, but only for a short time. Office space was found on Forty-second Street in Manhattan, and the talent hunt for men to staff the paper began. Every candidate's résumé had to indicate that (1) he was combat trained and fit for action if need be; (2) he was an enlisted man, for the paper was to be put out by enlisted men for enlisted men; and (3) he had to have a special talent—with the typewriter, camera, or artist's pencil.

Morriss's orders arrived in early May 1942 and simply specified that he report to an address on Forty-second Street in New York City. He had been recommended along with two of his friends, John Hay and Ed

Cunningham, by his old boss at the PRO, Lieutenant White, later to be on Gen. Douglas MacArthur's staff in the Southwest Pacific. The orders could not have come at a better time. Morriss's fortunes were at a low ebb. Marriage had accentuated his loneliness; he was uncertain as to what course to take regarding his army career; and in an incident a few weeks earlier at a dance in Columbia, a cop hit him flush in the face with a billy club and he was in the hospital for more than two weeks. Little wonder that when he arrived in New York, he told Ward Morehouse of the *New York Sun* that "he was the luckiest man in the army."[4]

With the others, Morriss settled down in the middle of Manhattan to create a GIs' paper from scratch. It was not an easy job under any circumstances, and in some respects, the summer of 1942 was as frustrating as the summer before when Morriss and the others had waited to see if they were to go home or be retained in the service. What Morriss really wanted was an overseas assignment, and in October, he got his wish. During the last week of the month he was put on call for duty in the South Pacific theater where army ground and air forces were being thrown into the battle for Guadalcanal. He felt "at once a great sense of relief, and a great dread," he wrote. The relief was in getting away from New York, which he described as a "center of bickering, of meanness, of phonies." Other than dreading the waiting, he had what he called "two sub-fears." One was that he would "be where there is no danger," the other that he would find more danger than he could survive. A few days later he was on his way to San Francisco with *Yank* artist Howard Brodie, who had been with the *San Francisco Chronicle*. It was the beginning of a lifelong friendship.

The two *Yank* staffers followed the usual route to the war in the South Pacific: an army transport to Auckland, New Zealand; another transport, navy this time, to Nouméa, New Caledonia; air transport to Espíritu Santo in the New Hebrides, the jumping-off place for Guadalcanal. On Christmas Eve, they hitched a ride in a B-17 to Guadalcanal, codename "Cactus."[5]

Morriss and Brodie stepped off the plane at Henderson Field into the sweltering heat and heard the dull rumble of artillery to the west. The Japanese, about to admit defeat in the battle that had raged since August, were dug in on the steep hills behind Point Cruz. Three American divisions—the 2d Marine, the Americal, and the 25th—along with the unattached 147th Infantry, were preparing to take the offensive against them. On the day after Christmas, Morriss rode up to the front and, on the way, passed the first casualties he had seen, one wounded and one dead. "The first boy was pale; the second's face was covered, but his pants were covered with blood," he wrote in his diary. "He was the first American I've seen killed in action."

Morriss and Brodie spent the next six weeks on Guadalcanal, billeted at XIV Corps headquarters, which was on a low ridge just east of the Lunga River. Looking north, Henderson Field was to the east, Fighter No. 2 airstrip was across the river to the west. Morriss used the press tent with the civilian press corps and typed his stories on a borrowed typewriter.[6] During Japanese air raids, both he and Brodie shared the nearby dugout known as the Cave. In his diary, Morriss recorded sixteen night bomber attacks, two large daylight raids, and one daylight "sneak" raid by a single Japanese bomber. The sneak bomber was destroyed quickly in full view of the cheering men by Capt. John Mitchell, who in April would plan and lead the mission that would shoot down Adm. Yamamoto Isoroku; and the heavy daylight raids were intercepted by Allied fighters before the Japanese got to Henderson Field. But in the absence of night fighters, the night raids got through and a number of men were killed and wounded.

Military spit and polish was at a minimum on Guadalcanal, and the press was given considerable independence. A few days after he arrived, Morriss hitched a ride on a PBY-5 Catalina flying boat for a night harassing mission against the Japanese airfield at Munda, New Georgia, and both men made a number of trips to the front, which ran from Point Cruz along the western bank of the Mataniko River and into the steep hills known (because of their shapes on aerial photographs) as the Galloping Horse (the setting for much of James Jones's novel, *The Thin Red Line*), the Sea Horse, and the Snake. The most rewarding trip in terms of experience and work for both Morriss and Brodie was their overnight stay with the 35th Infantry on the Sea Horse in mid-January. Not only were they able to witness the mortar preparation for the attack on the Japanese positions and the actual infantry attack itself but they became participants as well. On the first day, Brodie helped set up the loudspeaker used to appeal to the trapped Japanese troops to surrender—a futile effort—and on the second day Morriss helped a lieutenant colonel and others guide a boat of wounded down the Mataniko in chest-deep water in what was known, in a takeoff on Japanese ships' names, as the Pusha Maru.

Without doubt, both Morriss and Brodie produced their best Guadalcanal work as a result of this experience. Morriss's description of the action, which he titled "The Story of a Battle" and which, much to his disgust, the *Yank* editors changed to "Jap-Trap," helped establish his reputation for accurate detail in reporting. Here is his description of night on the line:

> Darkness on the battalion's line was softened by the light of a half moon. Occasionally from other ridges, other positions, shots popped and echoed with a hollow sound in the ravines. A mortar blasted from time to time, and now and then came the fast chatter of a Jap automatic weapon, higher pitched and more brittle than our own fire. From out of nowhere ricochets whined overhead. Once, twice, red rockets from Very pistols [used for firing pyrotechnic signals] sailed skyward, fire signals from an OP [observation post].[7]

Brodie's sketches, some published with Morriss's article as illustrations, some published separately as the cover and feature spread "Last Days at Guadalcanal," were among the most poignant to come out of the war in the Pacific. James Jones wrote later about his and his comrades' reaction to the Brodie sketches when a copy of *Yank* arrived at a New Zealand hospital: "We were astonished. Somebody had understood. We *did* exist after all."[8]

With the high hills cleared, the fighting moved west toward the Poha and Bonegi Rivers where the Japanese rearguard put up a heroic resistance, buying time for the evacuation of the rest of the forces. Then suddenly it was over. "I'd write Hallelujah! all the way across this page if I could just get it in my head that this afternoon at 4:30 the forces moving west and the forces moving east on the north side of Guadalcanal met and between them there were no Japs," Morriss recorded in his diary for Tuesday, February 9, 1943. While the American High Command had been preparing for another Japanese counteroffensive, the Japanese had silently and successfully evacuated the sick and beaten remnant of their forces from the place they called Starvation Island.

During the remainder of February and all of March, there was a lull in the fighting in the Solomon Islands. Morriss and Brodie decided to give themselves some rest and relaxation (R and R) in Auckland, New Zealand and arrived there on February 19 for a two-week stay. Morriss described Auckland as the "Army's liberty town," and indeed American servicemen were everywhere. Even though they were enlisted men, Morriss and Brodie were allowed to stay in a hotel—the Royal—and to buy liquor. It did not take the two men long to get accustomed to civilization again and to join in on the Battle of Queen Street, as the drinking, eating, and womanizing was called. As it turned out, however, the trip was not totally R and R. While in Auckland, Morriss and Brodie had gotten to know some of the B-17 crews flying from Guadalcanal; now their plan was to cover the air war.

By April 5 both men were back on Guadalcanal: Brodie in the Twentieth Station Hospital with malaria, Morriss billeted with the 31st Bombardment Group (H) near the beach. They had arrived just in time for Admiral Yamamoto's "I" Operation, an attempt to retard the Allied buildup on Guadalcanal, and Morriss was able to watch some of the action during the great air raid of April 7, which he described in his diary as "better than a $1.50 seat at the movies." In terms of experience, if not in productivity, the highlight of the second tour was the mission to bomb the Japanese airfield at Kahili in southern Bougainville, which Morriss and Brodie flew on the night of April 9–10 with the Burton Burns crew in an old B-17, a veteran of the Battle of Midway. An overcast sky and a new, inexperienced navigator combined to render the mission a failure; the planes failed to find the target and all returned with their bombs. Great for mood, but not much in the way of a story was Morriss's assessment. Still, the second tour must be reckoned a success because the two *Yank* staffers put into the record a little-known episode of the war in the Solomons—the operations of the heavy bombers of the Thirteenth Air Force. Brodie's contribution was a set of sketches of the Burns crew done on the ground and on practice runs over Tulagi that made a two-page spread in *Yank*. What Morriss needed was an angle, and he got it when the entire crew of the B-17, "My Ever Lovin' Dove," shot down in early February of that year, and a carrier torpedo bomber (TBF) crew member, shot down in August of the previous year, all made it back safely to Guadalcanal. Morriss's account, minus any mention of the role of the Coast Watchers, a still highly secret organization, was published as "66 Days Missing in Action" in the June 11 issue.

Morriss and Brodie left Guadalcanal on April 23 for New Caledonia. Although neither man realized it at the time, their South Pacific tour was nearing its end. Rumor had it that New Georgia in the central Solomons was the next Allied target, but for the moment things on the ground were quiet. In mid-May, Brodie was ordered home. He was seriously ill; and when he arrived in New York, he was immediately hospitalized with hepatitis. Morriss went as far as Honolulu with him and shortly after the two men said their good-byes, he came down with malaria. On the day he got out of the hospital, June had all but passed, and news arrived that the Allies had indeed invaded New Georgia. Morriss was torn between heading south immediately or waiting in Honolulu for news from

Helen, who was nearing the end of her pregnancy. In early July, a cable came, announcing that the baby had been stillborn, but that Helen was doing fine under the circumstances. Morriss closed out his diary on July 19, 1943, and left it with the Honolulu *Yank* office; on the next day he was on a C-47 headed south.

Sgt. Mack Morriss (*left*) and Sgt. John Bushemi take time out for lunch, September 13, 1943, on Arundel Island, part of the New Georgia group, Solomon Islands. *Courtesy of* Yank *and the U.S. Signal Corps*

He was in a hurry to get to New Georgia before the fighting ended and before the orders for his recall, which he knew to be imminent, caught up with him. By July 24 he had reached Fiji where he joined up with *Yank* photographer Johnny Bushemi, a former Gary, Indiana, sports photographer, and by August 11 the two correspondents had made it back to Guadalcanal. On August 14 they were aboard a landing craft tank on a slow and hot voyage to New Georgia. They were aware that the situation was extremely fluid. Munda, the main objective of the campaign, had fallen on August 5, and troops of the 25th and 43rd Divisions were pushing the Japanese on New Georgia Island west toward Kolombangara where the bulk of the enemy forces were preparing to make their stand. On August 15, however, the day Morriss and Bushemi arrived, the Allies bypassed Kolombangara and landed on Vella Lavella, which was undefended and had a suitable airfield site.

Morriss sensed an immediate difference between the situation at Munda and the experience he had had on Guadalcanal. There were rumors of low morale, which Morriss later narrowed down to the large number of "war neurosis" cases that had cropped up in one unit of the 43rd during the push on Munda. Military regulations were not as lax as they had been on Guadalcanal. "Want to get away from this particular area," Morriss wrote. "Example why: requested that I tell Bushemi to shave and get a haircut. This, in midst of place [that] looks like hell's corner. Small matter, but typical." Censorship also appears to have been tighter. Morriss did his first major story on the 73rd Seabees and their work on Munda Field, but the entire story was killed at army headquarters. The sensitivity no doubt was due to the fact that Munda was destined to play a major role in the final campaigns that defeated the Japanese in the South Pacific—it was to form the hub in the wheel of bases from which Allied aircraft neutralized Rabaul in late 1943 and early 1944.

What saved the tour and turned it into a highly successful venture was Morriss's credibility—going back to his work on Guadalcanal—with the officers of the 25th Division, especially Col. James Dalton III, who commanded the 161st Infantry on New Georgia. Dalton arranged for Morriss to interview and for Bushemi to photograph his men, who had taken part in the assault on Munda Field, and for one of his officers to take them on a tour of the battleground. The result was two feature stories, "Infantry Battle in New Georgia" and "The Five-Day Attack on the Japs at Hastings Ridge," both of which ran complete with Bushemi photographs. The first had a Bushemi cover. Morriss was one of the first to describe how close the fighting was in the rain forest east of Munda Field: "In the jungle, war is always a personal sort of thing, one man pitted against another. On Hastings Ridge it reached a point where individual action and individual courage were knitted together in two- and three-man units of assault, pitted against similar little units of Japs crouched in pillboxes. And the best fighters won because they cooperated with each other the best."[9]

Both Morriss and Bushemi knew that they were stretching their stay to the limit. Sure enough, on September 1, letters arrived informing Morriss that his replacement was on the way and telling Bushemi "to get the hell back to Oahu." Nevertheless, they took their time in obeying and, before leaving, managed to get themselves pinned down by mortar fire with the 2d Battalion, 27th Infantry, on Arundel, which resulted in a photographic spread and a cover for Bushemi in the November 26 issue of *Yank*.

But it was time to obey orders. The two men made it back to Nouméa, New Caledonia, where they separated. They never saw each other again. In February of the following year, Johnny Bushemi, who had written Morriss the month before that he would like to go to Europe because "the civilized war is the only deal for a cameraman," was killed on Eniwetok by a mortar shell.

Morriss arrived back in New York in October 1943 and spent the rest of the year and the first six months of 1944 in the States. He found that a great deal had changed. Like the rest of the American war machine, *Yank* had become a global enterprise and was well on its way to achieving the greatest circulation of any magazine in history: 21 editions and 250 million copies printed by the end of the war.[10] It had achieved its purpose of becoming the enlisted man's paper. GIs read it for the feature stories, for the cartoons and pinups, for the gripe sessions in the Letters to the Editor section, and for advice about matters important to them such as how to form a "Brush-off Club" when a Dear John letter arrived. CBS's Doug Edwards put it well during an interview with Morriss on *Report to the Nation* in early November. "Several million young Americans are in a new and difficult business these days," he said. "It's the business of being a soldier. Like nearly all businesses this soldier work has a trade paper. It's called *Yank, the Army Weekly*."

During the nine months Morriss was in New York, he and Helen were able to set up housekeeping again. In an East Eighty-seventh Street brownstone, just across from Gracie Mansion, they found a first-floor apartment that had a living room with a piano, a bedroom with a pull-down Murphy bed, a small kitchen, and a bath; they considered themselves extremely lucky. New York was an expensive place to live, especially on a sergeant's pay, and winter clothes for Helen from her mother and all-you-could-eat spaghetti houses like Ralph's helped them get by. In early 1944, Helen, who had been the social editor at the *Star*, went to work for *Parade* magazine, which eased their finances considerably. They were able to go to the theater; join the *Yank* crowd at Costillo's, a well-known watering place on Third Avenue; and, when Morriss was traveling on assignment as he frequently did, Helen could buy a dollar seat at the Metropolitan Opera.

Morriss worked in the *Yank* editorial offices when he was not on assignment. He went to Aberdeen for a feature on enemy vehicles, to Charleston for a story on the return of a hospital ship, to Atlantic City for a piece on a redistribution center, to Washington, DC, for a story on mental breakdowns (something he had promised himself to do when he first encountered the illness in New Georgia), to Louisville for an interview with a Medal of Honor winner, and to Camp Butler, North Carolina, for the return home of a Ranger outfit.

The Stateside interlude came to an end in the late spring of 1944. While the Allies planned to invade Europe, *Yank* was planning to set up shop in Paris. In mid-May, Morriss was tipped off that he would be going soon, but it was late July before he arrived in England and the end of August before he got to Paris. If the bureaucratic red tape he encountered in England suggested that his stay in the European theater was going to be considerably different from his free-wheeling days in the South Pacific, his reception in Paris dispelled any doubt. The major in charge of the office sent him by Jeep to bring rations from Brittany, a two-day trip, and since Morriss was leaving the next day for the front, he took what he considered to be his allotment. This act led to a scene. "You may be a good writer and you may have been hot stuff in the Pacific but you're just another sergeant in the Army," the major told him and continued with a list of accusations so ridiculous that Morriss was left dumbfounded.

More serious were what the official historian termed the "inflexible policies of the Public Relations offices of the SHAEF [Supreme Headquarters Allied Expeditionary Forces]." Four in particular hampered the *Yank* correspondents: (1) a correspondent or photographer could only be accredited to one headquarters at one time, which strained the limited number of available correspondents; (2) only one correspondent would be accredited to an army, destroying the team concept of writer-artist or writer-photographer; (3) transportation was assigned to three correspondents at a time, which put the *Yank* correspondents at a disadvantage because they needed more time for a magazine story; and (4) most troublesome of all, "the discrimination shown between civilian newsmen and the enlisted correspondents of *Yank*" tended to keep the latter in the dark about major events.[11] On the other hand, if Morriss's case is typical, the *Yank* men were superbly adept at getting around the restrictions.

Morriss, in fact, did some of his finest work in Europe. During the autumn of 1944 he covered the First Army's pursuit of the Germans, the assault on the Siegfried Line, and the capture of the old imperial city of Aachen. A number of his stories were featured in *Yank*. But it was his story about the 4th Division's ordeal in the Huertgen Forest that many consider to be his finest work. Reprinted on a number of occasions, included in anthologies of war reporting, and cited by historians writing about it, the article described in detail the battle that some have compared to the Civil War's Battle of the Wilderness and which Morriss compared to New Georgia: "Men of the 25th, 43rd, and 37th Divisions would know Huertgen—it was like New Georgia. Mud was as deep, but it was yellow instead of black. Trees were as thick, but the branches were stemmed by brittle needles instead of broad jungle leaves. Hills were as steep and as numerous, but there were mines—S mines, wooden shoe mines, tellermines, box mines." And what about the progress of the infantry—not just that of the 4th but of the other divisions fed into a battle that left some army officers and military historians wondering why it was ever fought in the first place? "The infantry went through Huertgen's mud and its splintered forest growth and its mines and its high explosives, mile by mile, slowly and at great cost. But it went through, with an average of perhaps 600 yards gained each day."[12]

During his time with First Army he worked initially out of Maastricht and then, when the Allied front was reorganized, at the press camp at Spa. What Bushemi had called "the civilized war" was considerably different from the island war. "Ernest Hemingway just walked through the room without any pants on," Morriss began a letter to his wife. "No underwear either, just a shirt." At one point, he warned Helen that she might see a photograph of him kissing a good-looking Red Cross woman in *Life* magazine (she did, in the February 5, 1945, issue). The occasion had been a wedding that had been turned into a major PRO event so that Morriss told Helen he was "still half blind" from all of the flashes going off. Only the slowness of the mail reminded him of the South Pacific, and when the letters did arrive they brought good news—and bad. A batch caught up with him in mid-October, and one written in August confirmed that Helen was pregnant; another that got through more quickly in December told him that Helen's younger brother, Kenneth, a tail gunner in a B-24, had been killed in action over Yugoslavia.

During the first two months of 1945, as the Allied armies reduced the Bulge and put pressure on the Germans all along the front in preparation for the invasion of Germany, Morriss worked back and forth between Ninth Army and First Army. Only two articles can be dated from that period, and from his letters home, it seems to have been a relatively lax time for him. Uppermost in his mind was the approaching birth of their child, and he was put even more on edge by hints that he might be able to return home. Twin girls were born on February 16, and Walter Winchell, probably the most famous columnist in America, announced the event to the world on March 5. Meanwhile, Morriss was on his way home, arriving in Elizabethton a month after he left Paris. He found mother and daughters healthy and was able to enjoy a quiet furlough far from the war, interrupted only by being sent to Lynchburg, Virginia, to cover the passage of the train carrying President Roosevelt's body from Warm Springs, Georgia, back to Washington. Morriss estimated that four hundred people had turned out at 2:00 A.M. to watch as two hours later the darkened train went coasting by.

Exactly a month after he came home, he was back in Paris. The war had moved east and the front was deep in Germany. He went there, arriving in time for the link-up of the American and Russian forces. Every correspondent had one thing in mind—to get to Berlin, which had just fallen—but the Russians did not care for the idea. As Morriss told Helen, "They would say, 'Sit down and let's talk about it,' and then they'd get us so drunk it was impossible to go anywhere." But Morriss and a *Stars and Stripes* correspondent, Ernest Leiser, did go, and after a hair-raising trip, they became the third and fourth American correspondents to make it into the center of the city. For their effort, all four were suspended and Morriss and Leiser were threatened with courts-martial, but nothing came of the threat. Here is Morriss's description of conquerors and conquered:

> There were Russians in the square, dancing, and a band played. In Unter den Linden were the bodies of civilians, the dust of their famous street like grease paint on their faces. And by the Brandenburg Gate, in a small building that had spilled its guts inward on the floor, was an old woman, alone. She lay on the debris, trying to support herself on an elbow. She had stockings, but no shoes, on her feet. Her hair was gray, and the grayness of it matched the gray dust on her dress. The woman slowly moved her head from side to side, dying.[13]

Berlin was Morriss's last adventure. In June he was assigned to cover the 4th Infantry Division as it left Europe for the States for redeployment in the coming invasion of Japan, and he sailed home with that unit in July. By this time, he had been in the army for nearly five years and had the necessary points for discharge. He could not have known that two atomic bombs would shortly end the war in the Pacific and

negate the need for the 4th Infantry Division to face the appalling casualties it had suffered in Europe. But he had seen his share of the war.
And there was a wife and twin daughters waiting for him at home. He
was discharged on July 26, 1945.

Although Morriss landed a job with *Life* in the fall of 1945, he
chose to give it up and return home to Tennessee. His novel, *The Prov-
ing Ground* (1951), was not a financial success; and although he published a number of stories in leading magazines, these were not enough
to support a family. He worked briefly for his old newspaper and then
went into broadcasting at the Elizabethton radio station, WBEJ, where
he remained until his death at a relatively early age in 1976.

Nonetheless, his reputation as "a top combat correspondent for the
Army magazine *Yank* in both Europe and the Pacific" seems secure.[14]
Even before he had gone on his final adventure to Berlin, he got his first
widespread exposure to the civilian audience when *The Best from YANK,
The Army Weekly* was published in the spring of 1945. Altogether six of
his stories were included, and Ira Wolfert, a Pulitzer Prize–winning correspondent, singled Morriss out in his review. "Mack is present throughout this anthology as a journalist, but so good a one that he makes his
work seem quite like that of an artist," Wolfert wrote. "There are few,
very, very, few indeed, of the internationally famous war correspondents
who can match this youth's work in its passion for meaningful detail."[15]
Since then to the present day, Morriss's stories have been a part of a
succession of *Yank* anthologies and most recently were included in the
Library of America's classics of war reporting, *Reporting World War II*,
published in 1995.

Notes

1. Unless otherwise noted, this chapter is based on the collection of letters, papers, notebooks, and unpublished diaries of Mack Morriss now in the possession of his
family. For travel to archives and battle sites, the author gratefully acknowledges major
funding from the Research Development Committee, East Tennessee State University,
and supporting grants from the Office of International Programs, East Tennessee State
University.

2. Dan Calfee, "This and That," *Johnson City Chronicle*, September 24, 1940.

3. "An Army Newspaper: Report of Special Committee of the Joint Army and
Navy Committee on Welfare and Recreation," February 25, 1942, RG 407, National
Archives and Records Administration.

4. Ward Morehouse, "Broadway after Dark," *New York Sun*, June 4, 1942.

5. In addition to the private collection cited above, the section on the South
Pacific and Guadalcanal is based on Mack Morriss, *South Pacific Diary, 1942–1943*,

ed. Ronnie Day (Lexington: University Press of Kentucky, 1996). Quotations may be found by the date given in the text.

6. Morriss had managed to secure a typewriter—a precious commodity at this stage of the war—but he gave it to a staff officer of the 172d Infantry who had lost his when the *Coolidge* sank in Segond Channel, Espíritu Santo.

7. Mack Morriss, "Jap-Trap," *Yank*, March 5, 1943.

8. James Jones, *WWII: A Chronicle of Soldiering* (New York: Grosset and Dunlap, 1975), 58.

9. Mack Morriss, "The Five-Day Attack on the Japs at Hastings Ridge," *Yank*, November 19, 1943.

10. Capt. C. H. E. Stubblefield and Lt. Col. Jack Weeks, "Yank," January 17, 1946, p. 1, in History of Army Information Branch, Information and Education Division, War Department, 2 vols. (Center of Military History, Washington, DC), vol. 1.

11. Ibid.

12. Mack Morriss, "War in the Forest," *Yank*, January 5, 1945.

13. Mack Morriss, "Berlin Death Rattle," *Yank*, June 15, 1945.

14. "Mack Morriss, 56, Combat Reporter, Yank Correspondent Dies—Covered Fall of Berlin," *New York Times*, February 20, 1976.

15. Ira Wolfert, "The Army's Magazine Reflects a Vivid Picture of the War," *PM*, April 29, 1945.

Suggested Readings

Kennedy, William V. *The Military and the Media: Why the Press Cannot Be Trusted to Cover a War*. Westport, CT, 1993.

Kluger, Steve, ed. *Yank, the Army Weekly: World War II from the Guys Who Brought You Victory*. London, 1991.

Knightley, Phillip. *The First Casualty: From the Crimea to Vietnam: The War Correspondent as Hero, Propagandist, and Myth Maker*. New York, 1975.

Maslowski, Peter. *Armed with Cameras: The American Military Photographers of World War II*. New York, 1993.

Oldfield, Barney. *Never a Shot Fired in Anger*. New York, 1956.

15

Justice M. Chambers
An American Cincinnatus

Donald F. Bittner

Unlike the Marines of World War I, who had fought as part of the American Expeditionary Force in the trenches in France, their World War II descendants saw the entirety of their action in the Pacific. All six Marine divisions were committed to amphibious assaults to drive the Japanese off the coral atolls of Micronesia and the jungle islands of the Southwest Pacific. The final Marine campaigns aimed at the capture of Iwo Jima and, with the U.S. Army, Okinawa—two staging points close to Japan that would have been critical had an invasion of the home islands proved necessary.

The war against Japan, waged for more than three years, was unusually grim and merciless. During the first American offensive at Guadalcanal in August 1942, Marines were shocked at the fanaticism of the enemy soldiers who almost invariably fought to the death while disregarding international conventions regulating warfare. The Japanese often shot American wounded and medics or, feigning surrender, would kill those who tried to take them prisoner. From then on, Marines took terrible casualties but few prisoners. For example, on the three-hundred-acre island of Tarawa, Marine attackers in November 1943 lost 3,000 men in three days to 4,700 Japanese, only 19 of whom survived the battle as American captives. Eleven months later in the fearsome 115-degree heat of Peliliu, the Japanese, skillfully concealed in underground defenses, inflicted frightful losses on the American attackers. Eugene Sledge, a Marine whose rifle company suffered 64 percent casualties, later remembered, "A note from the commanding general was read to all units stating that we didn't need Army help to finish the job. It was met with curses and fervent hopes that the commanding general would burn in hell."

The desperate struggle at Peliliu presaged the more famous battle for Iwo Jima. The Marine victory on that volcanic island only five hundred miles from Japan was forever engraved in the American memory by Joe Rosenthal's photograph of six Marines raising the American flag atop Mount Suribachi. If that vision became the lasting image of Marine arms triumphant, the combat deaths soon afterward of three of the six Marine flag-raisers symbolized the cost of what one commander called "the toughest fight in the 169 years of our Corps." On Iwo Jima, Marine losses of 24,961 killed and wounded exceeded, for the first time in the Pacific war, the total number of Japanese defenders and gave a frightening preview of what an invasion of the home islands might cost.

The top naval officer in the Pacific, Fleet Adm. Chester Nimitz, remarked, "Among the Americans who served on Iwo Jima, uncommon valor was a common virtue." During the course of World War II, the highest award bestowed by the United States for bravery was the Medal of Honor, given a serviceman for "gallantry and intrepidity at the risk of his life above and beyond the call of duty." Of the 16 million Americans who wore their country's uniform, 433 won the Medal of Honor, more than half (245) at the cost of their lives. Broken down by organization, 256 medals went to U.S. Army soldiers, 38 to airmen of the Army Air Forces, 57 to sailors in the U.S. Navy, 1 to a Coast Guardsman, and 81 to Marines. One of those Marines was Justice M. Chambers, a lawyer and Marine Corps reservist who saw combat from Guadalcanal to Iwo Jima where he earned his nation's highest award for heroism.

Relating Chambers's war in the Pacific is Donald F. Bittner, professor of history at the Marine Corps Command and Staff College, Quantico, Virginia. A Marine officer from 1963 to 1989 when he retired as a lieutenant colonel, Bittner earned his Ph.D. in history from the University of Missouri in 1974. Among his numerous publications is *The Lion and the White Falcon: Britain and Iceland in the World War II Era* (1983).

In World War II an estimated 16,354,000 Americans served in uniform in the fight against the Axis powers. Whether draftees or volunteers who joined before or after Pearl Harbor, or reservists or National Guardsmen who had come on active duty before December 7, 1941, almost all were nonregulars. Hence these men and women were "citizen soldiers" who left civilian life, served on active duty, and, after 1945, resumed their lives in the everyday world. During World War II the U.S. Marine Corps evolved into a fourth de facto coequal member of the armed forces of the United States. As such, it eventually fielded two amphibious corps, six combat divisions, five aircraft wings, twenty defense battalions, four raider battalions, and two parachute battalions, and various supporting units while also maintaining ships detachments and manning barracks at naval stations. To build this formidable force, the corps also relied upon nonregulars, that is, Marine Corps reservists. In World War II almost 600,000 Americans wore the globe and anchor emblem of the nation's "soldiers of the sea." Of these, 68–70 percent were reservists.[1]

Col. Justice M. Chambers (1908–82), U.S. Marine Corps Reserve, was one of them. He enlisted in the naval reserve in 1928 and the Marine Corps Reserve in 1930, and was commissioned a second lieutenant

Col. Justice M. Chambers, U.S. Marine Corps Reserve (Ret.), wearing what was called the Summer Service "A" Uniform. Note the eagles denoting his colonel's rank. The ribbons are (*from top to bottom, left to right*) Medal of Honor, Silver Star, Legion of Merit with Combat "V," Purple Heart (three awards), Presidential Unit Citation (four awards), American Defense Medal, Asiatic-Pacific Campaign Medal, American Campaign Medal, World War II Victory Medal, and the Organized Marine Corps Reserve Medal (three awards). *Courtesy of the U.S. Marine Corps Historical Center, Washington, DC*

in 1932. Before mobilization in 1940 as a Marine reservist, he was a "weekend warrior." Between 1942 and 1945 he fought in the Solomon, Marshall, Caroline, and Volcano Islands. A combat Marine, he was awarded the Silver Star, the Legion of Merit with Combat "V," and finally the Medal of Honor for heroism. Wounded three times, Chambers was medically retired from the Marine Corps on January 1, 1946, and returned to civilian life.[2]

Justice Marion Chambers was born on February 2, 1908, in Huntington, West Virginia, the son of Arthur and Dixie Chambers. As Chambers later recalled, in Huntington, "you either had money or you didn't. We didn't." Raised by supportive parents, along with one brother and two sisters, Chambers experienced in his youth a bout with polio, a brief sojourn in Kentucky, employment with a road construction company, and familiarity with outdoor life. Violence and death were not part of these early years, and there was no emphasis on firearms, shooting, or hunting. In January 1925 he entered Marshall College for three years, paid his own expenses, studied prelaw, and left with 81 of the 90 credits required for his degree. As he recalled, "[I] left in part because I sort of led a students' revolt against the dismissal of two professors who we thought were top-side [outstanding] people." The president of Marshall had told him that some faculty would not want him in their classes.

Chambers's career in the Marine Corps began in May 1928 when he joined the U.S. Naval Reserve, prompted by a rumor of the benefits: "I was working for the federal government and somebody told me that I could get two extra weeks' vacation with pay as military leave." And what a vacation: one seasick summer on a World War I destroyer with miserable living conditions and gamblers as his companions. He returned to Washington, saw his commanding officer, and requested "out"—only to be told he had signed a contract and had a four-year obligation. However, there was an escape: transfer to the Marine Corps Reserve. His response: " 'What are the Marines?' . . . So I ended up in the Marine Corps where you could really get seasick in a small boat tossing around reef lines."

He served another two years as an enlisted trooper in the Marine Corps Reserve. Drills were held once per week, and he attended two two-week summer camps, both in Virginia. Chambers later recalled one lowlight of his life as a trooper. At a time when boxing competitions were a major part of service life, he had a career as a pugilist that lasted two fights. Thrown into the ring, he won his first fight but lost his second, felled after his eighth knockdown! However, the event had one beneficial effect: His battalion commander noted that "the thing that really caught his attention was the fact that I kept getting up even though I was getting the hell beat out of me."

Chambers then decided that he wanted to be an officer. Remembering his decision later, he said, "I guess it was just my instinct, trying to better myself. If I was going to be in the outfit, I wanted to go as far as I could." After appropriate training, he appeared before an examining board on July 5, 1932, was found qualified, and commissioned as a second lieutenant on July 18, 1932. Promotions soon followed. In 1935 came his advancement to first lieutenant and in 1938 to captain. Education and study were crucial to his success. As he later recollected, "I was studying in the Marine Corps once I got my commission. . . . Over a period of seven years I completed all of the correspondence courses that the Marine Corps gave. . . . They stood me in good stead when we were mobilized." His official record is full of completion certificates, including the nonresident courses for the Basic School (for second lieutenants) in 1936 and the Junior Reserve Course (for captains) in 1937, plus others for individual military subjects.

Drills during the year, two weeks of annual active duty, and occasional other active service were now part of his life. He described this period as one of "hard work, of tremendous interest in the company, and of even more interest in the schools." At this time, his company numbered about fifty officers and men. Still, because of funding and equipment shortages, the weekly reserve training was of limited practical value. The sessions consisted in part of rifle marksmanship and close order drill, the latter for public relations reasons: "We all had to have a lot of close order drill for it was our chore to be in parades, so we had to look right."

Chambers also had duty with regular units at Quantico where he had temporary command assignments, became familiar with weapons, and met many regular officers who would lead the Corps in World War II. In 1938 he temporarily commanded "C" Company, 1st Battalion, 5th Marines, permanently commanded by Capt. Samuel B. Griffith.[3] In June 1940, while at Quantico, Chambers returned to the battalion to fill a temporary vacancy in one of the companies; the battalion commander asked for Captain Griffith, then with the 3rd Battalion, who commented, "They've got a reserve captain over there who has forgotten more than I'll ever know about this business. Why don't they use him?" Thus, Chambers commanded a regular company reinforced by a machine-gun platoon and two 81 mm mortars during an amphibious exercise on the Potomac River.

However, not everything went well. During one training period at Camp Ritchie, Cascade, Maryland, he laid out a battalion maneuver and assault problem, distinguishing himself, as he later noted. But then because of an embarrassing mishap, one of the worst fears of any young officer became a reality. Chambers took the battalion commander, most of the staff, and the company commanders up the side of Mount Quirack: "There was only one trouble: I got them all lost. We kicked around for three hours before we finally lucked our way off the side of that hill, and it took me a long time to live that down."

In retrospect, he evaluated his ten years of Marine Corps Reserve training as of limited value: "We learned a lot in our summer training, but none of it was realistic." However, he did absorb key tenets of leadership—one of which was "the need to try to develop within your men a sense of responsibility. They would be able to go ahead and do their jobs even if you were not looking over their shoulder. I also found early on that you weren't going to get very far if you simply told the men what to do. You had to do it with them. . . . [This lesson] paid off later under combat conditions."[4]

During the years that Chambers was serving in the Marine Corps Reserve, he had been also making changes in his personal life, earning a living, and had once again enrolled in college. In 1927 the future Marine had left Huntington for Washington, DC, and entered the federal civil service, initially with the Federal Bureau of Investigation and a year later with the Department of Agriculture. On December 25, 1932, he married Johanna W. Schmutzer, whom he had met at a Labor Day party at the home of his Marine Corps Reserve company commander. He spent two years (1933 and 1934) working for the Acacia Life Insurance Company but returned to the government because he saw a dull future in insurance. By September 1936 he was at the Treasury Department, followed by service with the U.S. Maritime Commission. In Washington, Chambers attended The George Washington University for two years, joined Sigma Phi Epsilon fraternity, and was elected president of his law class. He neglected his studies and voluntarily withdrew; later he enrolled in National University, which he noted "was a refuge for many people who couldn't make it at G.W. and Georgetown." Chambers humorously recalled that later this school was taken over by The George Washington University and that his law degree of 1931 came from the latter!

On November 10, 1940, Chambers was called to active duty with the rest of the Marine Corps Reserve. When the Japanese attacked Pearl Harbor, he was with the 1st Marine Division in North Carolina. At the time, the Marine Corps was raising American equivalents of Britain's commandos, called raider battalions. Lt. Col. Merritt Edson commanded the 1st Raider Battalion, and the unit's executive officer was Sam Griffith, both of whom Chambers knew. Despite his age, family, and reserve status, he volunteered for this new unit.

When he joined the 1st Raiders in March 1942, he initially received command of its weapons company. The unit then moved from Quantico, Virginia, to San Diego, then to American Samoa, and finally to New Caledonia. In his training, Chambers emphasized personal leadership, physical conditioning, terrain analysis, handling of boats, and tactical and weapons skills. His demands were rigorous and his standards high; he expected his enlisted and officer leaders to be knowledgeable about the battalion and its capabilities, and to give close personal attention to the troops and to lead from the front. Edson was an influence on Chambers, who later recalled, "Eddie's theory was that every officer in that battalion should know how to do everything. . . . To Eddie, you were supposed to be a jack of all trades."[5]

Then in the summer of 1942 came the first U.S. amphibious operation of the war—the landing on Guadalcanal and the supporting assault on Tulagi—which the 1st Raider Battalion would seize. In New Caledonia, Chambers, after having trained the Weapons Company, received command of "D" Company, a rifle unit. This was also the last company to join the 1st Raiders, and hence the least trained. Because there was a shortage of ships, his officers thought they would be left behind; however, Edson told Chambers, "I just came to tell you if any of our companies go, you go."

The initial baptism of fire came on August 7. The 1st Raider Battalion landed, unopposed, on Tulagi and proceeded inland. As his men made their way through the harsh and heavily vegetated terrain, Chambers's emphasis on physical conditioning on similar ground in American Samoa and New Caledonia reaped its dividend. The Japanese defense was anchored in a ravine near the former British resident's house, firefights began, and Chambers, now under enemy fire, personally supervised his troops. He later recalled the initial incident: "There were some snipers in back of us. I know I was leaning my head around a big coconut tree and a Jap laid a round right alongside my head. That's when I thought they were using explosive bullets." Later, armed with a

Reising submachine gun, he entered a clearing about twenty-five or thirty feet wide; "as I came out of one side a Jap stepped out of the other. It was just a question of who was the most scared, I reckon. I dove to my left and started firing my weapon as I went down. I don't know whether I got him or not; I didn't see him again."

Eventually, Chambers was hit. He was adjusting fire from his own weapons when "all of a sudden there was this great flash of fire right in front of me, oh, maybe ten or fifteen feet up in the air. It smashed my left wrist, broke my right wrist, and took a chunk out of my left leg." Initially he believed the cause was a premature burst from one of his own 60 mm mortars; later he concluded it was a shell from a Japanese knee mortar. Chambers retained command for a time, moving extensively and personally directing his men, until relieved by his executive officer. He later summarized the situation: "All I had was a piece of shrapnel in the back of my kneecap. I was bleeding pretty good in my wrists and was sore as hell, but I was ambulatory. If they shot at me hard enough I could move real fast."

Chambers, now at an aid station within the combat zone, had only been in combat for one day—but already he had the veteran's feel. Anticipating a Japanese counterattack, knowing there were pockets of enemy defenders within and around his position, and hearing the enemy's approach, he ordered the medical personnel and wounded to move to a better position. Before they could complete the move, the Japanese attacked. It was after midnight, and the aid station was now caught between both forces: "My only concern was [to] get these people out of there. Another thing, the Marines up the hill were shooting down the hill, and Japs were shooting up the hill, and there we were. It was a mess." As the wounded withdrew to the Marines' fighting positions, Chambers was the last in line.

While recuperating in the United States, on October 30, 1942, Chambers assessed the war in the Pacific for the *Washington Star*. The Japanese were ferocious and ruthless soldiers who would shoot the American wounded: "I've seen them do it, and I suppose they logically believe that a wounded soldier, if left alive, will return to fight again. They are tough fighters and the only time I ever saw one attempt to surrender he was shot by his officers before he had gotten five steps from his own lines." The next day, the *Washington Times-Herald* reported a comment he made about being caught between the Japanese and Marines in the night counterattack, "Boy, was I scared."[6] In August 1943,

Chambers was awarded both his first Purple Heart for wounds received in action against the Japanese on Tulagi and the Silver Star.

For Chambers, another legacy remained from Tulagi: Edson's concept of leading from the front. When Chambers and his company first encountered enemy resistance, he found his battalion commander standing behind him on the front line, smoking a cigarette and observing his troops. Chambers later reflected upon this incident: "I think that episode was probably responsible for me getting wounded later on so many times as I became a battalion commander because I thought this was the way battalion commanders should act."[7]

After he recovered from his wounds, Justice Chambers took command of the 3d Battalion, 25th Marines, on May 1, 1943, and remained its leader until severely wounded on Iwo Jima on February 22, 1945. His initial action with this unit, part of the newly raised 4th Marine Division, occurred in the Marshall Islands in early 1944. The division's mission was to capture the twin islands of Roi-Namur at the northern tip of Kwajalein atoll, one of many steppingstones on the road to Japan.

Chambers's battalion had to seize two off-shore islands, Ennumennet and Ennugarret, near Namur, then prepare supporting arms for the assault on the main island. On January 31 his unit took Ennumennet. Despite this success, Chambers's battalion confronted problems: the landing on Ennugarret was behind schedule; amphibian tractors that were needed to transport his troops had received no orders, suffered from fuel shortages, and then disappeared; and no air, artillery, or naval gunfire support was available. As one official Marine Corps history noted, "This left Chambers in the position of having to assault a defended island [Ennugarret] over water without landing craft and with no support other than the weapons under his own command."[8]

Decision time had arrived for Chambers. He commandeered four amphibian tractors that had come into his area, packed 120 troops in them, and launched an assault wave toward the beachhead. The assault on Ennugarret was supported by the battalion's own weapons, now erected on the previously seized Ennumennet. By evening, the Marines held both islands. Then Chambers commenced erecting supporting arms for the next day's assault on Namur by other troops of the 4th Division. After that, between February 4 and February 7, 1944, his Marines participated in mopping-up operations on Kwajalein atoll. The battalion had performed well and suffered light casualties, with losses of 6 officers and 72 troops killed, and 5 officers and 94 men wounded. After occupation duty, the command moved back to Hawaii for further training and recovery for the men from amoebic dysentery. Another operation soon loomed, one that would be more difficult than the Marshalls: Saipan and Tinian.

A major change now occurred in the character of the war in the Pacific as it shifted from small jungle-covered isles to larger islands on which there was space to maneuver. Because of the difference in terrain, the Japanese changed their defensive approach, increasing the numbers of tenacious and skilled defenders fighting to the death from prepared positions against increasingly larger numbers of Marine and army invaders. As the 4th Marine Division's history candidly admitted, "On Roi-Namur, Marines of the 4th Division had not experienced enemy artillery or anything like the savage resistance which the Saipan Japanese put up on the ground. The men of the 4th were still, in a sense, green."[9] This inexperience they soon lost, courtesy of more than 30,000 defenders awaiting them on Saipan and more than 8,000 on Tinian. Chambers ruefully noted nineteen days after landing on Saipan that of 1,050 men in the 3d Battalion, 25th Marines, who had landed "in reserve" on June 15, 1944, he had only 468 left.[10]

His battalion landed on D day and remained engaged on Saipan for almost a month. As the battle raged, the terrain heavily influenced the ensuing combat: "Each of the intermediate objectives were ridges that ran down to the beach. The Japs had organized defenses back up in each of the gullies. It got rougher and rougher as we went along." This situation, combined with Japanese skill and a value system of no surrender, ensured that a high cost in blood would be extracted before Saipan was won.

Saipan thus became a major killing ground. This type of combat placed a premium on leadership, and Chambers not only wanted to be where the action was—but also had to be so as to command. Mistakes occurred, and Chambers later cited one that happened the day after they landed. The regimental headquarters had "bunched up" with too many officers too close together near trees that were Japanese artillery reference points. He warned them, but he was too late as incoming fire killed the regimental personnel officer and wounded several others. Six days later, Chambers himself was wounded when the Japanese blew up a large ammunition dump. Scheduled for medical evacuation, he refused to leave and the next day (June 23, 1944) rejoined his battalion.

Chambers's approach to command—leading from the front—continued to bring him under direct enemy fire. He once peered over a ridge; "within twenty-five to thirty yards, I was looking right down the muzzle of an 88 mm antiaircraft/antitank gun. It was pointing right up the damn hill at me!" He dropped down, the gun fired, and "the shell tore through the parapet and took the head halfway off the Marine to whom I had been talking . . . then detonated behind him, wounding several other Marines." Other close calls came from machine guns. One bullet struck his radioman—not hurting the trooper but cutting the spare batteries in half. In another instance, an enemy machine gun opened fire on Chambers and another officer of "K" Company, with the latter charging the gun with a pistol. As Chambers remembered, "This duel didn't last very long. After a few moments, you could see him just sag and slump down to the earth. There must have been eighty-some slugs in him."

Saipan exposed Chambers and his men to the full horrors of war. High casualties were incurred when a skilled, but defeated, foe refused to surrender. The reality of the situation soon was brutally apparent to everyone. As Chambers later recalled, "The Jap soldiers were not surrendering, and they were not permitting the civilians to surrender. I saw, with my own eyes, women and children come out of caves, start for our lines, only to be shot down from behind by their own weapons." He also witnessed voluntary suicide: Japanese civilians, including women, threw their children and themselves off cliffs into the sea or huddled together and detonated explosive charges.[11] Time and lives were wasted trying to induce Japanese troops to surrender. The enemy also tried a deadly lure: One of his company commanders told him that "some of the Japs had smeared blood on themselves and played dead as the Marines came up. Our instructions were that 'if it didn't stink, stick it.' . . . This was the sort of thing you had to do."[12]

Death abounded on Saipan. After the last major banzai attack, Chambers noted, "I never saw so many dead bodies in such a confined area. These were the remnants of the counterattack, and I understand that even though only 2,000 were supposed to have made the attack, over 4,000 bodies were counted." Unforeseen horrors occurred. Chambers later remembered his second night on Saipan: "It was dark and the Jeep was blacked out. Somewhere along the way, we started running over dead bodies. As we rolled across them, they would burst. All of us were vomiting, and we had maybe 300 yards of bodies to go across. By the time we got back to the CP [command post], no one there would let us, or our Jeep, anywhere near them."[13]

In such an environment, casualties came from both enemy and friendly fire. After his battalion captured Hill 500 at a relatively light cost, its supporting artillery fired on the fleeing Japanese. However, the guns also accidently fired on his men, and thirty-three unnecessary wounded and dead resulted. An emotional reaction followed: "Later, the forward observer told me that he had made it a point to stay as far away from me as he could. I suspect, if I had gotten my hands on him, I would have killed him."

Combat on Saipan was quickly followed by the assault on Tinian. Historians and practitioners of amphibious warfare call Tinian the "classic" amphibious operation. After the landing on a narrow beach, which the Japanese believed would never be the primary one, the Marines launched a highly successful ship-to-shore movement and subsequent operations that lasted from July 24 to August 1. However, Tinian also represented further fighting, more losses, and lessons learned.

The increased complexity of the war included coordinating supporting arms, especially close air support. On Tinian, Marine aviation was not present. Instead, there was an Army Air Force squadron of P-47 Thunderbolts. Chambers recalled: "They were going to have to fly up against steep cliffs to our immediate front. . . . These kids would dive right at those cliffs, firing away, and then they'd pull out and zip straight up the face of those cliffs, vertically. They were flying over so close that their empty shells were raining down all over us. How effective they were, I don't know, but they tried and that's all we could ask for."

In preparation for the assault, Chambers flew over Tinian in a B-24 Liberator, closely examining the beaches over which his troops would land. He correctly concluded that the approaches and beaches were mined. More important, he insisted that in the assault waves, his 37 mm guns land with his troops, for he expected a major Japanese counterattack, which indeed occurred. After the attack, more than five hundred enemy dead lay in front of his lines. The personal cost was revealed in front of two dead Marine machine gunners. Chambers recalled: "Those two kids had stayed at their gun, and in the morning, we discovered a cone of dead bodies leading right up to their gun. There must have been seventy-five dead Japs in that cone. The two boys were dead by their weapon with the body of a Jap officer in there with them."[14]

Further lessons lay ahead. One involved the tank-infantry team, with the tank often as important to the Marine on the ground as an aircraft overhead. After realizing that tanks were especially vulnerable when operating alone, Chambers "passed the word as strongly as I knew how that the rifle companies were never to allow the tanks to be without infantry support." Senior officers were also casualties, and Chambers realized that these were the result of command and control techniques of modern war: "One of the reasons battalion commanders were getting knocked off was because the Japanese could always see several antennas [of radios] sticking up wherever the battalion commanders went."

For the 3d Battalion, 25th Marines, operations in the Marianas had been costly. Of the original battalion landing team of more than 1,600 men, only 400 to 500 were left; of Chambers's own 900-man battalion, 24 officers and 658 men had been killed, wounded, or taken ill. He decided to acknowledge this sacrifice: before departing Tinian, the survivors lined up, and roll call was held. All were accounted for, either by the men calling out "present" or by buddies answering "killed in action," "wounded in action," or "wounded and evacuated." This process took an hour and a half. Later, Chambers concluded, "I think that gesture bound those guys together with a bond that could never be broken. I didn't do it for that purpose. To me, I had to do something to acknowledge the guys we left there."[15]

The Marianas were a sobering experience for Chambers, who was later awarded the Legion of Merit with Combat "V" for his duty there. The experience prompted this comment: "[Civil War General William T.] Sherman was right about war. The best way to get a war over with is to kill off a bunch of the enemy and make things terrible for them in the process. You can only hope they will eventually surrender, or die."[16] The Marianas were bad, but something worse was literally just over the horizon: Iwo Jima. There, as on Saipan and Tinian, the enemy would not surrender but only die—and there Chambers reached the pinnacle of his Marine Corps career.

In August 1944, Chambers and his command returned to Hawaii, where they trained for Iwo Jima, the archetype of Pacific battles. By the battle's end, the 3d Battalion, 25th Marines would suffer 760 casualties: 36 officers (10 killed) and 724 troops (222 dead).[17] One of the wounded was Chambers. He was only on the island five days before he fell, shot through the collarbone, lung, and chest. How did he become a casualty? Immediately after hitting the volcanic sands of Iwo Jima on February 19, 1945, the Marines, amid great disorganization, were subjected to intense mortar and rocket fire—and Chambers took action. In the words of Capt. Herbert E. Ing Jr., an officer in his battalion, "The gallant and intrepid action of Colonel Chambers, during the initial period of utmost confusion in ranks, resulted in the reorganization of his battalion and the reestablishment of confidence in our ability as Marines to move forward and secure that portion of the battalion's assigned zone of action." In Ing's opinion, Chambers's action restored effectiveness, saved men's lives, and precluded the envelopment of the 4th Marine Division's right flank.[18]

On that day much of the murderous enemy fire came from cliffs on the right of the beaches.[19] Chambers reorganized his rifle companies and directed his 81 mm mortars to fire on this high ground, thus reducing the enemy resistance from that area. Later, one of his companies seized this ground. As its commander and then Chambers's successor as battalion commander, Capt. James Headley, later wrote, "The seizure of the high ground made it possible for us to overrun and destroy enemy positions from which fire on the beaches had been received."[20] Lt. Col. James Taul, the battalion's executive officer, recalled: "During the entire time Lieutenant Colonel Chambers remained in the immediate front line, directing, exhorting, and by his own fearless example, encouraging the battle-weary troops to push forward against the most fanatic resistance." A direct observer of what occurred, Taul drew the only possible conclusion: Chambers's actions contributed to the early establishment of the force beachhead, and "it is my firm opinion that had the high ground not been seized promptly on D day, the subsequent operation ashore would have been seriously threatened."[21]

On February 21, with his battalion in reserve, Chambers made another personal reconnaissance of his area. He was in the observation post of the first battalion when its commander, a friend from prewar reserve days, was wounded. Chambers took control until a replacement arrived; recommended that his own battalion, despite its severe casualties, be returned to the line; and found a gap in the lines, which he had filled. Such a charmed existence could not continue indefinitely—and an enemy round finally found its mark. On February 22, Chambers occupied an almost completely exposed position on the enemy main line of resistance, directing fire and aiding the advance on the left. He was hit by enemy machine-gun fire, severely wounded, and evacuated from Iwo Jima.

Justice M. Chambers's most notable exploits in World War II occurred on Tulagi in the Solomon Islands (1942), at Roi-Namur in the Marshall Islands (1944), on Saipan and Tinian in the Marianas (1944), and on Iwo Jima in the Volcano Islands (1945). However, his total combat time of sixty-five days was only a small part of his almost six years of active service in that conflict. His military record for the period between 1940 and 1945 also included service in the United States and for a short time at Guantanamo Bay, Cuba. Promotions continued: to major in May 1942 and to lieutenant colonel in March 1943.

After Chambers came back to the United States from the Solomon Islands, the U.S. Maritime Commission requested his return to that organization. The Marine Corps denied the request, stating he would be assigned to duty where the benefits of his experience in combat with the enemy could be utilized. His expertise was called upon often. He spoke to army personnel at Camp Edwards, Massachusetts, about the plans for the Tulagi operation, and he forcefully stressed the absolute necessity of hard training to prepare the troops for the conflict. In May 1943 he was at Fort Monroe, Virginia, addressing the U.S. Army's Coast Defense Artillery School on gunnery subjects. Other duties also devolved upon him. In March 1943 he became commander of the 15th Replacement Battalion. Then on December 23, 1944, he assumed command of 85 officers and 1,209 troops, to embark aboard ship "for transportation to further duty beyond the seas." Things indeed had changed in four years for the reserve officer who in 1940 commanded a unit of just over 50 Marines.

Ironically, Chambers ended the war in school—between June 20 and September 18, 1945, he attended the Command and Staff School at Quantico, a three-month abbreviated wartime version of the peacetime one-year course for career field grade officers. While there, he received the Navy Cross for his actions on Iwo Jima—and his evaluation at that time was "excellent" in regular duties and tactical handling of troops—a surprising mark for an experienced combat officer and former battalion commander! The school director, however, also wrote, "Finished course in the upper third of class. He clearly although unconsciously, attempted to dominate any group in which he worked."[22] To attend this course, he had to pass a medical examination, which found him physically qualified for the school but unfit for combat duty. Chambers's physical condition reflected the rigors of his wartime service in the Pacific.

Chambers's gallantry and effectiveness in combat led to the recommendation for the Medal of Honor. In his forwarding endorsement for this award, the commanding officer of the 25th Marines, Col. J. R. Lanigan, wrote, "By continued example of his outstanding and personal courage, he fearlessly inspired his numerically weak battalion to continue to press the attack under the most adverse conditions against the unbelievably strong and fanatically defended Japanese emplacement."[23] Chambers had already received the Navy Cross (in 1945), the nation's second highest medal for gallantry. However, the nation's highest award for valor was not conferred until five years later—in 1950. The matter was raised by the commandant of the Marine Corps, Gen. Clifton B. Cates: "The continued interest in this case by officers and members of the 25th Marines . . . and my own firm conviction regarding the nature of the services of this officer at Iwo Jima, it is earnestly recommended that Colonel Chambers's case be reconsidered for the award of the Medal of Honor in lieu of the Navy Cross previously awarded him."[24] Accordingly, in that year the Navy Cross was rescinded and Col. Justice M. Chambers was awarded the Congressional Medal of Honor. President Harry S. Truman bestowed the medal on him at a White House ceremony at noon on November 1, 1950, with Chambers's wife and children in attendance.[25]

During World War II, Chambers was an exemplary combat leader of Marines. When asked what role fighting had played in his prewar years in preparing him to be a leader, he recalled, "I never wanted to get in fights for I was afraid of getting hurt, but I did fight but only as a last resort. When I did fight, I went in to win. There were no holds barred, and that was that."[26]

With the war over and a medical board declaring Chambers permanently incapacitated for service, he returned to civilian life. Because of his awards for valor, he was promoted to colonel on the retired list in June 1946. Chambers reentered government service. In 1954 he established a private consulting firm specializing in foreign trade and international finance. In 1962 he joined the Kennedy administration as the deputy director of the Office of Emergency Planning.[27] In August 1965 his marriage to Johanna was dissolved; he subsequently married Barbara C. Fornes. One of his sons, "Mike" Chambers, graduated from recruit training at the Marine Corps Recruit Depot, Parris Island, South Carolina, in September 1960.[28] Chambers also received continuous medical treatment for his war wounds. According to his son, "In the mid-1960s we were still digging shrapnel out of Father."[29] On July 29, 1982, at seventy-four years of age, in Bethesda, Maryland, Col. Justice M. Chambers died of a stroke.

His time in the Marine Corps meant much to him. As Chambers prepared to return to civilian life, on December 21, 1945, he wrote a letter to the commandant of the Marine Corps, which concluded: "I have learned much from the Corps in the way of loyalty, sacrifice, and endurance which will carry me through my future life where perhaps before I would have failed. The Corps was an exacting job, but one that brought forth the best that was in me and in those with whom I served. Just boiling it down to language which I can perhaps use best, I am proud to have been one of you."[30]

Sources

No biography of Justice M. Chambers exists, although in books and journals on the Medal of Honor there are references to him, his actions on Iwo Jima, and the accompanying citation. Also, in operational histories, his personal and units' actions are addressed within larger contexts. This profile of Colonel Chambers is based on primary unpublished sources. These include his official Marine Corps records retained at the Federal Records Center, St. Louis, Missouri; his Biographical Reference File, Marine Corps Historical Center, Washington Navy Yard, Washington, DC; and personal papers held by the Chambers family, including an oral history, an unwritten memoir, and papers from World War II. Interviews were also conducted with his son, Lt. Col. J. M. "Mike" Chambers, USMC (Ret.), and members of the Fourth Marine Division Association who served with Colonel Chambers.

To reduce the number of citations, the following are noted:

1. Chronological and factual material pertaining to Chambers's military career, such as promotions, awards, and postings, are based on material in his official records and his biographical reference file.
2. Quotations by Chambers from his early life through Tulagi are from *Oral History Transcript: Colonel Justice M. Chambers, U.S. Marine Corps Reserve (Ret.)*, 2 vols. (Washington, DC: History and Museums Division. Headquarters, U.S. Marine Corps, 1998), Vol. 1, abbreviated as Chambers, *Oral History*, Vol. 1, for the few citations.
3. Quotations from the operations on Saipan and Tinian are from Justice M. Chambers, "Informal History," n.d. (original text retained by the Chambers family, with copies in the author's possession), abbreviated Chambers, Informal History, "Saipan" or "Tinian," respectively, for the noted citations.
4. Iwo Jima material (plus one fitness report citation) are from Chambers's official record of service, with quotations from witnesses to his actions in support of the Medal of Honor, abbreviated Chambers, Official Record.

Notes

1. Specific figures are vague. This percentage is from the official history of the U.S. Marine Corps Reserve: Public Affairs Unit 4-1, *The Marine Corps Reserve: A History* (Washington, DC, 1966), 82; see also 59. These were confirmed by the Marine Corps Historical Center: Danny J. Crawford, Head, Reference Branch, to author, e-mail of September 1, 1998, 2:56 P.M. Crawford noted that "nearly 400,000 of the men (68 percent according to one source) were reserves."

2. A chronological overview of Chambers's military career, based on his biographical reference file in the Marine Corps Historical Center, is in Kenneth N. Jordan Sr., *Men of Honor: Thirty-Eight Highly Decorated Marines of World War II, Korea, and Vietnam* (Atglen, PA, 1997), 43–51. Jordan also includes the full Medal of Honor citation and excerpts from those for the Silver Star and Legion of Merit with Combat "V."

3. Griffith retired as a brigadier general and later translated into English, for Oxford University Press, the Chinese military classic *The Art of War*: Samuel B. Griffith, trans. and intro., *Sun Tzu: The Art of War* (Oxford, 1963).

4. Chambers, *Oral History*, 1: 207, 209.

5. Ibid., 1: 275–76.

6. "Japs Learn Marines Are Tough, Says Wounded Solomons Officer: Maj. J. M. Chambers Returns to Capital to Recuperate," *Washington Evening Star*, October 30, 1942, and repeated in the *Washington Star,* October 30, 1942. Also see similar comments in "Shot in Back: U.S. Major Saw Jap Kill Own Private," *Washington Post,* October 12, 1942, and "D.C. Marine Home, Hailed as a Hero, Maj. Chambers Also Finds He's a Father," *Washington Times-Herald,* October 31, 1942.

7. Chambers, *Oral History*, 1:306. This is also recounted, with the Chambers quotation, in Jon T. Hoffman, *Once a Legend: "Red Mike" Edson of the Marine Raiders* (Novato, CA, 1994), 179. Chambers was exaggerating; he already had this leadership style.

8. Lt. Col. Robert D. Heinl Jr., USMC, and Lt. Col. John A. Crown, USMC, *The Marshalls: Increasing the Tempo* (Washington, DC, 1954; reprinted Nashville, TN, 1991), 51.

9. Carl W. Proehl, ed., *The Fourth Marine Division in World War II* (Washington, DC, 1964; reprinted Nashville, TN, 1988), 64.

10. Chambers, Informal History, "Saipan," 113–14. Maj. Carl Hoffman, USMC, *Saipan: The Beginning of the End* (Washington, DC, 1950; reprinted Nashville, TN, 1988), Appendix III: "Casualties," gives the total casualties of Chambers's unit as 27 officers (6 dead) and 375 troops (78 dead).

11. Chambers, Informal History, "Saipan," 124. This, and other aspects of the Marianas operation, has been captured on film, in the *Victory at Sea* episode titled "The Marianas Turkey Shoot."

12. Chambers, Informal History, "Saipan," 93, 118.

13. Ibid., 120, 87.

14. Chambers, Informal History, "Tinian," 138–39.

15. Ibid., 158–59.

16. Chambers, Informal History, "Saipan," 125.

17. Lt. Col. Whitman S. Bartley, USMC, *Iwo Jima: Amphibious Epic* (Washington, DC, 1954; reprinted Nashville, TN, 1997), Appendix III: "Casualties."

18. Cap. Herbert E. Ing Jr., USMC, letter to commandant of the Marine Corps, March 13, 1950. Chambers, Official Record.

19. In 1950, Lt. Col. James Taul, USMC, described this event: "From the heights on the ridge, the enemy enjoyed unrestricted observation of the entire 'V' Amphibious Corps front; moreover, from these positions, the enemy poured withering and ever-increasing volume of fire directly onto the troops already ashore and onto the craft in succeeding waves. The fire was so heavy and so accurate that casualties mounted at an alarming rate." Lt. Col. James Taul, USMC, letter to commandant of the Marine Corps, March 1, 1950. Chambers, Official Record.

20. Statement of Cap. James G. Headley, USMCR, n.d., enclosure (b) to commanding officer, 25th Marines, letter to the secretary of the navy, April 7, 1945. Chambers, Official Record.

21. Lt. Col. James Taul, USMC, letter to commandant of the Marine Corps, March 1, 1950. Chambers, Official Record.

22. Lt. Col. Justice M. Chambers, USMC[R], "Report of Fitness of Officers of the United States Marine Corps," September 18, 1945. This is only one of two (the other a report from 1949) in Chambers's personnel file. Chambers, Official Record.

23. Commanding officer, 25th Marines, letter to the secretary of the navy, April 7, 1945. Chambers, Official Record.

24. Commandant of the Marine Corps, letter to the secretary of the navy, July 25, 1950. Chambers, Official Record.

25. The recommendation was sent to President Truman for approval and a decision on his personally awarding the Medal of Honor; he assented to both. File 1285-C, Marine Corps. Harry S. Truman Presidential Papers, Harry S. Truman Library, Independence, Missouri. Published accounts of the ceremony can be found in "Twin Babies Spar with Truman as Father Gets Medal of Honor," *Washington Post*, November 2, 1950; and "Marine 'Caught' Doing His Job Gets Top Medal from Truman," *Washington Evening Star*, November 1, 1950; and repeated in the *Washington Evening Star*, November 2, 1950.

26. Chambers, *Oral History*, 1: 53.

27. A brief summary of Chambers's postwar career is in "War Hero in Line as Planning Aide," *New York Times*, March 20, 1962.

28. Three other sons, John, Paul, and Peter, also graduated from Parris Island. His enlisted service conformed to Colonel Chambers's belief, "You cannot lead until you learn to follow." Lt. Col. Justice M. "Mike" Chambers Jr., USMC (Ret.), interview with author, Quantico, Virginia, March 16, 1999.

29. Lt. Col. Justice M. "Mike" Chambers Jr., USMC (Ret.), interview with author, Triangle, Virginia, March 9, 1998.

30. Lt. Col. J. M. Chambers, USMCR (Ret.), letter to commandant of the Marine Corps, December 21, 1945. Chambers, Official Record.

Suggested Readings

Many official and unofficial histories of World War II and the role of the Marine Corps in that conflict have been written. For a historical overview of the war in the Pacific, see Ronald H. Spector, *Eagle against the Sun: The American War with Japan* (New York, 1985). Analyses of the operations in which Chambers participated from the perspectives of the assaulting American forces and the defending Japanese are given in Joseph H. Alexander, *Storm Landings: Epic Amphibious Battles in the Central Pacific* (Annapolis, 1997), and Theodore L. Gatchel, *At the Water's Edge: Defending against the Modern Amphibious Assault* (Annapolis, 1999).

Combined personal and tactical perspectives can be found in the Marine Corps Historical Center's "Marines in World War II Commemorative Series" published during the fiftieth anniversary of that conflict. Those associated with operations in which Chambers was involved are Henry I. Shaw Jr., *First Offensive: The Marine Campaign for Guadalcanal* (1992); Maj. Jon T. Hoffman, USMCR, *From Makin to Bougainville: Marine Raiders in the Pacific War* (1995); Capt. John C. Chapin, USMCR (Ret.), *Breaking the Outer Ring: Marine Landings in the Marshall Islands* (1994), and *Breaching the Marianas: The Battle for Saipan* (1994); Richard Harwood, *A Close Encounter: The Marine Landing on Tinian* (1994); and Col. Joseph H. Alexander, USMC (Ret.), *Closing In: Marines: Marines in the Seizure of Iwo Jima* (1994).

Also of interest are Eric Bergerud, *Touched with Fire: The Land War in the South Pacific* (New York, 1996); Richard B. Frank, *Guadalcanal* (New York, 1990); and Eugene B. Sledge, *With the Old Breed at Peleliu and Okinawa* (New York, 1981).

16

George A. Lincoln
The Evolution of a National Strategist

Charles F. Brower IV*

By the spring of 1945, the Axis was crumbling fast. Allied forces advancing up the Italian peninsula reached the Alps; the puppet regime of Benito Mussolini collapsed, and the dictator was killed by his own people. In Germany, Soviet armies surrounded the Nazi capital while British and American troops poured into the country from the west. Hitler's suicide on April 30 was followed quickly by the unconditional surrender of all German forces.

At that point, Japan was in a hopeless position by any rational benchmark. Bereft of allies, the Japanese found their homeland under naval blockade and fierce aerial bombardment. The single great fire raid on Tokyo of March 9-10 killed over one hundred thousand people, more than either atomic bomb at Hiroshima or Nagasaki. American air superiority over Japan was virtually absolute. B-29s dropped leaflets over target cities giving civilians warning of coming attacks. With their supplies from the Asian mainland almost totally disrupted by submarine blockade and mines, the Japanese people faced literal starvation. Many, perhaps most, of the civilian population hoped for a quick end to the war; so did some Japanese diplomats.

However, these people did not make the decisions for the Japanese government. In the imperial cabinet, radical army and navy officers argued for continued resistance, hoping that a prolonged and bloody campaign would lead to better terms from the Americans. Indeed, some Japanese leaders were willing to starve children and the elderly in order to feed those men carrying arms. Japanese fanatics were heartened by the ghastly losses that their conventional forces and their suicide weapons had inflicted at Okinawa. U.S. Army and Marine casualties totaled almost 40,000. The U.S. Navy lost 400 ships between those sunk and those damaged. More than 4,900 sailors died; as many were wounded, making Okinawa the bloodiest battle in U.S. Navy history.

---

*The views expressed herein are those of the author and do not purport to reflect the position of the U.S. Military Academy, the Department of the Army, or the Department of Defense.

Despite the total American conquest of Okinawa, U.S. planners were deeply depressed by the terrible cost of that campaign. If the Japanese could inflict 50,000 casualties on Americans attacking islands 150 miles south of Japan, what would an invasion of the homeland cost? Easier terms might bring an early capitulation by Tokyo, but Washington strategists also had to consider an American public opinion hardened against the Japanese by the bitterness of the recent fighting and revelations of atrocities such as the Bataan Death March. (During the march, American prisoners in the Philippines had suffered grim mistreatment at the hands of the Japanese.)

George Lincoln was one of those planners who tried to balance the necessity of obtaining America's announced war aims with the desire to avoid the heavy bloodshed that an invasion of the Japanese home islands would inevitably entail. This portrait of Lincoln is drawn by one of his students at the U.S. Military Academy, Charles F. Brower IV. A professional army officer, Brower earned his doctorate in history at the University of Pennsylvania. His scholarly work has focused on the U.S. Joint Chiefs of Staff in World War II; his most recent book is *World War II in Europe: The Final Year* (1998).

Lincoln Hall lies on the northeastern edge of the Plain at West Point, situated to observe both the Academy and the world beyond the gaps slashed through the Hudson highlands by the river. The man for whom the building is named, Brig. Gen. George A. Lincoln, would have appreciated the vantage point, for few of West Point's graduates better exemplify the breadth and balance of politico-military perspective that Lincoln applied over a lifetime of national service.

Born in Michigan in 1907, Lincoln, after a year at the University of Kansas, entered the Military Academy in 1925, where he distinguished himself academically and militarily. Graduating fourth in the Class of 1929 and commissioned in the Corps of Engineers, he won a coveted Rhodes Scholarship and for three years studied philosophy, politics, and economics at Oxford's Magdalen College. This broad Oxford background helped to lay a foundation for a sophisticated appreciation for the interrelation of political and military factors in strategy making. Following his years at Oxford, Lincoln served as an engineer company commander in Colorado, constructing New Deal Civilian Conservation Corps camps, before returning to West Point in 1937 to teach economics, government, and history.

In the aftermath of Pearl Harbor, Lincoln quickly found his way to London as a logistics adviser in Maj. Gen. John C. H. Lee's headquarters where his vast talents soon caught the eye of Maj. Gen. Thomas T. Handy, the assistant chief of staff in the War Department's Operations

Brig. Gen. George Lincoln, U.S. Military Academy, Class of 1929, during his service as professor and head of the Department of Social Sciences at West Point. *Courtesy of the Special Collections and Archives Division, U.S. Military Academy Library, West Point, New York*

Division (OPD) under Army Chief of Staff Gen. George C. Marshall. Over Lee's strenuous objections (he argued that Lincoln's Oxford background greatly facilitated Anglo-American communications), Handy reassigned Lincoln as deputy chief of OPD's Strategy and Policy (S&P) Group in May 1943. As one of Lincoln's associates later recalled, Handy had agreed that Lee's assessment of Lincoln's value in the Anglo-

American strategic debates seemed to be on the mark, but he had concluded that "such competence could be better used to draft cables for Mr. Roosevelt to send to Mr. Churchill."[1]

Service at the summit of the Anglo-American war effort played right to Lincoln's considerable strategic and political talents. Located on the Pentagon's third floor, adjacent to the offices of the secretary of war and army chief of staff, the S&P Group served as the brain trust of the army, coordinating the operational concerns of the various theater commands with the strategic concerns of the joint and combined staff systems. The deputy chief position was known to be the training post for promotion to the chief's position in the S&P Group, and the deputy substituted for the chief when required. Lincoln therefore had regular interaction with Marshall and his senior assistants in the course of his daily responsibilities from the beginning of his service in the Operations Division.

Appointed chief of the S&P Group in November 1944 and promoted to brigadier general at the age of thirty-eight, Lincoln was then the youngest general on the army staff. Exercising broad responsibilities in the arena of strategic planning, he served as a member of the Joint Staff Planners (JPS) and on the JPS's Anglo-American counterpart, the Combined Staff Planners (CPS). Marshall expected the S&P Group to have analyzed every staff paper introduced into the joint and combined staff committees, and Lincoln or his designated representative usually discussed the pertinent issues with the chief of staff before every meeting of the Joint Chiefs of Staff (JCS) or Combined Chiefs of Staff (CCS). In addition, Lincoln accompanied Marshall to the JCS and CCS meetings in Washington and attended most of the crucial wartime conferences of 1944 and 1945—Quebec, Yalta, and Potsdam. After the State-War-Navy Coordinating Committee (SWNCC) was established in December 1944 to improve the machinery for coordinating politicomilitary matters among the three departments, Lincoln served also as principal military adviser to the War Department's SWNCC representative, Assistant Secretary of War John J. McCloy.[2]

After the war, Lincoln continued to lead the S&P Group when Dwight D. Eisenhower became the army chief of staff, playing a central role in organizing the new Department of Defense. In 1947 he voluntarily surrendered his brigadier general's stars and returned to West Point as a professor in the Department of Social Sciences. He subsequently became head of the department and remained in that position until his retirement from active duty in 1969. Under his tutelage the department drew the best and brightest of the army's young officers to its faculty by way of distinguished graduate programs, after a few years returning them to the field army to leaven its corps of future leaders. Through his chairmanship the department moved to the forefront of American national security studies. Lincoln introduced economic analysis into the West Point curriculum and took the lead over the next two decades in raising public consciousness about the economic dimensions of national defense policy.[3]

From time to time he was called away from West Point to serve at the highest levels of American government. He served in the Truman administration as military adviser to Secretary of State James F. Byrnes, as deputy undersecretary of the army, and as a special assistant to the secretary of defense responsible for designing the new Mutual Security Program. In 1950 he advised his old friend Averell Harriman in the latter's role as chairman of the North Atlantic Treaty Organization (NATO) committee laying the ground rules for effective politico-military collaboration among its members. President Eisenhower, another alumnus of the War Department's Operations Division, called on him to serve on the Gaither, Rockefeller, and Draper panels, and in 1964 President Lyndon Johnson appointed him for a year-long stint as a special adviser for the Agency for International Development, surveying American aid missions in Latin America. In 1969, after his retirement, President Richard Nixon named Lincoln director of the Office of Emergency Preparedness (responsible for the stewardship of the nation's strategic stockpiles) and a member of the National Security Council. As the senior administration official charged with the difficult management of the ninety-day wage-price freeze initiated in 1971, Lincoln earned national recognition and acclaim for his performance. He held these positions until 1973. In all these capacities Lincoln selected, trained, and served as a mentor to a whole generation of army and air force staff officers who over the years came to be known as the "Lincoln brigade." His influence on this generation of West Point cadets and professional military officers is undoubtedly his true legacy to the nation. According to the Military Academy's first postwar superintendent, Gen. Maxwell Taylor, Lincoln's mentorship role over that time was "a greater contribution to national defense than that made by most general officers of the line."[4]

Lincoln assumed his duties as the chief of the Strategy and Policy Group in 1944 at a time when the politico-military nature of the strategic questions facing General Marshall's Washington command post was coming into full bloom. Although many military officers remained convinced that political questions should not be persuasive in the formulation of military recommendations to the commander in chief, others such as Lincoln better recognized the inseparability of political considerations from strategic matters and took on the outlook of a national—as opposed to military—strategist. Lincoln's activities in the S&P Group during the last months of World War II in the debate over the final strategy for the defeat of Japan and in the efforts to induce a Japanese surrender by clarifying the meaning of unconditional surrender are more suggestive of the politico-military role subsequently played by military officers in national security affairs in the Cold War era than that played during World War II. He assembled an unusually talented group of officers to work exclusively on such issues and channeled their sophisticated work into broader national issues through his membership in top-level committees. The S&P Group became in effect a kind of clearinghouse for national security issues, presaging the role to be later played by the National Security Council staff. In this way Lincoln was far more than a military strategist: He was the prototype of a national strategist par excellence, seeking to provide well-grounded politico-military advice to coordinate a variety of instruments of American power toward the accomplishment of the political aims of the country and the establishment of a sound peace.

Lincoln's accession as chief paralleled the creation of the State-War-Navy Coordinating Committee in December 1944. Consisting of three civilian assistant secretaries representing State, War, and Navy, SWNCC's raison d'être was the coordination of the views of the three departments on politico-military issues, "especially those involving foreign policy and relations with foreign nations." The S&P Group directly supported the various SWNCC subcommittees and was increasingly involved in the SWNCC's deliberations and decisions. In March 1945, at the insistence of McCloy, the S&P Group assumed for SWNCC initiatives the same staff-coordination role it played within the joint committee system. Lincoln acknowledged the implications for the S&P Group of this broader mandate, characterizing the group's role in those last months of the war as that of consummating the "official marriage of political and military policy of the State Department and the War Department."[5]

As the new army planner, the chief of the S&P Group found himself in late 1944 at the center of the interservice debate within the Joint Chiefs of Staff over the final strategy for the defeat of Japan. Opponents in the wartime debate generally aligned themselves along service lines, with navy and army air force planners favoring blockade and bombardment and army planners believing an invasion of the Japanese home islands was necessary. But the assault versus siege debate was only superficially a military question; its essence was profoundly political, and key American planners knew it. The Joint Chiefs appreciated the pervasive influence of political considerations on strategy and struggled hard to reconcile American strategy with them. And because these political considerations included elements fundamentally in tension, key subordinates such as Lincoln were forced to wrestle with that dilemma throughout the last year of the war.[6]

Two important and related political considerations guided Lincoln during his tenure as the chief of the S&P Group. First was the policy of unconditional surrender that had been enunciated by Roosevelt (FDR) and Winston Churchill at the Casablanca Conference in January 1943. The Joint Chiefs of Staff interpreted FDR's announcement as a political guideline for their military strategy. Unconditional surrender defined the nature of the victory that FDR wanted to obtain and was thus very much a commentary on the nature of the postwar world the president sought to create.

Second, the Joint Chiefs were intensely aware of the political need to maintain the commitment of the American people to the president's grand strategy. FDR's military advisers were deeply concerned about the ability of the public to sustain a protracted war and thus felt compelling pressure to develop strategies that would deliver unconditional surrender in a speedy fashion. Marshall's assertion after the war that "a democracy cannot fight a Seven Years' War" is well known; his navy counterpart's concerns about the stamina and commitment of the home front reveal even more clearly the depth of the military's concerns. Adm. Ernest J. King's fear about the war, voiced in 1944, was that "the American people would weary of it quickly, and that pressure at home will force a negotiated peace, before the Japs [*sic*] are really licked." This specter of a long, costly, and inconclusive war haunted military planners and shaped their strategic choices.[7]

The strategic dilemma emerging from these political considerations was clear: A long attritional war placed the aim of unconditional surrender at risk by straining the patience of the home front; a speedier war of annihilation risked excessive casualties and consequent domestic pressure for a negotiated settlement. After the war Fleet Adm. William D. Leahy, who served as the ad hoc chairman of the Joint Chiefs of Staff, starkly summarized the dilemma he and his colleagues faced. In

American strategic assessments, he wrote, "the urgency of time was always present. The quicker your enemies are defeated, the smaller the costs in dead men, wounded men, and dollars. The plan was . . . to force Tokyo to surrender at the earliest possible moment and at the same time hold casualty lists to a minimum."[8]

At the Quebec Conference in September 1944 the Combined Chiefs of Staff adopted a new strategy for the defeat of Japan. Unconditional surrender was to be forced upon Tokyo, first, by lowering the Japanese ability and will to resist by bombardment and blockade and, second, by invading the industrial heart of Japan. This outline of operations, later code-named Downfall, called for a two-phased invasion in the fall and winter of 1945–46. Phase one, Operation Olympic, envisioned seizure by fourteen divisions in September 1945 of an intermediate objective on Kyushu, the southernmost of the home islands. If Olympic failed to produce unconditional surrender, Operation Coronet three months later was to finish the task by assaulting the industrial heart of Japan on the main island of Honshu with twenty-five divisions. Although on the surface this concept seemed an endorsement of an invasion strategy, in fact nothing had really been settled. Siege proponents still believed that phase one would deliver Japanese surrender certainly short of an invasion of Honshu and that an early surrender forestalling the Kyushu operation remained a good possibility. No important navy or army air force figure had yet truly embraced the new strategic concept. Indeed, the debate was just beginning.

In the spring of 1945, Lincoln led the attack on the resilient siege strategy, arguing that it played to the strength of the Japanese strategy. Tokyo's desperate hope was to raise the cost of the final defeat of Japan to such a level that it would stimulate war-weariness in the American public and thereby create the conditions for a negotiated settlement. Given that strategy, Japan would not likely be induced to an early surrender through a siege. Indeed, the Joint Intelligence Committee concluded surrender would probably not occur before "the middle or latter part of 1946" and perhaps not even before "a great many years."[9]

Adopting a broader national outlook, Lincoln and his fellow staff planners boldly called in April for a definition of unconditional surrender "in terms understandable to the Japanese," perhaps through a "declaration of intentions" by Washington. Treading on decidedly political ground, they argued that the failure to define unconditional surrender in terms acceptable to Tokyo would mean "no alternative to annihilation and no prospect that the threat of absolute defeat would bring about capitulation." Only "force of arms"—invasion—would then be able to deliver unconditional surrender.[10]

Lincoln's interest in clarifying the definition of unconditional surrender had been stimulated earlier when Maj. Gen. George V. Strong, the senior army member of the Joint Post War Committee, suggested that the State Department consider a call for a Japanese surrender under terms that left open the possibility of a lenient peace. Although SWNCC subsequently modified the Strong proposals to bring them more into line with the public policy of unconditional surrender, Lincoln had studied the Strong initiative closely in his role as McCloy's senior adviser and had been impressed by its logic.[11]

Modifying unconditional surrender policy was political dynamite, however. The new president, Harry S. Truman, had had that point hammered home to him in his first address to Congress on April 16 when his reaffirmation of Roosevelt's policy received a standing ovation from the members in joint session. Nonetheless, some effort to clarify the meaning of unconditional surrender for the Japanese and thus induce surrender short of invasion—the goal sought by Lincoln in his call for a declaration of Washington's intentions regarding Japan—soon emerged from the Truman White House. Truman's V-E Day press conference on May 8 echoed FDR's assurances to Tokyo that unconditional surrender did not mean the enslavement or extermination of the Japanese people, but the president then went on to make the important distinction that unconditional surrender applied to the *armed forces* of Japan, not *Japan*, as FDR had insisted previously at Casablanca and elsewhere.[12]

Although pressed throughout May by Acting Secretary of State Joseph C. Grew to accept the idea that a clear American commitment to the retention of the imperial dynasty would prompt Japan's surrender, the president instead referred the matter to the JCS and SWNCC for further study.[13] Lincoln played a prominent role in both arenas. His perspective emerged clearly in the preparations for the now-famous June 18, 1945, meeting in the White House in which the president reviewed the Japanese campaign with his senior military advisers. Reading from notes prepared for him by Lincoln's staff,[14] General Marshall argued forcefully for Olympic to be undertaken as scheduled. He now believed that the operation was a prerequisite for both the siege and the invasion strategies and "offered the only way the Japanese could be forced into a feeling of utter helplessness." In line with this rationale, Marshall sketched out for Truman the alluring possibility that Japan might capitulate "short of complete military defeat in the field" if faced by "the completely hopeless prospect occasioned by (1) destruction already wrought by air bombardment and sea blockade, coupled with (2) a landing on Japan indicating the firmness of our resolve, and also perhaps coupled with (3) the entry or threat of entry of Russia into the war."[15]

Convinced now that Olympic was essential to the success of the siege strategy, Adm. Ernest J. King stood solidly with Marshall in urging the president's approval of Olympic, as did for the same reason Lt. Gen. Ira C. Eaker, who was representing the Army Air Forces.[16] Leahy alone among the Joint Chiefs remained unconvinced. Frustrated that Marshall and King had concluded that Olympic was necessary to deliver speedy unconditional surrender, he pushed Truman to reassess the meaning of the unconditional surrender policy. Truman demurred, indicating that he had considered such a reassessment but felt he could not "take any action at this time to change public opinion on the matter," although "he had left the door open for Congress to take appropriate action."[17] For their part, the Joint Chiefs could only conclude that their objective remained the speedy unconditional surrender of Japan.

Because Marshall believed that the siege strategy placed the aim of unconditional surrender at risk, the task of resolving the problem of how to deliver speedy unconditional surrender while minimizing casualties fell largely upon Lincoln and the S&P Group. Army strategists were naturally concerned about the high human cost of the invasion strategy. The Okinawa campaign, the bloodiest thus far in the war, was drawing to a close, with casualties approaching the fifty thousand figure, including dead, wounded, and missing. Various joint committees had estimated the American cost of Olympic-Coronet at between twenty-five thousand to forty-six thousand killed and an additional one hundred thousand wounded; and others, including Admiral Leahy, feared even higher casualties.[18] The specter of one bloody Okinawa-like campaign after another through the Japanese main islands haunted American strategists.

Marshall had presented the S&P Group's logic at the June 18 meeting with Truman: The invasion of Kyushu, with air bombardment and sea blockade and perhaps Soviet entry or threat of entry, might deliver a Japanese surrender without the Honshu invasion and the resulting battle of annihilation. Marshall's comments previewed his strategists' efforts to steer a course between embracing the siege strategy and rushing into Honshu at the risk of Okinawa-like casualties unacceptable to an unsteady home front. Given the fanatical resistance of the Japanese as the Allied forces approached the home islands and the assumption that they would fight even more tenaciously for their homeland, it is likely that Marshall and most in the S&P Group remained skeptical that anything short of Japan's complete military defeat could deliver unconditional surrender. No one appreciated more than they did the soldier's knowledge that there is no easy, bloodless way to victory in war. "We had to assume that a force of 2.5 million Japanese would fight to the death, fight as they did on all those islands we attacked," Marshall told reporter John P. Sutherland. "We figured in their homeland they would fight even harder. We felt this despite what generals with cigars in their mouth had to say about bombing the Japanese into submission."[19] But concerns about the will and stamina of the American people to see the war through to unconditional surrender also increasingly tempered the army strategists' judgments.[20] Lincoln sought to reconcile these concerns by devising a strategy aimed at maximizing the military, psychological, and political pressures on Japan to create the best conditions for unconditional surrender short of a Honshu invasion. In the event that these pressures failed to bring about Japanese capitulation, Lincoln knew the armed forces of the United States would be in position to assault the Kanto Plain and directly impose unconditional surrender upon Japan by force of arms.[21]

In Lincoln's view, maximizing the military pressures on Japan went far beyond the siege strategy and included securing a lodgment on Kyushu. Bombardment and blockade would continue, for sure, and would be extended to include atomic bombs as they became available. But Tokyo had to be convinced of the firmness of American resolve. A secure beachhead on Kyushu might be just the psychological lever to persuade Japan to surrender and to make Coronet unnecessary. By exploiting the support given by Admiral King and Army Air Force Chief of Staff Gen. H. H. Arnold to the Kyushu invasion as requisite to the success of the siege and bombardment operations, the Lincoln approach had the additional advantage of putting a "foot in the invasion door." And since the S&P Group viewed Olympic as essential to Coronet's success, King and Arnold's acceptance of it made Olympic—and thus Coronet—more credible to the Japanese. To put it another way, opposition to Olympic by the other members of the Joint Chiefs of Staff would have very likely put the invasion strategy at risk; the King and Arnold endorsement of Olympic, even in the context of the siege strategy, allowed Marshall and Lincoln to maximize the psychological effect of military pressures on Japan as well as keep the Honshu invasion option open.

Under Lincoln's leadership, the army's planners also sought other nonmilitary ways to intensify the pressures on Japan to surrender short of a battle of annihilation on Honshu. Truman had directed Stimson, Grew, and Secretary of the Navy James Forrestal to study the question of a surrender demand, the implication being that they were to explore how unconditional surrender might be defined in such a way as to induce Japan to surrender short of invasion. The committee's composition was further broadened to include Marshall and King, and a working committee headed by McCloy was given the task of drafting the surrender demand. The S&P Group, with careful guidance from Lincoln, prepared the document.[22]

Lincoln characterized his task as a curious one of "stating the conditions of unconditional surrender," carefully wording them so that they would not be negotiable and including in them "items which will give hope to the Japanese people as a whole."[23] Stimson had shared with him and the S&P Group a draft of a memorandum to the president laying out ways for achieving American objectives without having to incur the heavy casualties resulting from an invasion. Lincoln's thinking had clearly been influenced by Stimson's notion that a carefully timed warning and call for surrender that also clarified what amounted to the terms of surrender would "secure . . . the equivalent of an unconditional surrender of [Japan's] forces." Stimson's terms were remarkably liberal: elimination of the authority and influence of the Japanese militarists; limitation of Japanese sovereignty to the home islands; maintenance of an economy, "purged of its militaristic influences," that could provide a reasonable standard of living; willingness to allow "trade access to external raw materials"; and assurance of the end of Allied occupation once Allied objectives were accomplished and a peaceful government representative of the Japanese people established. Most significantly, the secretary of war added that he believed that the chances of acceptance would be substantially increased if the Allies left the door open for a "constitutional monarchy under [Japan's] present dynasty."[24]

The S&P Group's surrender draft ran into stiff opposition from elements in the State Department who believed the elimination of the imperial dynasty to be a requirement for the full rehabilitation of Japan. As Brian Villa demonstrated in his seminal work on the army's role in preparing the Potsdam Proclamation, this opposition was reinforced by a number of events in late June and July. First, although the stubborn and bloody Japanese resistance on Okinawa had ended on June 21, any clarification of the meaning of unconditional surrender could easily embolden further Japanese resistance and reduce, not encourage, their inclinations to surrender. Second, when James F. Byrnes was sworn in as secretary of state on July 3, Grew, the department's strongest supporter of clarification, receded into the background. Sensitive to the domestic risks of modifying unconditional surrender, especially with regard to the emperor's status, and persuaded that the proposed surrender demand smacked of appeasement, Byrnes emasculated it, eliminating any mention of the imperial dynasty from the proclamation.[25]

Lincoln accompanied Marshall to the Potsdam Conference in July and worked assiduously on the issue of when best to time the issuance of the declaration. Lincoln believed that "two psychological days" remained in the war: "the day after we persuade Russia to enter" and "the day after we get what the Japs [*sic*] recognized as a secure beachhead in Japan." Providing the Japanese understood what surrender meant, Lincoln believed that they might capitulate "around either of those times." The S&P Group's thinking was that the surrender demand's greatest psychological impact required it to be coupled with other significant blows to the Japanese, such as Soviet entry into the war, a successful landing on Kyushu, and the beginning of "a more drastic phase" of the bombing campaign, the latter an oblique reference to atomic attack. Truman's decision in June to go ahead with Olympic was a stride toward a secure beachhead on Kyushu. Marshall's consistent championing of early Soviet entry into the war because of the strategic and psychological blow that Soviet intervention would inflict on Japan is also well known.[26] The War Department's serious—but ultimately unsuccessful—attempts to prompt an American clarification of the meaning of unconditional surrender had been the final item in the Lincoln-spearheaded initiatives to induce a Japanese surrender by measures short of invasion.

When the Potsdam Proclamation was issued on July 26, a subtle softening of the unconditional surrender policy had clearly occurred. To be sure, tough language abounded in the warning, but no careful observer—American or Japanese—could have missed the logical implications of section five, which began: "The following are our terms," phraseology reminiscent of Lincoln's "conditions of unconditional surrender." Moreover, the proclamation emphasized that the surrender applied to the armed forces of Japan and included some of the items Stimson and Lincoln had thought would encourage more thoughtful Japanese to accept this new definition of unconditional surrender.[27]

Premier Kantaro Suzuki's rejection nonetheless followed, revealing the latent strength that the militarists retained over the direction of Japanese policy. Barton Bernstein has recently concluded that it would have taken American concessions not only on the issue of the emperor but also on postwar occupation, self-disarmament, and war crimes trials to deliver a speedy surrender. No important American policymaker (and certainly not the American public) would have believed such conciliatory terms justified the investment of American blood and treasure in the war against Japan.[28]

After the war, Lincoln summarized the nature of the counsel he and the S&P Group provided Marshall and the Joint Chiefs as they strove to bring the Japanese war to a conclusion. That the army's strategists supported what has been labeled an invasion strategy has misled some critics to dismiss their contributions as parochial in outlook. In fact, the S&P's counsel reflected an ecumenical appreciation that ranged far beyond narrow service considerations. Lincoln and the S&P Group understood—and successfully persuaded Marshall—that Japan's defeat would result from the cumulative application of "military, psychological, and political pressures at a continually increasing tempo as the means became available." The S&P Group advocated continuously tightening the blockade; it supported the relentless bombardment of Japan with conventional and atomic weapons; it actively sought to induce an early surrender short of invasion through a clarification of the meaning of unconditional surrender; it strongly and successfully advised Marshall and Stimson to urge two presidents to seek Soviet entry into the Pacific war; and it initiated preparations for what would have been the largest amphibious assault in history, the invasion of Japan proper and the seizure of the Kanto Plain.[29]

That the cumulative effect of these pressures produced Japan's unconditional surrender short of invasion was precisely the point of these efforts. The army strategists in the S&P Group were not thirsting to invade Japan, although they knew that an invasion might be necessary to deliver the political aim of the war. As Lincoln put it, "The final outcome was certain and the broad strategic concept was clear." However, he was less certain about how best to orchestrate the various pressures against Japan or to understand just how much influence each would have on the Japanese. The timing and effect of the entry of the Soviet Union, the nature and effectiveness of the Potsdam Declaration, and the military capabilities of the atomic bomb were cases in point.[30]

After all, the Japanese decision to surrender ultimately rested in Tokyo, not Washington. Lincoln and his colleagues had concluded that since V-E Day the Japanese had been searching for the best time to terminate the war "with the best arrangements from their standpoint." One line of strategic logic led Lincoln to conclude that the Japanese might decide to stubbornly brave invasion with the aim of raising the costs to a level that would persuade the Americans to terminate hostilities "under terms short of unconditional surrender." Lincoln believed that short of imposing American will through Olympic and Coronet, the best strategy was to coordinate this variety of pressures in such a way that a sense of utter helplessness would grip Japan's leaders and bring their acceptance of unconditional surrender. He hoped that these pressures would force the Japanese to accept what he called "a negotiated unconditional surrender" without invasion, but he understood fully that the United States must be militarily and psychologically prepared to invade the Japanese homeland. There was, as Marshall had reminded Truman in their June invasion planning meeting, the "grim fact that there is not an easy, bloodless way to victory in war."[31] Without a Japanese acceptance of unconditional surrender, only invasion could ensure it.

The broad and multifaceted contributions of the S&P Group in the last year of the war against Japan clearly reflected Lincoln's appreciation that military considerations must not be divorced from the grander considerations of national policy. One cannot help but be struck by the quasi autonomy of the S&P Group in those months, its broad interaction with the State Department and other agencies within the Executive Office of the President, and its increasingly prominent role in ensuring the integration of politico-military issues. After the war John J. McCloy, certainly one of those best positioned to assess the substance of the S&P Group's contribution to national security concerns, characterized the officers of the group: "They exhibited balanced judgment and keen powers of analysis. They are the sort who would disabuse anybody of the impression that Army officers lack flexibility of mind and capacity to deal with new problems imaginatively."[32] As Lincoln understood so well, these new problems were more than ever broad national ones, and their strategic horizons had to be adjusted accordingly. In this way, Lincoln and the S&P Group anticipated the requirements that led to the National Security Act of 1947 and provided a model of excellence for successor national security staffs. It may be the most important of the many contributions to postwar national security policy made by the remarkable George A. Lincoln.[33]

Notes

1. Roger H. Nye, "George A. Lincoln: Architect of National Security," in *Issues of National Security in the 1970s: Essays Presented to Colonel George A. Lincoln on His Sixtieth Birthday*, ed. Amos A. Jordan Jr. (New York, 1967), 4. Other biographical information on Lincoln comes from Wolfgang Saxon, "Brig. General George Lincoln Dies: Top Military Planner Was 67," *New York Times*, May 26, 1975, A18; and "Biographical Summary of George A. Lincoln," Box 1 (Personal Papers), folder 1/1, George A. Lincoln Papers, U.S. Military Academy Library, West Point, New York (hereafter Lincoln Papers).

2. On Lincoln's and the S&P Group's responsibilities, see Ray S. Cline, *Washington Command Post: The Operations Division* (Washington, DC, 1951), 136, 204–5, 326–27.

3. Robert Cuff, "From the Controlled Materials Plan to the Defense Materials System, 1942–1953," *Military Affairs* 51 (January 1987): 2–3.

4. "Biographical Summary of George A. Lincoln," Lincoln Papers.

5. This and the following discussion of the relationship between SWNCC and the S&P Group rest heavily on Cline's chapter "Military Planning and Foreign Affairs," in *Washington Command Post*, 312–32, esp. 326–30. The first quotation is from p. 326. Lincoln's quotation is found on p. 330.

6. The following discussion of Lincoln's role in shaping the final strategy for the defeat of Japan elaborates on my own "Sophisticated Strategist: General George A. Lincoln and the Defeat of Japan, 1944–1945," *Diplomatic History* 15, no. 3 (Summer 1991): 317–37.

7. Marshall interview, July 25, 1949, cited in Maurice Matloff, *Strategic Planning for Coalition Warfare, 1943–1944* (Washington, DC, 1959), 5; Perry to Barnett, February 18, 1944, in Glen C. H. Perry, *"Dear Bart": Washington Views of World War II* (Westport, 1982), 249.

8. Fleet Adm. William D. Leahy, *I Was There* (New York, 1950), 219. Leahy, who held the post of chief of staff to the commander in chief, served as the president's representative to the JCS and CCS.

9. Lincoln's attack began in March and continued through the month of April. See Minutes of JPS 192d Meeting, March 10–16, 1945, CCS 334 Joint Staff Planners Meetings (September 20, 1943), Record Group 218, National Archives, Washington, DC; JIC 266/1, "Defeat of Japan by Blockade and Bombardment," April 18, 1945; and JIC 268/1, "Unconditional Surrender of Japan," April 25, 1945, both in Record Group 165, ABC 387 Japan (February 15, 1945), National Archives, Washington, DC.

10. JPS Report, JCS 924/15, "Pacific Strategy," April 25, 1945, Record Group 165, ABC 384 Pacific (January 1, 1943), sec. 9, National Archives, Washington, DC.

11. On the Strong proposals, see Brian A. Villa, "The U.S. Army, Unconditional Surrender, and the Potsdam Proclamation," *Journal of American History* 63, no. 1 (January 1976): 75–76.

12. Harry S. Truman, *Memoirs*, vol. 1, *Year of Decisions* (Garden City, 1955), 207.

13. Joseph C. Grew memorandum of conversation, "Appointment with the President, 12:35 P.M., May 28, 1945," Grew Papers, Houghton Library, Harvard University, Cambridge, Massachusetts; Grew memorandum of conversation, "Possible inclusion in President's forthcoming speech of statement on Japan," May 29, 1945, Grew Papers.

14. Report by the Joint Staff Planners, JCS 1388, "Details of the Campaign against Japan," June 16, 1945, ABC 384 Japan (May 3, 1944), Record Group 319, National Archives, Washington, DC.

15. JCS minutes of a meeting held at the White House, June 18, 1945, CCS 334 Joint Chiefs of Staff Meetings (February 2, 1945), Record Group 218, National Archives, Washington, DC.

16. On Arnold's support for the Kyushu invasion, see Barton J. Bernstein, "Understanding the Atomic Bomb and Japanese Surrender," *Diplomatic History* 19, no. 2 (Spring 1995): 250.

17. JCS minutes of a meeting held at the White House, June 18, 1945, CCS 334 Joint Chiefs of Staff Meetings (February 2, 1945), Record Group 218, National Archives, Washington, DC.

18. Barton J. Bernstein, "A Postwar Myth: 500,000 U.S. Lives Saved," *Bulletin of Atomic Scientists* 42 (June-July 1986): 38–40.

19. John P. Sutherland, "The Story General Marshall Told Me," *U.S. News & World Report*, November 2, 1959, 52–53.

20. On American war-weariness, see Charles F. Brower, *The Joint Chiefs of Staff and National Policy in American Strategy and the War with Japan, 1943–1945* (Ann Arbor, MI, 1987), 320–22, 326–37.

21. For the fullest explication of this thinking, see Lincoln memorandum for Ray S. Cline, subject: Comment on Study Prepared by P[lans]&O[perations] Historian Concerning Historical Facts Related to the Use of the Atomic Bomb, October 11, 1946, Box 2, September–October 1946 folder, Lincoln Papers, West Point, New York (hereafter Lincoln Comments on Special Historical Study).

22. Villa, "The U.S. Army," 87.

23. Lincoln memorandum for General John E. Hull, subject: Immediate Demand for Japanese Surrender, June 28, 1945, Box 2, May–June 1945 folder, Lincoln Papers, West Point, New York.

24. Stimson draft memorandum for the president, subject: Proposed Program for Japan, enclosed in Lincoln memorandum for Gen. John E. Hull, June 28, 1945, Box 2, May–June 1945 folder, Lincoln Papers, West Point, New York.

25. Villa, "The U.S. Army," 85–89.

26. Lincoln to Gen. A. C. Wedemeyer, July 10, 1945, Box 5, Wedemeyer folder, Lincoln Papers.

27. "Proclamation by the Heads of the Governments of the United States, China, and the United Kingdom," July 26, 1945, in *Foreign Relations of the United States: The Conference of Berlin (The Potsdam Conference), 1945*, 2 vols. (Washington, 1960), 2:1474–76.

28. Bernstein, "Understanding the Atomic Bomb and Japanese Surrender," 241.

29. Lincoln Comments on Special Historical Study; Brower, 336–37.

30. Lincoln Comments on Special Historical Study.

31. Ibid. Marshall quoted in JCS minutes of a meeting held at the White House, June 18, 1945, CCS 334 Joint Chiefs of Staff Meetings (February 2, 1945), Record Group 218, National Archives, Washington, DC.

32. McCloy memorandum for OPD, November 14, 1945, in Cline, *Washington Command Post*, 329n. See also McCloy, "In Defense of the Military Mind," undated [April 1947], Box 4, Speeches folder, Lincoln Papers, West Point, New York.

33. On this linkage, see especially Wilson Miscamble, *George F. Kennan and the Making of American Foreign Policy, 1947–1950* (Princeton, 1992), 8–9, which links Marshall's creation in 1947 of the State Department's Policy Planning Staff to replicate an organization modeled on the S&P Group within the State Department.

Suggested Readings

Chappell, John D. *Before the Bomb: How America Approached the End of the Pacific War*. Lexington, KY, 1997.

Cline, Ray S. *Washington Command Post: The Operations Division*. Washington, DC, 1951.

Pogue, Forrest C. *George C. Marshall: Organizer of Victory, 1943–45*. New York, 1973.

Stoler, Mark A. *George C. Marshall: Soldier-Statesman of the American Century*. Boston, 1989.

Index